ormatio

TRADITION. EXPERIENCE.
TRANSFORMATION.

Formatio books from InterVarsity Press follow the rich tradition of the church in the journey of spiritual formation. These books are not merely about being informed, but about being transformed by Christ and conformed to his image. Formatio stands in InterVarsity Press's evangelical publishing tradition by integrating God's Word with spiritual practice and by prompting readers to move from inward change to outward witness. InterVarsity Press uses the chambered nautilus for Formatio, a symbol of spiritual formation because of its continual spiral journey outward as it moves from its center. We believe that each of us is made with a deep desire to be in God's presence. Formatio books help us to fulfill our deepest desires and to become our true selves in light of God's grace.

A Guidebook to Prayer

Twenty-four ways to walk with God

MaryKate Morse

Foreword by Joshua Choonmin Kang

IVP Books

An imprint of InterVarsity Press
Downers Grove, Illinois

InterVarsity Press
P.O. Box 1400, Downers Grove, IL 60515-1426
ivpress.com
email@ivpress.com

InterVarsity Press® is the book-publishing division of InterVarsity Christian Fellowship/USA®, a movement of students and faculty active on campus at hundreds of universities, colleges and schools of nursing in the United States of America, and a member movement of the International Fellowship of Evangelical Students. For information about local and regional activities, visit intervarsity.org.

Scripture quotations, unless otherwise noted, are from the New Revised Standard Version of the Bible, copyright 1989 by the Division of Christian Education of the National Council of the Churches of Christ in the USA. Used by permission. All rights reserved.

While all stories in this book are true, some names and identifying information in this book have been changed to protect the privacy of the individuals involved.

The closing chapter is adapted from "The Problem of Prayerlessness" by MaryKate Morse in Giving Ourselves to Prayer, © 2007 PrayerShop Publishing. Used with permission.

Cover Design: Cindy Kiple
Interior Design: Beth Hagenberg

Images: sheep at sunset: Peter Adams/Getty Images
* sailboat in storm: o-che/Getty Images*

ISBN 978-0-8308-3578-2 (print)
ISBN 978-0-8308-6464-5 (digital)

Printed in the United States of America ∞

Library of Congress Cataloging-in-Publication Data

Morse, MaryKate, 1948-
 A guidebook to prayer : 24 ways to walk with God / MaryKate Morse.
    pages cm
 Includes bibliographical references.
 ISBN 978-0-8308-3578-2 (pbk. : alk. paper)
 1. Prayer—Christianity. I. Title.
 BV215.M67 2013
 248.3'2--dc23

                                                        2013024159

P	19	18	17	16	15	14	13	12	11	10	9	8	7	6	5
Y	29	28	27	26	25	24	23	22	21	20	19				

To my dad,
Vaughan Palmore,

and my husband,
Randy Morse,

two men who have inspired me
with their lives of prayer.

Contents

PART THREE: GOD THE HOLY SPIRIT

Foreword

Dr. Morse is inviting us to the deep and mysterious world of prayer. It might sound a bit strange, but Almighty God also prayed. If anyone asks me why we should pray, I would answer them that we have to pray because God prays. Our God is the God of prayer. Our Father God listens to our prayers. Even at this moment, Jesus is praying for us (Rom 8:34; Heb 7:25). The Holy Spirit helps our weakness through intercession and prays for us in accordance with God's will (Rom 8:26-27). Prayer is the divine principle through which God operates the cosmos. Thus, the spiritual world is the prayer world.

Dr. Morse invites us to pray with the triune God. What an amazing invitation! The greatest honor for a Christian is to have fellowship with the triune God. To pray means to fall in love with God. To pray means to enjoy the privilege of conversation with the triune God. To pray means to desire the Triune God and enjoy fellowship with him. It is to thirst for God.

The author not only invites us to the deep prayer world, but also helps us to lay a good foundation of prayer. She teaches us about the One to whom we pray, what we pray for and how we should pray. The Chinese word for *laying foundation* means taking care of or checking out the roots. To pray is to send one's roots deeply to Jesus, the source of living water. Prayer spirituality is the spirituality of growing *down*. Only when the tree sends its roots deeply down into the ground can the branches grow up outwardly and bear abundant fruit. Our souls grow and bear the fruit of the Spirit by the living water that we absorb from the roots through prayer. True prayer is an encounter between heaven and earth.

Dr. Morse teaches us various ways of enjoying intimate fellowship with God by introducing twenty-four prayers. Just as a skillful and competent surgeon uses many different scalpels, depending on the part of the body being operated on, Morse helps us to come closer to God through many different ways of praying. A doctor who knows only one method to cure a patient is not a good doctor. An excellent doctor not only knows several ways to treat a patient, but also knows how to apply these treatments. In that perspective, the author is like a soul doctor, teaching us twenty-four ways to cure and heal our wounded souls.

She also serves as a spiritual guide into the deep prayer world. Since the prayer world is full of mysteries, we must have a guide. A person who tries to enter into the world of prayer without a guide is like a person who hikes into a wilderness alone or tries to climb Mount Everest without the help of a Sherpa. That is very dangerous.

Jesus' disciples asked him to teach them how to pray. We must go before Jesus and learn how to pray from him. We need to receive help from the spiritual guide who has experience with deep prayer. The author of this book is an excellent spiritual guide. Her soul is calm and quiet. Her character reminds us of that of Jesus. She has sharp intelligence and a gentle heart. Dr. Morse has a very bright and pure spirit. This book is a holy masterpiece of her long prayer and study. Before they entered the land of Canaan, the spies first drew a map of the land. Just as they could not enter into the land without a proper map, we need a spiritual map like this book to enter into the Promised Land.

The world of prayer is not only a world full of mysteries but also of grace. We cannot be saved without God's saving grace, nor can we enter into the school of prayer without his special favor. We cannot experience the depth of the world of prayer without the help of the Holy Spirit, who is the spirit of prayer. The author invites us into the world of God's grace. If you have this book in your hand, that's a great incident of God's grace. An encounter with a good book is an incident of grace. Good books help us to fall in love with God, and leave us wanting to be more like him. This book is a good book!

I recommend this book as a guide for those who want to pray but don't know how. And I wish to recommend this book for those who want to go deeper into the world of prayer. Read this book slowly and prayerfully. As you do, you will find yourself falling in love with God.

Rev. Joshua Choonmin Kang

Acknowledgments

I am grateful to so many who accompanied me on the journey of writing this book. Before I began writing I attended a Writer's Retreat sponsored by IVP and led by my editor, Cindy Bunch. Cindy thought it would inspire her "baby" writers (those of us who hadn't written many books) to see writing as a calling. She also wanted us to learn from each other and hear from some seasoned writers about the craft of writing. I remember when we Skyped in a conversation with Richard Foster. I couldn't believe that here I was ready to embark on the writing of a prayer guidebook, and I was getting writing advice from one of the most-read authors on prayer and formation. Of course, he didn't know about my project, but it still felt holy to me. During that time, I came to know Cindy as more than my editor. She was on a mission to develop and nurture writers for the sake of God's kingdom. Every morning and evening she would open her tablet and lead us in prayer. She created an experience after which I felt newly inspired to bring my very best to the writing task. Thank you, Cindy, for caring about us writers. Thank you, Anne Grizzle, for the hospitality and love of your retreat home and the amazing food.

I am also grateful to George Fox University for giving me a year sabbatical in which to write this book. I am aware that a yearlong sabbatical is a rare gift, a treasure I wanted to steward. I created goals and had a schedule; I dedicated myself in prayer and industry to the writing of this book. I hope I make the "family" proud. Thank you, George Fox, for the opportunity to write without interruption and teaching duties.

Of course, I am grateful for the people who over the years have shared their prayer lives and experiences with me. So many stories I was unable to include, but so many continue to inspire me. Thank you all for your insight, adventure and courage while trying these many ways to pray. Thank you for sharing honestly about your experiences and allowing me to share your stories with others. I'm especially sending a shout-out of love to all my students and former church members.

Finally, one of the fruits of my time at the Writer's Retreat was the idea of having a small group of people to pray for me while I wrote and to hold me accountable. When you are alone writing, it is easy to feel isolated. It is also easy to take too many breaks and get behind. So, I chose a group of women. I chose women whom I have known and loved over the years, and who know and love me. I chose women who pray. These women are Sandy Bass (church worship leader and artist in Portland, OR), Margaret Duggan (professor at Redcliffe College in Gloucester, England, and missions worker in Asia with Navigators), Lu Hawley (ministering with Co-Serve in Thailand and Kazakhstan), Deborah Loyd (church planter, blogger, and adjunct professor in Portland, OR), Una Lucey-Lee (leadership trainer for InterVarsity in Chicago, IL), Carol McLaughlin (in the ordination process for PCUSA Teaching Elder and seminary adjunct in Gig Harbor, WA) and Miriam Mendez (American Baptist pastor and church planter in Portland, OR). Every week I sent them an email on Friday afternoon with a status report, my draft chapters and prayer needs. They prayed for me, and I am so, so thankful to each one of them.

At the end of my sabbatical I traveled to Seoul, Korea, with some doctor of ministry students. It struck me that I began my journey on retreat with Richard Foster sharing about his writing ministry and ended my journey in South Korea with Rev. Joshua Choonmin Kang, who is the "man of prayer" in South Korea. We attended a 6:00 a.m. prayer service at Myungsung Presbyterian Church with five thousand men, women and children in attendance. When we walked to our seats, the sanctuary was completely quiet as people prepared in contemplative silence. The people of South Korea were a persecuted church, and so they prayed. I am humbled to contribute a small work on prayer in light of the contributions made by such saints as these.

Introduction

Prayer as *Roadness to God*

The root of all prayer, and indeed all life itself, is desire for God.
All things are made to desire God.

ROBERTA BONDI

The difference between talking about prayer and praying
is the same as the difference between blowing a kiss and kissing.

G. K. CHESTERTON

Many of us lament, why is prayer so hard? We want to pray but we don't pray as consistently and as meaningfully as we might like. The problem is increasing as we are formed more and more by media and technology than we are by prayer. Americans watch TV an average of twenty-eight hours a week,[1] and 50 percent of all adults spend time using social media.[2]

Prayer is the most fundamental avenue for connecting us to God and growing in faith. Through prayer we know who we truly are and who this God is who loves us. Prayer:

Wrestling, agonizing, sweating, working, asking, fulfilling a duty—this is what prayer has been for me. I have found, along with comfort and help, both confusion and frustration. The same questions lurk like shadows in the back of my mind year after year. Why is prayer so hard? Why do I lose interest? Why does God feel distant? Is this all that prayer really is? Intuitively, I felt that prayer should be more and take me deeper, but I did not know what was missing or where to look for answers.

—Shane Gandara

- draws us to experience love and to be love

- increases our faith

- expands our vision of God

- helps us grow in self-understanding

- gives us perspective on life and death, on gardens and deserts

Through prayer, we experience forgiveness, guidance and peace. We are healed physically and emotionally. We experience the mystery of God, see truth and receive spiritual gifts. We receive vision and courage for God's mission. Faith becomes more beautiful, more real.

The purpose of this guidebook is to move from the lament to the joy of praying. Whether you are a beginner or a lifetime person of faith, the journey of prayer enriches our relationships with God and others. Prayer is more than a practice. It is a living adventure with a relational and risen Lord. God created us to be in a relationship with God expressed in the Trinity. God is the Creator and Covenant Maker. Jesus Christ is the living embodiment of God's love and is the Redeemer who heals and forgives us. The Holy Spirit empowers us and intercedes on our behalf.

Within this book you will find comments from people who have walked different prayer paths with me. Julie Hopper is one such person, and she describes prayer this way:

> If God were a city, prayer would be ways into the city. Some would be freeways, others boulevards. There would be avenues, alleys, sidewalks, train tracks, bike paths, and winding dirt trails. All of these obviously participate in *roadness*, yet by merely looking, one might see very little likeness between a freeway and a hiking trail. . . . Looking closely at prayer, I see God has provided many means for us to approach him.

Discovering these roadways is the purpose of this prayer guidebook. The aim is more than simply having various ways to pray. The aim is to have a more meaningful prayer experience and to know more authentically God, yourself and others with whom you pray.

A MOVEMENT OF PRAYER

George Barna, the founder of a research group that studies American beliefs, stated that the only constant his researchers ever found between effectiveness of the kingdom of God and some other element was not a gifted person or special program, but prayer.[3] I believe that prayer is the tipping point for the church.

A tipping point, a term made popular by Malcolm Gladwell in his book *The Tipping Point*, is any idea that becomes contagious, comprises little causes that yield big effects, and creates change in a dramatic moment.[4] Every reformation had a tipping point in Christian history, beginning with the first one in Acts. An idea becomes contagious: "For God so loved the world that he gave his only Son, so that everyone who believes in him may not perish but may have eternal life" (Jn 3:16). This Son lived among us, gave himself on behalf of us, and rose from the dead to live again. Hundreds and then thousands of individuals and families believed, becoming a movement that began to threaten the very structure of the Roman government and Jewish religious system. It was contagious, especially the love Christians had for each other. The dramatic moment came in two steps: an open tomb and tongues of flame. The tomb was empty. Jesus appeared alive. The disciples and followers were continuously praying and waiting as the risen Jesus instructed them. Then the Holy Spirit fell with power on the band of believers. They went out with prophetic courage and healing gifts to change the world.

With prayer we can experience afresh the mystery of a life on fire for God and a life set free from the tomb. The contagious idea is that with prayer—that connection with the Trinity—we can flourish spiritually despite circumstances. Many people make small changes to incorporate prayer into their lives. The change is not about right behavior or thinking, though that happens. The change is about a people of God who love the world as God loves the world. The dramatic moment is in the hands of God. We wait and pray and respond as the Holy Spirit leads us.

Today is a serious time especially with the divisions and animosity found among believers. For Jesus and his first followers, the identifying mark of the church was the love believers had for each other. This is the very fundamental nature of Christ: "Beloved, let us love one another, because love is from God; everyone who loves is born of God and knows God" (1 Jn 4:7).

Love happens in relationship. Prayer is the space where time and words and silence are given to God as a holy offering of love. It is the first place where problems between Christians are examined in the sacred gaze of God. How can we hate, if we have been on our knees in humble prayer interceding for each other?

The world also needs Christians committed to Jesus' kingdom mission. Jesus proclaimed, "The Spirit of the Lord is upon me, because he has anointed me to bring good news to the poor" (Lk 4:18). Our mission is Jesus' mission. We are to go and do likewise (Mt 28:18-20). Because of distractions and busyness we can miss the places where Jesus is yearning for us to make a difference. Prayer is the space where we get close to the heart of God and are renewed in our priorities.

Prayer matters, but the difficulty is that we struggle with a meaningful prayer life, even though prayer is a universal and common practice. Whether male or female, young or old, educated or not, whatever race, region, or income, people report praying at a very high percent, eight to nine out of every ten adults. The problem isn't whether people pray or not. The problem is that people don't experience God very often when they pray. Of those who reported that they prayed, 43 percent never felt led by God and 39 percent never received a spiritual insight. Only 26 percent regularly experienced God's presence and only 32 percent regularly had a sense of peace.[5] That means that for most people there is a disparity between the act and the experience of prayer. Those with the lowest value in their prayer experience felt the most distant from God, and those with the highest prayer experiences felt closest to God.[6] Therefore, the urgency is for vitality in prayer.

WHAT IS TRUE PRAYER?

Though there are benefits to prayer, we are sometimes motivated to pray for the wrong reasons. Prayer can lead to pride and religiosity, a feeling that we are particularly holy or special because of our prayers. On the pretext of praying, gossip can run through a congregation. We sometimes develop high expectations for how God is going to act, making it about our will and not God's. We can use prayer to scold, direct, shame and even manipulate. We say, "God told me to . . . while praying" and so little is left for discernment and discussion with others.

How do you differentiate the abuse of prayer from true prayer? Richard Foster defines prayer as "nothing more than an ongoing and growing love relationship with God the Father, Son, and Holy Spirit."[7] Prayer is not an event but a life. It is not a petition but a love relationship with one God, expressed as Father, Son and Holy Spirit. All three expressions of God bring imagination and possibilities to the character of the love relationship.

Some of us are inhibited in prayer because of limited views of God as judging father, or the Son as everyday buddy, or the Spirit as ecstatic confirmation of our value. Prayer is a love relationship expressed and known in many ways. In the same way that people who love each other delight in finding ways to express that love, prayer is how we delight in the Lord and the Lord delights in us.

Ched Myers, a theologian and activist, offers another dimension to the definition of prayer. He writes, "To pray is to learn to believe in a transformation of self and world, which seems, empirically, impossible—as in moving mountains."[8] Myers notes that prayer is a love relationship and more. True love leads to observable transformation. The result of prayer is changes in ourselves and in how we engage in the world. Prayer is trusting God to act despite the obstacles, to work miracles, moving the immovable in our lives and the world.

> **Prayer and I have** endured a relationship not unlike that of junior high would-be lovers. It's great, then awkward, then I stop texting and we drift apart. This cycle repeats *ad infinitum*. The busier my life becomes, the less time and space I create for prayer. And then I feel empty, yet emptiness is the crux of our humanity precisely because it creates space for us to be filled with God's Spirit. This is the great battle of the desert: our dual longing for and requirement of love. Love is the space in which we can cup our hands to contain enough small water to wet our faces in God's stream of life.
>
> —Pete Garcia

Prayer is a love relationship involving the interdependent union of the Trinity. Because it is a love relationship there is commitment and change. Researchers evaluate prayer most often on its frequency and outcomes such as guidance or peace, but rarely do they consider the relational aspects of a prayer life. Rather than asking ourselves, "Am I praying each day?" we should ask ourselves, "Am I in a love relationship with God today? Am I living like Jesus today? Do I smell the sweet breath of the Spirit today?"

All of life is a gift of love to believers and thus all of our life experiences can be ways to actively or passively experience the love of God. For most of us the issue is not the abundant presence of God but our limited attention to it. Thus, much as a beloved is wooed with texts, flowers, meaningful glances, meals and walks together, we engage with a God who loves us. And when we truly love, we are changed. Our primary struggle is not a focus on prayer as routine but rather a belief that prayer really matters and that anyone can pray.

Those who study behavioral change suggest that there are two questions that must be answered *before* an authentic change can occur: "Is it worth it?" and "Can I do it?"[9] These questions are about motivation and ability. These are two fundamental questions that illustrate the problems with developing a satisfying prayer life.

Prayer doesn't *seem* to be worth it and very few know *how* to pray in creative and meaningful ways. Prayer as modeled in the church is sometimes highly structured, or delivered by the pastor or "saint," or is charismatic and requires a Holy Spirit gift. If we pray because we should or because we need something, the motivation for a life of prayer is weak. However, if we pray to experience God and to grow, the motivation is stronger. Prayer can redirect anxiety to hope, bitterness to freedom, insecurity to courage, and stuck-ness to vision. We feel ourselves in the living water of Christ. We hear the whisper of the Holy Spirit guiding us. We know the presence of God.

The answer to the question "Can I do it?" is yes. We can all pray. Prayer is not a skill leading to better and better results because one is praying rightly. Prayer is the simplest and most elegant of spiritual disciplines. Nothing is needed. It is the

> **I struggled with** the notion that I had to get everything right in order to pray. I imagine if I were a pilgrim, working my way through the dusty paths of the desert to find an Abba to listen to my plaintive question, the exchange might go something like this. "Abba, I have tried so often to prepare myself for prayer, yet I never seem able to do well enough to pray." The Abba would smile at me and offer, "Prayer itself is preparation; through it alone will you be made ready." Pressing the issue, I mumble, "But ready for what?" To which the wrinkled Abba responds, "Ready for everything."
>
> —John Ray

most primal avenue for reaching out and engaging with God and then being strengthened and directed in our mission in the world. Everyone can pray, anytime, anywhere, and in lots of ways.

This prayer guidebook is designed to respond to the motivation and ability questions. Change happens best when we are motivated by an outcome that elicits joy and future expectation. Prayer is a struggle but the expectation of a closer walk with God, a more mature self and a more committed community can transform the difficult to the desirable.

THE SHAPE OF THIS BOOK

This guidebook introduces many ways for Christians to pray. It is not a definitive guidebook. There are still other ways to pray. Each person and community can discover new paths in which God is known and present through prayer.

By approaching prayer as a love relationship, the guidebook is set up to explore our relationship to God as expressed in the Trinity. Each chapter has content and then a prayer practice. The prayer practices are developed for individuals as well as for larger groups and prayer partners. Accountability and community are essential for any type of lasting change to occur.[10] By praying with a friend or with a group, we stretch and grow together. We can ask questions and learn together. The experience of God is communal, not just personal. So when one person in a group has an answer to prayer or an experience of blessing or forgiveness, the entire community is blessed and encouraged. Sharing stories and experiences helps us walk together as we journey with God.

Prayer connects us with our entire being and with each other. Prayer is not simply a mental or spiritual exercise. It is physical, mental, emotional, relational and spiritual. Prayer is more than words spoken in sacred spaces. Prayer gives us access to the breadth of God's sovereignty over all things and God's presence in all things. With Jesus Christ in us we experience prayer as a multifaceted life journey that affects all of our bodies, minds, hearts and actions. In the life practice of prayer we become naturalized into our forgotten citizenship in Christ's kingdom. We are on the journey with the Holy Spirit and friends.

> **I have come to** realize how expansive prayer is. It is as if we launch off in a little boat onto a very slow moving stream, which is our prayer. We can stay on this little stream our entire life, talking to God as we paddle safely around. Or we can be adventurous and paddle downstream, where it widens into a river. Effort is needed to paddle our boat, but the river begins to carry us and in time we reach a vast ocean that is the very heart of God. There we can rest and be with him.
>
> —Pam Kelsay

The introduction of various prayer types is connected to the role of the Trinity in prayer—God in the Old Testament for the design and nature of prayer, Jesus in the Gospels as the practice and breadth of prayer, and the Holy Spirit in the New Testament as the guide and power of prayer. The chapters begin with an introductory section connecting an attribute of the Trinity to prayer. Each chapter has several true stories that I have collected over many years of teaching, leading retreats and speaking on prayer. Then there are specific prayer practices for groups, partners and individuals.

In Hawaiian culture, there are four ways of knowing. It is through one's mana'o (head), puu'wai (heart), na'au (gut, deep knowledge), and kino (body). These four ways of knowing correlate with Mark 12:30, where we are called to love God with all our heart, soul, mind and strength. This allows me to help others to see and experience God in whatever context I find myself in, whether cultural, spiritual or personal. This is the incarnation of Jesus—that he came to our contexts and allowed us to come into contact with God, the divine Presence.

—Ryan Hee

- *Group experience.* Any type or size of faith group can go through the various practices to expand understanding of God's multifaceted love and to grow together in faith.

- *Partner experience.* You can also choose one to three prayer partners to meet with regularly and practice prayer together. Accountability and support exponentially encourage us on our prayer journeys.

- *Individual experience.* I encourage you to pray as an individual at least four times a week for at least fifteen minutes a day as you begin. If you are already a person of prayer, then this will be an opportunity to explore new avenues into the city of God.

This guidebook may be used as an occasional tool for different ways to pray, but it is primarily designed to help us become people of prayer. There is no particular order to how you might use this book, and there is no particular pace. You may complete a chapter each week going straight through the guidebook, or you may move around in the guidebook and stay with a practice as long as you like. Some practices will be truly helpful and will awaken life in you. Some chapters might not be helpful at all. This guidebook is designed for anyone whether you are a new believer or a saint for fifty years.

THE PRAYER JOURNEY

At the end of each chapter you will find prayer stories. The storytellers are people ranging in age from twenty to eighty. There are men and women, new Christians and lifelong believers, pastors, business people, students, mothers and fathers, ordinary folk representing a wide variety of ethnic diversity and Christian back-grounds. Some have told me their stories. Others have written them down for me. I have collected these stories over the years hoping to share them one day with a wider audience. They have inspired me. I hope they inspire you. These are people who have found their own "roadness to God" through prayer. Some have asked that their real name be disguised to protect others.

MY STORY

Though I felt called to serve God as a little girl and though I made a confession of faith at a neighborhood Good News Bible club at the age of ten, I struggled with following Christ. My family life was dysfunctional with an unfaithful and distracted mother. My father traveled often as an Air Force pilot. When we lived on Guam, my mother finally left when I was eleven, leaving five children behind between the ages of two and twelve. My dad kept us together, but it was not easy. The most vivid picture I have of him at that time was praying on his knees every morning by his bed. My father prayed.

I took on the role of caregiver, but I was confused and lonely. I lived to leave home. As I look back now, I believe the prayers of my father kept us all from going over the cliff. When I did leave for college, I was as lost as could be in every sort of way. I was searching for what I hadn't experienced—someone who saw me there alone, knew me and loved me.

During my first summer home, my new stepmother arranged for me to be a counselor at a Christian high school camp. I was appalled. I wasn't sure I even be-lieved in God anymore. I tried to get out of it, but in the end there I was assigned to a group of teenage girls. Every night there was an altar call—the very same one every night. On the last night I was desperate to have a different life. I wanted the joy of the young people around me. I accepted Christ.

I vividly remember going back to college and walking to class thinking, "What now? I guess I should talk to God. How do I do that? What do you say?" I just started talking to God. It felt awkward but real. No one discipled me or taught me how to walk this new life in Christ. I stumbled along, and God watched over me as I learned about this new journey.

Since that day it has become my passion to walk with people in prayer and to remove all the obstacles that I can and to pray in faith that God will remove others. In some ways I still feel like that college girl haltingly talking to God as I walk. In other ways, I feel like a wounded warrior after many personal difficulties and after walking with people who have had horrific challenges. But I still pray. I believe in prayer. I've seen it work in my life and others. Healings, forgiveness, visions, quiet deserts, worship, wisdom, intercession, blessing and new life have all come from praying. I've practiced every prayer in this book. Some I've developed. Others are classic ways of praying. The stories I tell are true stories from real people like you and like me. Some of the stories are mine, but except for two times I have chosen to use aliases. In the end I am a companion with you, still discovering what it means to be in a love relationship with God the Father, Son and Holy Spirit. Enjoy the journey. It is worth every step.

FURTHER READING

Bondi, Roberta C. *To Pray & to Love: Conversations on Prayer with the Early Church.* Minneapolis: Fortress, 1991.

Foster, Richard J. *Prayer: Finding the Heart's True Home.* New York: HarperSanFrancisco, 1992.

Hybels, Bill. *Too Busy Not to Pray: Slowing Down to Be with God.* Downers Grove, IL: InterVarsity Press, 1998.

Willard, Dallas. *Hearing God: Developing a Conversational Relationship with God.* Downers Grove, IL: InterVarsity Press, 1999.

Yancey, Philip. *Prayer: Does It Make a Difference?* Grand Rapids: Zondervan, 2006.

PART ONE

God the Father

1

Community Prayer

The God revealed in the Christian Scripture is,
in essence, plurality in oneness: three persons in one being,
Father, Son, and Holy Spirit, all eternally bonded together in
the original community of oneness, in the embrace of the
interpersonal dynamics that the Bible describes best when it
summarily affirms that "God is love" (1 John 4:8, 16).

GILBERT BILEZIKIAN

Insects crawl
Fish swim
Birds fly
Humans pray.

LEONARD SWEET

GOD AS ONE IN COMMUNITY

When you meet people for the very first time, you immediately begin gathering impressions about them. Are they quiet? Outgoing? Content? Sad? If you were to open the Bible for the very first time and you knew nothing about God, you would meet the God of Genesis 1 and 2. In the beginning of Scripture, God is known as the Creator in Community. God creates out of nothing and makes it good. And God creates in community and for community. The very first way that we know God is that God made us and made us for connection.

> Then God said, "Let us make humankind in our image, according to our likeness; and let them have dominion over the fish of the sea, and over the birds of the air, and over

the cattle, and over all the wild animals of the earth, and over every creeping thing that creeps upon the earth."

So God created humankind in his image, in the image of God he created them; male and female he created them. (Gen 1:26-27)

Then the LORD God said, "It is not good that the man should be alone; I will make him a helper as his partner." (Gen 2:18)

Being made in the image of God, we are designed for relationship with our Maker and with each other. It is not good for us to be alone. God desires connection with us, and we desire connection with God and others. Prayer is the simplest and most intimate way in which we can connect to God. Because we are made in God's image and God is manifested in the Trinity as God the Father, the Holy Spirit, and Jesus Christ, one in three Persons, we too are most alive and most true to ourselves when we are in community. C. Baxter Kruger, trinitarian theologian (and fishing lure designer) wrote this:

A few years ago I asked my friend June (one of the women I call on Mother's Day every year, a devoted Christ-follower, a professor of psychology and a counselor). "June," I said, "can you put something in clinical terms for me?"

"Anything I can do," she said—already laughing.

"How do you say, 'when people hang out, they rub off on each other' in clinical speak?"

"It looks something like this: In the *natural* and normal course of human interaction, attitudes and behaviors are mutually modified at both a high and a low level of awareness."

That God seeks our friendship is astounding. It is indeed motivated by divine Love. It is our only hope of transformation on all levels.

—Wilson Parrish

God is not some faceless, all-powerful abstraction. God is Father, Son and Spirit, existing in a passionate and joyous fellowship. . . . The Trinity is a circle of shared life, and the life shared is full, not empty, abounding and rich and beautiful, not lonely and sad and boring. The river begins right there, in the fellowship of the Trinity.[1]

Psychologists and social scientists have conclusively observed that the emotional attachment of a healthy, loving parent with his or her child results in a healthy, loving child. When we are unable to attach for whatever reason, our mental health is unstable and our outlook on the world and on ourselves is skewed. God is perfectly whole and loving, and when we relate to God our lives begin to resonate with God's character and nature. When we pray with others, we become in tune to each other. In the Garden of Eden, God would walk and talk with Adam and Eve. They would visit each day. It was a completely natural and even ordinary relationship.

We are created to be in relationship with God and others, so we are always seeking stabilization with others. Our humanity is precisely this—that we are most human when we connect. God as our Creator is most able to provide a foundation of love and worth in the midst of life's challenges when we connect regularly to God. In the same way that we greet our loved ones each day, we greet God. In the same way we call and check in, we connect to God. With prayer we are bonded to our Maker and Sustainer.

Before the fall, prayer was not called "prayer." Adam and Eve walked and talked with God. They had conversation and time together. After the fall when our natural connection was broken, prayer became more occasional. The first mention of prayer after the fall is found in Genesis 4:26: "At that time people began to invoke the name of the Lord." People in the Old Testament *began* to pray after the fall. Throughout the Old Testament there are many forms of prayer—daily routine prayers, desperation prayers, guidance prayers, celebration prayers and petition prayers. The most basic of prayers are the prayers done together in community, often called "liturgical" or written prayers.

COMMUNITY PRAYER

Worship in the Old Testament tradition involved saying prayers aloud in community, especially using the Psalms. Deuteronomy 11:13 describes the nature of prayer for the Jewish people: "If you will only heed his every commandment that I am commanding you today—loving the LORD your God, and serving him with all your heart and with all your soul." To love and serve God with all your heart and soul meant to pray. It was called the *avodah sheba-lev*, service from the heart. The structure for prayer is called the *Shemoneh Esrie*, which consists of eighteen (later nineteen) blessings. The prayer structure contains the basics of prayer: praise, petition and thanksgiving.[2]

Prayer was a part of life experienced in worship and by praying three times a day. The prayers were a combination of written words that included Scripture verses and words that brought to remembrance God's character and promises and the people's covenantal response. Always there was a place for people to pray their own personal prayers during the recitation of the *Shemoneh Esrie*. Three times a day, morning, afternoon, and evening, Jewish people would stop to pray, men and women. There were extensive prayer versions and shorter ones to accommodate individuals' prayer time frames.

> The purposefulness of saying each word aloud, to God, stirred something I don't know how to describe. I love listening to God, but speaking to him doesn't come easily, and I don't know why. Praying a liturgy of psalms aloud makes a difference for me. I feel more connected in my prayer time. The repetition allows the meaning of the words to soak in. I stay focused rather than let my thoughts stray. I want to keep praying like this and see how my relationship with God grows through it.
>
> —Cheryl Flaim

It is not clear where the habit of praying three times a day originated. However, it probably corresponded with the temple sacrifices, which were offered three times a day, and it recognized the three patriarchs, Abraham, Isaac and Jacob. We also know that David and Daniel prayed three times a day. For us, it is clear that prayer is a regular way to connect with God and be reminded of God's grace and goodness. It is a time to adore God and bring our concerns to God, and also for God to love us and respond to us.

Prayers were said standing, kneeling, lying flat on the ground, sitting or raising hands. Prayers were said in the temple or in one's bedroom or by the roadside. Not many contemporary Christians have a habit of praying three times a day, but we can choose to have regular times to connect with God and others. Time, place and manner help create space for prayer. Another necessary element is *attentiveness* to God. Attentiveness is an awareness that we are in God's presence, and God is in ours. The Jewish people call it *kavanah*, a proper concentration or focus. Simply put, it is a sincere desire to enter God's presence. We give our attention to someone with whom we are talking. We focus on the person. In the same way, we focus on God.

> **I have always** enjoyed praying Scripture aloud to God. It helps me form pictures in my mind that I may have never been able to conjure given all of the noise in my head or trouble in my heart. This was an especially trying week for me emotionally, so it was wonderful to have a set, structured way to approach God with some very powerful words of praise to him. I worked over each word in my mind and heart as I read them aloud, trying to focus on him. This prayer was very powerful for me.
>
> —Michael Mahon

In the Jewish tradition, psalms are prayed aloud. The faithful stand as individuals together in worship and surrounded by all the faithful throughout time. There is a very present nature to prayer and also a timeless aspect. Those from the beginning and millions since David have prayed the psalms. And into the future, people will pray these prayers. Saying written prayers such as the psalms or prayers written by faithful men and women in the past has several advantages.

First, we become part of the great community of faithful from the Old Testament people to Jesus to today. We are not alone or isolated. We also become part of the community of faithful all around the world in every country and tongue. We might not understand their words, but when we say psalms together we are saying the same words for that day.

Second, we are challenged to pray things we might not normally pray. The psalms cover the full gamut of human experiences. Some we would rather avoid. Some psalms we love and others cause discomfort. By praying all the psalms we are stretched by God's Word and we allow God to teach us and shape us. Many of the psalms shift from lament to praise. We are invited to experience all the emotions and challenges of our humanity such as betrayal, illness, confession, anger, pleading and thanksgiving. Praying prayers written by the faithful connects us to God and each other.

COMMUNITY PRAYER GUIDELINES

- The term *community prayer* is also referred to as "liturgical" prayer. Liturgical prayers are written prayers used by a community of believers to connect together to God.

- The phrase *liturgical prayers* can suggest to people staleness and ritualism without faith. However, praying authentically in this manner is personal and full of meaning. These prayers require a sincere desire to enter into God's presence together.

- The psalms, prayers written by saints or prayers written for special occasions by participants are all possible forms of liturgical prayers. They invite us into common human experiences.

- Liturgical prayers are often assigned to specific days of the year with Scripture verses and sometimes meditations.

- These prayers can be said privately, but the backdrop is people everywhere using the same prayers to come together with God. The point is to experience God together. The purpose is to remember God throughout our days.

- All aspects of our life are brought to God, and the prayers remind us of God's sovereignty and goodness. The psalms and written prayers protect us from hyper-individualism, which can create God in our own image.

- Community prayers are prayers of trust that God is good, present and yearns to be with us.

- Community prayers are especially helpful when one is struggling with despair, ill health or difficult circumstances. The community of the faithful surrounds us.

COMMUNITY PRAYER EXPERIENCE

Group Experience

- In the Talmud it reads, "Whoever recites Psalm 145 three times a day is assured of a place in the time to come." This doesn't mean that saying the psalm saves us, but that the words are so powerful they remind us over and over about the true character of God, and thus we are changed.

- Instructions: The group leader prepares a handout with the *Shema* and Psalm 145 printed out so everyone has a copy. Explain the prayer before experiencing it.

- Everyone stands with feet together facing in the same direction. (If you desire, you can face toward Jerusalem to remember the land and place where God led the chosen and where Jesus came in the flesh.)

- Begin by reciting together the *Shema* (a central prayer for the Jews and a declaration of faith in one God). A partial version is below (Deut 6:4-9).

Sh'ma Yisrael	Hear, O, Israel
Adonai Elohaynu	Adonai is our God
Adonai Echad	Adonai is one
Baruch Shem	Holy One of Blessing
Kavod malchuto	Your Presence radiates glory
l'olam va-ed	now and forever

- Move to the *Amidah*—the experience of standing and praying together in community when we are seeking God. We each seek a special place to experience our
  own "burning bush." During this part of the prayer, speak the psalm out loud but
  to yourself. We each audibly say the psalm at our own pace. We enter into the
  experience as individuals but with others saying the same verses at their own
  pace. The pray-er can take three steps forward and bow, signifying respect for
  Almighty God. Upon conclusion of each reading of Psalm 145, the pray-er takes
  three steps back. When ready, move forward again three steps and repeat the
  process until you have said Psalm 145 three times. The experience is over when
  everyone has finished and a designated leader says, "Amen."

- After the prayer discuss in small groups about the prayer time. What was meaningful?
  What was difficult? How did you experience God and the others who were praying?
  What aspects of community prayer might enhance your personal prayer life?

Partner Experience

- For Jewish people each day of the week has a particular psalm: Sunday is Psalm
  24, Monday Psalm 48, Tuesday Psalm 82, Wednesday Psalm 94, Thursday Psalm
  81, Friday Psalm 93 and Saturday Psalm 92. Start by using these psalms. If you
  want to continue for subsequent weeks you can choose your own psalms to pray,
  or you may begin with Psalm 1 and complete one each day, or follow the psalms
  in the daily lectionary.

- Stand and say the psalm aloud three times (unless you have chosen one of the
  longer psalms, then adjust which sections you plan to read aloud). If you would
  like, take three steps forward at the beginning of the psalm, and three steps back
  at the end of each psalm as preparation for entering God's presence.

- Plan to meet with your prayer partner as many days of the week as you can to
  pray the psalm for the day together. If you cannot meet physically, pray the psalm
  together on the phone or Skype or with an electronic device that allows for a
  face-to-face encounter.

- Remember these psalms were prayed by Jesus and in worship together with his
  disciples. Discuss your experience together. Did any words or phrases resonate

with you? Did anything cause you confusion? Sometimes God speaks to us in the quiet and sometimes in the questions.

Individual Experience

- Pray the psalm for the day by yourself and aloud following the same pattern of standing, taking three steps forward and then back at the end of the psalms as explained in the group experience above. Journal about your experience. What drew you to God today or helped you with your spiritual walk?

- You may also use the Book of Common Prayer and follow the prayers for the day. There are many wonderful books with daily prayers and Scripture, such as *Common Prayer: A Liturgy for Ordinary Radicals* and *Celtic Daily Prayer.* A suggested list is found at the end of the chapter.

- If you like the idea of praying with others but are unable to, you may find a prayer place online, such as missionstclare.com, which has a recorded choir and music for hymns. Sacredspace.ie is an online site that guides you through small prayers, questions and meditations. Many others such as Christian-prayers.com and prayergroup.org respond to your prayer requests and allow you to pray with persons around the world. Pray-as-you-go.org allows you to download daily prayers.

THE PRAYER JOURNEY

Mark Franklin

When you pray, you are never alone. These simple words at the end of the daily prayers on *sacredspace.ie* launched me on a new perspective on prayer. The totally obvious yet mind-shattering revelation that other people, perhaps a great number of people, were concurrently participating in prayer with me shook me out of my fixed view of prayer. It is not, after all, between me and God—it is between me and God and everyone else in the world who is praying. I am humbled because I am now unable to pray without re-membering I am but one of a vast multitude before the throne of God. I am encouraged for exactly the same reason.

Experiencing prayer in this way made my daily experiences less frustrating; it mattered less if I felt the presence of God in the way I thought I "should" during prayer. Instead, I felt the power of the community of believers. As time went on God used conversation with others to teach me that I truly participate in the communion of all the saints when I pray. God has been teaching me that when I am speaking to him, I am speaking in concert with everyone who ever cried out to God throughout history. I was experiencing God in a new and bigger way.

As I prayed in the shadow of all the saints, I began to experience what I will call unintentional prayer. Whenever I gathered with my brothers and sisters in Christ, I found myself praying. Not aloud, not as some kind of ritual, but as an internal reflex. My thoughts took on a quality of speaking to God, rather than to myself. The most shocking change was that I listened for a response from God in the voices of my brothers and sisters—and found it. God really was speaking through his people, and he had given me eyes to see it. I was again forced to re-evaluate what prayer was. I had already discarded the idea that prayer was just between me and God. Now I found myself questioning if prayer is communication in the way I thought of it. If my internal voice is becoming prayerful by God's grace, is prayer communication—or transformation? The frustrations of my prayer life faded in the wonder at God's transformational ability. He had made prayer an experience of community beyond any I had before and transformed an internal part of me where I hid sinful attitudes like envy and anger—using one line on a prayer website from Ireland.

Rick Adams

One August I heard a rabbi teaching that if we would promise God that we would do something at the same time every day for the rest of our life, it would change us. I once more began a process I hoped would bring about a change in me for the better. I read that a pious Jew would read Psalms 145–150 every day before prayer, just to get into the right attitude. I promised the Lord that this is what I would do every day at 5:00 a.m. for the rest of my life. Of course I have started these kinds of projects before only to find that I couldn't fast one day, certainly not forty days.

The first three weeks were difficult. I started writing down prayers for people and reading these after I finished my psalm ritual. This was great because it kept me from praying for the things I wanted. As my list grew longer I found more and more people and their situations coming to my mind instead of my usual financial fears about the future.

After a couple of months I noticed a kind of satisfaction developing in me. I eventually recognized this as pride that I was following through with my promise. One morning I felt like God just wanted me to be still. This was a real issue because I had my routine and I kept track of my consecutive mornings, and I was now in the seventies. I felt like God was asking me if my routine was the main reason why I was getting up or if it was just to be with God. Sheepishly and reluctantly, I did not turn on my laptop. I sat still for about ninety minutes. I had no revelation and I did not hear God say anything, but I felt like I had a personal breakthrough.

My mornings have become precious to me, despite no breakthroughs and some prayers not answered. Mostly I do my routine, but every now and then I will feel like I am just supposed to be still or read Scripture. I wait expectantly, not knowing exactly what I am waiting or hoping for, but nonetheless happy that I am waiting.

I have learned that it is quite all right to use my lists, read, pace or lie across the ottoman downstairs, as long as I don't come to believe that any one or combination of these things is somehow necessary.

I don't see any changes in myself, but my wife says I have changed dramatically. She says I am more relaxed, easygoing and attentive. All I know for sure is that when the alarm goes off at five I get up with expectancy, as though a friend is waiting for me. Speaking of a friend, my everyday prayer used to be for godly wisdom, discernment and understanding. I would finish my praying by telling God when I die it would be great to hear God say, "Well done, good and faithful servant." Now the desire of my heart is that when I breathe my last, I so much want to hear God say, "Welcome home, old friend."

FURTHER READING

Claiborne, Shane, Jonathan Wilson-Hargrove and Enuma Okoro. *Common Prayer: A Liturgy for Ordinary Radicals.* Grand Rapids: Zondervan, 2010.

Peterson, Eugene. *Praying with the Psalms: A Year of Daily Reflections and Prayers on the Words of David.* New York: HarperCollins, 1993.

The Northumbria Community. *Celtic Daily Prayer: Prayers and Readings from the Northumbria Community.* New York: HarperSanFrancisco, 2002.

Tickle, Phyllis, compiler. *The Divine Hours,* pocket edition. New York: Oxford University Press, 2007.

2

Creative Prayer

God, our Creator, has stored within our minds and personalities,
great potential strength and ability.
Prayer helps us tap and develop these powers.

<small>Abdul Kalam, Indian statesman</small>

In the beginning when God created the heavens and the earth,
the earth was a formless void and darkness covered the face of the deep,
while a wind from God swept over the face of the waters.
Then God said, "Let there be light"; and there was light.
And God saw that the light was good;
and God separated the light from the darkness.

<small>Genesis 1:1-4</small>

GOD AS CREATOR

The world and universe are an extraordinary reflection of the creativity and diversity of our Creator. Who can fathom the number of stars in the heavens? Who can name the hidden creatures in the deepest oceans? How do we comprehend the complexity, beauty and terror of life in the dark jungles? Who can stand on the highest icy peaks and embrace the majesty of God? God created an amazing universe.

In Genesis God is the creator of all things. God made all things out of nothing, and it was good. Then God made us in God's image, and it was good. By inference we connect with God when we are creative, and it is good. Because we are made in the image of God, one of our primary drives is the desire and the ability to create. Many of us believe that being creative or "artistic" is a special gift, something you either have or don't have. Often we get the unwritten message that our creative efforts are okay for display on the home refrigerator but not for display in an art gallery. We often see creativity as a profession rather than as an expression of being fully human.

As we grow, this message becomes even more ingrained. A grade school teacher once wrote on Walt Disney's report card, "Walt has no imagination." Walt obviously ignored this assessment of his gifts. However, many of us accept such messages and do little to stretch our creative potential or use creativity as a means of prayer. This is tragic and has unintended consequences for our spiritual lives.

Without creativity we can develop a fixed pattern of responding and thinking in a formulaic manner. The brain learns through patterns of repeating messages established with neuron connections over and over. When we learn to read we recognize an *A* by seeing it over and over. When we become proficient, we recognize the *A* in a variety of fonts and styles, but in the beginning the letters are simple and large. Creativity allows us to imagine many other possibilities. The *A* can be different colors, shapes and styles. Without creativity, rigid behaviors and thoughts become deeply enforced, and we miss the movement and mystery of God.

Some established patterns are necessary because from them we learn control and we live by our values. Just because sex on a first date is the norm in the media does not mean that it is the way we choose to behave in our relational lives. Over and over the value for the sanctity of intimacy in a committed relationship overrides the prevalent messages of our culture. Therefore, having deeply ingrained ways of responding and knowing is imperative to becoming Christlike.

On the other hand, sometimes deeply ingrained responses and ideas keep us from exploring and knowing the fullness of God and the depth of ourselves. As social and medical researchers have affirmed, doing new things stimulates the brain and opens us up to possibilities. Peter Steinke, a Lutheran pastor, author and church consultant, wrote, "A recent study indicated that children who are unimaginative are more likely to act violently than imaginative children. The unimaginative cannot imagine alternatives."[1]

By being creative we connect to God in new ways outside of the more controlled and structured part of our brains. As we get older we are less and less able to think creatively, not because we don't have the capacity, but because our environments often limit our options. A child is an open book, but an adult is less open. Many things are already figured out. We are less likely to entertain new ideas even if from God. Creative prayer gives us the opportunity to animate God's presence in us. By being creative we allow God to open up areas of our lives that are not controlled and managed.

Being creative simply means that we make something that wasn't there before, whether it's a watercolor, a poem, a tray of cookies or a refurbished car. Each creative expression is unique to its creator. To create means to bring into existence, and the goodness of that act blesses the one creating and others. Creativity is not about the outcome but the process, the experience of creation. Often when we are creating

Crayoned curves.
Stillness held
above
counter-curved chaos.
The wonder that
even here he speaks
through fumbling fingers
and fear of failure.
This too, so surprisingly, is prayer!

—Margaret Duggan

we experience what is called "flow," a mental state of complete immersion and focused energy.[2]

Creativity taps into our deepest inner emotions and thoughts. Ronald Rolheiser writes, "Creativity is not in the end about public recognition or outstanding achievement. It's about self-expression, about nurturing something into life, and about the satisfaction this brings with it."[3]

CREATIVE PRAYER

Creativity is one of the highest forms of prayer, and yet there is no quality standard to its expression. It simply connects us to one of God's primary impulses—to create good things. Not because the thing is beautiful or perfect—thus the armadillo or the squid—but because the thing reflects something of the nature and imagination of God and thus draws us to God. Creative prayer is giving God access to areas of our inner life often neglected. Being creative connects us with our essence and with God's nature.

Creative prayer requires solitude. In the same way that God created out of the deep silence of a formless and void environment, the creative act requires solitude of the heart. Sometimes we begin with a physical isolation, but in the end we can find solitude wherever we are when we transition into a creative place. Solitude requires that we get rid of the scaffolding we often use to prop up our lives. Constant connection equals constant distraction. In solitude there are no friends to talk to, no meetings and no internet access. An actor in the middle of a performance does not stop to text his friends. Henri Nouwen wrote, "Solitude is the place of the great struggle and the great encounter—the struggle against the compulsions of the false self, and the encounter with the loving God who offers himself as the substance of the

Creative prayer was a more multisensory approach to prayer, breaking my thought that only verbal words could be prayer. While drawing and listening to God, I was so attentive to catch something from God and find something on the white paper that my hand attempted to pursue the track of God's voice. It was not easy to create something, which belongs to God's area, but I realized that to create is also our calling to work with him. He loves to leave some places on the earth empty, expecting us to fill the places with our creativity because he really enjoys the creatures made by us.

—Sang Hee Moon

new self."[4] We can't be busy and create. We have to be present.

Solitude gives us "negative space." In art negative space is the place where there is nothing, no color or line. In Japan the word is *ma*, meaning pause or gap. Arthur Schnabel, an Austrian classical pianist, once said, "The notes I handle no better than many pianists. But the pauses between the notes—ah, that is where the art resides!" Therefore, creative prayer needs space in both time where there are no distractions and place where there is no intrusion. The result of solitude is compassion.

Creative prayer is a very sensory experience engaging our sight, touch, sound, smell and sometimes taste. Our physical

In preparation for Thanksgiving, I decided to bake as my creative prayer. As I got supplies out of the cupboard, I sensed a deep connection with God. With each ingredient, I could see the blessings of God being poured over all the people who would eat it. As I stirred and mixed, I could see God permeating and becoming an inseparable part of each person. As I cut and shaped, the thought of God covering each one with protection, love, grace and mercy was very visible. As the food baked, I thought of each person being refined as gold in fire. Throughout this very special time, though my apron was wet with tears, my heart was glad.

—Brenda Burg

I am a person who measures my worth by my performance. When I first experienced solitude in prayer something began to change in me. It was the most wonderful feeling of coming home. There was something so complete in "just being" before God without expectation of anything from him or from me. I began to feel an acceptance of who I am by the great I AM just because he created me to be. It was like the negative space in art: no one really looks at it or even realizes it is there, but art cannot exist without it. It was like the shadows in painting that define the light. It has been the beginning of new understanding for me of the silent part of God.

—Sandy Bass

bodies and the physical world connect with our interior world and with God in a way that very few other activities do. The only ingredient is you, fully engaged with any type of activity that evokes creative reflection. If drawing stick figures is creative for you, then draw stick figures. If planting a flower garden or writing a song or doing photography is your avenue of creative expression, then do that. You might also choose to try something new—cooking Indian food, doing watercolors, building a deck—which will take you into new sensory areas and create new pathways and expressions of experiencing God.

CREATIVE PRAYER GUIDELINES

- The simple elements of creative prayer are a creative activity you enjoy and a focus on God as a partner with you in the creating experience.

- Creative prayer connects us with God as our Creator. We are reminded of the mystery, complexity and beauty of God who made us to create. Our identity and God's are expressed in creating.

- Creative prayer is not just creating something. It is a combination of creation and conversation with God. The conversation might be active or an attentive silence.

- Everyone creates differently, though we are all creative. Therefore, it might take some experimentation to find the creative experience that absorbs you and draws you to God.

- There is no expectation of gain either of profit or praise when one engages in creative prayer. The point is to be with the Creator.

- Creative prayer usually needs enough time and solitude to distance us from our busyness and other distractions. Extroverts often enjoy creative prayer in community.

- Journaling or sharing your experience with others helps harvest the creative prayer experience for all its spiritual possibilities.

CREATIVE PRAYER EXPERIENCE

Group Experience

- For a simple creative prayer experience for a group, gather materials such as blank paper, paints, crayons, clay, beads, scissors, glue and magazines. When I lead people in creative prayer, I pass out blank sheets of paper and a few crayons to each person.

- It is often helpful with a group to have some instrumental, meditative or worship music in the background to mask the sounds of others creating.

- Explain that the creative expression can be whatever the person imagines in prayer—from simple figures to drawings to abstract features to words and lines.

- The leader can use a question to help guide individuals in the experience, such as, "Where is God most present in you at this time?" "What is your desire for God at this time?" or "What are the blocks in your spiritual life?"

- Another idea is to use an event such as a community or national concern or an event in the Christian calendar to pray to God with some other medium besides spoken words.

- To begin, the leader says a brief prayer such as, "God, our Father and Creator, we are listening." Instruct the group not to talk during the creative prayer experience.

- Allow at least thirty minutes for the prayer experience.

- At the end of the time the leader says a simple closing prayer such as, "God, thank you for making us creative and for being present with us."

- Have everyone get into small groups of two to four and share their experience and their finished piece. How was God present for you? Did you learn anything about yourself? Do you have any questions?

- Close with a simple prayer of thanks.

Partner Experience

- With your prayer partner, agree to do a creative project together. It can be anything from gardening, sewing, taking a walk with a camera, grooming a pet or building a bookcase. You could also learn something new together.

- Give yourselves at least an hour to be together with the project.

- Begin with silence and a simple prayer that you might listen to God.

- Try not to talk during the creative prayer time.

- When the allotted time is over, share with each other about your experience and pray for each other. How did the experience draw you or not draw you to God? Were you able to focus and experience the flow of God? How might you bring creative prayer into enriching your relationship together?

Individual Experience

- Decide what creative prayer project you might like to do. This can be something completely new and different that will stretch you, or you can do some creative activity you are used to doing.

- Decide how much time you will devote to this, whether fifteen to thirty minutes or one to two hours.

- Begin with silence to instill a reflective God-focused spirit in you. If you get completely immersed in the project and forget to think about God as part of it, don't worry. Simply come back to God's presence with you.

- At the end of the time, journal on your experience. Is this a form of prayer that might feed your soul? Did you feel close to God? Were there any blocks? How did you experience God?

THE PRAYER JOURNEY

Dominic Passarelli

I drew pictures for my prayer experience. It was amazing. I should back up. I have had negative experiences with "creative" prayer and worship. I work with a college ministry in Eugene, OR, and every time our students request a night of "creative" worship it ends up like a religious talent show or spiritual show-and-tell. Thus going into this prayer experience, I was apprehensive. When we were given our task of drawing a picture expressing our prayer for some students I had never met (a student was killed and several were injured in a car crash), I was uneasy. I've hated drawing and painting since before kindergarten. I do not express myself that way, especially to God.

But then I picked up the crayons.

What ended up on the paper was a scribbly, scrawly mess, but what ended up happening in me was a reflection that even in the darkest and most lifeless of times, God's light and life are breaking out. The darkness has not overcome. My paper was a prayer.

This past week was incredibly busy and hectic with lots of classwork and familial obligations. When I had a moment to read the Bible, reflections didn't come in neat, tidy journal entries but in scribbly, scrawly images. Something opened up for me and it's pretty exciting. I have a new way of communion with God.

Brad Rohr

I chose to cook for my creative prayer. I wasn't taking creative prayer very seriously because I dislike right-brain activities, but I actually had a profound moment with God. As I was sautéing some bell peppers in butter, I began thinking how death must occur for almost anything to happen in life. We must consume calories in order to live; a tree must die in order for a forest fire to sustain itself; a snake must die in order for an eagle to live. I know these thoughts sound pretty morbid, but I was focusing more on what takes place after death: resurrection

into something new. I realized how the bell peppers had to die in order for me to do something creative and how there are things within me that need to die in order for God's character to be resurrected within me.

So I asked myself, "What needs to die?" After I ate the food I prepared, I sat down with a pen and piece of paper to write out some thoughts. I realized how much I have grown over the past eight months and how many bad habits and patterns of thinking have come back with the busy season leading up to Easter. I need to reclaim a right view of who I am in Christ and an identity that is defined by who I am rather than what I do. This has given me a lot to think about, and I pray that God resurrects these things within me.

FURTHER READING

Henderson, Daniel. *Prayzing: Creative Prayer Experiences from A to Z.* Colorado Springs: NavPress, 2007.

Kincannon, Karla M. *Creativity and Divine Surprise: Finding the Place of Your Resurrection.* Nashville: Upper Room, 2005.

MacBeth, Sybil. *Praying in Color: Drawing a New Path to God.* Brewster, MA: Paraclete, 2007.

Sullivan, Michael. *Windows into the Soul: Art as Spiritual Expression.* New York: Morehouse, 2006.

3

Work Prayer

Men invent means and methods of coming at God's love,
they learn rules and set up devices to remind them of that love,
and it seems like a world of trouble to bring oneself into the
consciousness of God's presence. Yet it might be so simple.
Is it not quicker and easier just to do our common business
wholly for the love of him?

BROTHER LAWRENCE

The LORD God took the man and put him in
the garden of Eden to till it and keep it.

GENESIS 2:15

GOD AS ACTIVE

Humanity is bound together in our work. We get up each day, dress, hopefully eat breakfast and head out for our places of work or study, or begin our work in our homes. We are all one in this daily ritual of survival and meaning, and God is reflected in work. The creation narrative refers to God as "working." God's occupation was to create a good and loving world: "And on the seventh day God finished the work that he had done, and he rested on the seventh day from all the work that he had done" (Gen 2:2). We are made in God's image. We are people who thrive on community, people who create, and now people who make a contribution. We are people who work.

God did not create us and then leave. We see throughout Scripture that God is an active and engaged God. Throughout time and place God interacts and shapes the present and the future of people's lives. God created us and then blessed us. God's first act of grace toward us was a blessing. Blessing means that God gave humanity power. God recognized as good our capacities. God endorsed them. "God blessed them, and God said to them, 'Be fruitful and multiply, and fill the earth and subdue it; and have dominion over the fish of the sea and over the birds of the air and over every living thing that moves upon the earth'" (Gen 1:28).

Blessing can also mean that we are consecrated. We are set aside for holy purposes. God created us for relationship but also for partnership in the kingdom work God intended for this complex and beautiful world. The value of work is clarified by the very first command that God gives us. The command is not to bring people to God, but to be fruitful and multiply and have dominion over the creatures of the earth.

God commands us to be fruitful, to bear children, tend gardens and enhance the wonder of our world. We are to multiply and fill up the earth with good things. The double command to "have dominion" and "rule over" doesn't mean that we are to be the users and masters but that we have the power to be the caretakers, the stewards. God cares for us, and we in turn care for God's world. The picture of the Garden of Eden is one of bounty and beauty. In the same way, our "work" is to care for the earth and others, especially those who have little or no influence, such as children, the poor, the lonely, the afflicted and the sick.

God intended us to work. Work isn't the result of the fall. Work is part of the fabric of creation. The "betrayal of work" is the consequence of the fall.[2] The fact that work environments are sometimes oppressive, bosses and coworkers sometimes untrustworthy, institutions sometimes greedy, and workers sometimes undervalued and underpaid, is the consequence of sin. God created work and can redeem it in our lives. Beth Shulman, in her book *The Betrayal of Work,* tells this story about Cynthia:

> In our Cherokee beliefs we are taught that we are not above the rest of creation but simply part of the sacred circle of all created life. That said, our role is significant because we are the ones who have been given the responsibility by the Creator to keep the balance or harmony in creation. Each part of creation has a role to play. One of our jobs is to protect creation from abuse, i.e., overuse and depletion of resources.
>
> —Randy Woodley[1]

And yet, despite the frustration and the difficult conditions, Cynthia beams when she talks about her job. "I like helping people," she says. "I like talking with them, and shampooing their hair. I like old people. If they are down, I can really make them feel better. The patients say, 'Nobody loves me or comes to see me.' Sometimes I help the residents play dominos. Sometimes their hands shake but I hold them. It's a lot of fun for them. I tell them 'I love you' and give them a hug. I like being a CNA. I'm doing what I want to be doing."[3]

WORK PRAYER

Work is another way in which we experience the presence of God. When we bring prayer into our work we uncover other possibilities for being shaped and influenced by God. Work occupies a large portion of our waking lives even more so today. An average middle-income couple works seven weeks longer each year than they did just ten years ago.[4]

With work taking more energy and focus from people's lives and with a stressed economy, work becomes a survival environment that begs for the influencing presence of God. By bringing prayer into our work environments, whether we are students, homemakers, store clerks, bank presidents, gallery owners, farmers or manufacturers, God is walking and talking with us at work. God is part of our ordinary lives, not just when we are having devotional times. God is not just in the sacred spaces of worship, confession and holiness, but in the secular spaces of sweat, energy and productivity. Whatever we are doing, it can be bathed in prayer.

Because work requires our attention, bringing God into our work also requires finding ways to pay attention. Leighton Ford, in his book *The Attentive Life*, writes this:

> From the time we were children we were told to "pay attention," as if this were the simplest thing in the world. But in fact attentiveness is one of the most difficult concepts to grasp and one of the hardest disciplines to learn. For we are very distractible people in a very distracting world.[5]

Our perception of God's availability and capability comes through finding ways to pay attention to God in our work environments.

We don't intend to put God in our back pockets, but we inadvertently do when we become overly focused on work. The result is that we compartmentalize our spiritual lives. If we do think about bringing God to work, it's usually when we think we should witness about God to someone. We do need to witness, yet the greatest witness to God is a

> **I visited a friend** who ran a store and noticed that some of his stuff had stayed there for a long time without being bought. I decided to do something. I took a cleaning mop, looked at the spot where these goods had sat and said, "Lord, I am cleaning this portion for you to come and sit here (so I put a chair there) and be my friend today in this store." Immediately after cleaning there came a few people who went straight to where these goods were. At first I did not know the consequences of my little act. An hour or so after, I looked at the spot and a chill ran down me—all the stuff had been bought! I broke into tears. Is it not true that God really is found in the ordinary life?
>
> —Meshak Mwangi

person who is reflecting God's character and love. Therefore, praying in our workplaces connects us to God and helps us pay attention.

Paying attention also enlarges God's role in our lives. God is more than a "miracle worker" who we call on when the going gets tough. God designed us for significance, and the strange spiritual reality is that significance usually comes with attentiveness to God in the ordinary rather than the execution of something extraordinary. Dr. Simon Chan, a theologian in Singapore, explains it this way:

> Today's world is increasingly defined by the market economy. Thus work has become one of the most significant activities people pursue. In prayer, work loses its self-serving character and aims at serving God; *ad maiorem Dei gloriam* (to the greater glory of God). When we pray, we no longer see work solely in terms of profit and productivity; we begin to see it in terms of its ultimate intention in creation—to further the blessings of creation and counter the effects of wickedness. This view of work can only be achieved through prayer, which opens our vision to the interconnectedness of all things to God.[6]

WORK PRAYER GUIDELINES

- In the same way that we pray for someone's health, finances, children or the souls of others, we can also pray for our work. Work prayers bring God's blessing into the work environment.

- Work prayers are prayers for the people, the decisions, the customers, the products and the meetings. Yes, especially the meetings.

- Work prayers invite us to become attentive stewards of the things God has placed in our hands to do.

- These prayers are best if they are simple and ordinary. Small, short requests for blessing, help or guidance remind us that God is near. Here are three ways to pray:

  - *Daily habits of work prayer*: Establish a pattern for arriving at work and spending five to ten minutes in prayer before the day begins. Pray for the day and the people and the work in the day. These are simple prayers. If this is not possible, use five to ten minutes of your lunch time or break time. At the end of the day, take five to ten minutes to give to God all that happened during the day.

  - *Create a work prayer group or find a prayer partner*: Bring together one to three other people to meet weekly for ten to fifteen minutes only to pray for work. Again pray for the company or place, its decisions, its challenges, its meetings and the dear people who work there. Focus on work rather than personal needs.

- *Walking work prayer*: Wherever you go through your work day, walk and pray with God. "Lord, I'm going into a budget meeting. Guide us." "Lord, I'm walking this tool over to Joe, bless him." "Lord, I'm going to lunch with Amy, feed us." "Lord, I'm washing clothes, cleanse us."

- Work prayer is a prayer closet experience. We don't announce it or report on it. We simply become intentional and mindful that in this place God too wants to bless, shape, influence and guide us.

WORK PRAYER EXPERIENCE

Group Experience

- If you are a student group, men's or women's group, or an adult Bible study or spiritual formation group, decide together that you will each pray in your work environments five to ten minutes a day for four days one week.

- If you are a homemaker, then you will be praying for the home and those in the home. If you are a student, you will be praying for the teachers, students, learning processes and school needs. If you are retired, pray for a business in your town that is important to the town's economy. You can go to a large store or mall and walk around and pray for the employees and leaders or walk up and down your local downtown praying for the businesses and people. If you are self-employed, pray for your own business. Of course, if you are employed and going to work each day, you can pray in your workplace. These are closet prayers, prayers said silently and privately.

- Another option is to go together as a group to a place of business such as a shopping mall, business complex, social service and court buildings, or hospital. You can walk around individually praying and then meet together after fifteen to thirty minutes to share about your experience.

- A suggested prayer format is

  - *Blessing*: Begin by praying short prayers of blessings: "Lord, bless this business and the people who work here."

  - *Guidance*: Next pray short reminder prayers that the company or work place might be good stewards of God's creation and might contribute to improving the lives and environments around them. "Lord God, guide this X to care for its employees and the environment."

  - *Requests*: Then pray short petition prayers for any particular challenges the workplace might face. "Lord God, our school needs new equipment." "Lord, this home needs your peace." "Lord, help this company get financially stable."

  - *Personal requests*: Finally, pray for yourself in the workplace. "Lord, help me to be a blessing and a light in this place. Teach me how to reflect you."

- *Thanks*: Conclude by thanking God for work, blessings and provision.
- If you don't go as a group to one place, keep a short journal or notes and reflections on your personal work prayer experience. The next time you are together as a group, share about your experience. Do you have questions or insights? How did you experience God? What did you learn about prayer and work?

Partner Experience

- With your prayer partner, decide whether you want to pray individually at your places of work or pray together in a work environment.
- Pray together out loud following the pattern described in the group experience section. If you wish to walk together and pray silently, that also is effective. Spend time at the end of the week, reflecting on your experience.

Individual Experience

- Whether you are retired or a student or a working person, choose the work environment that fits your situation.
- Spend at least four days one week praying for that work environment while you are there. If you can, spend five to ten minutes at the beginning of the day or a few minutes two to three times a day, praying blessings, reminder prayers and specific petitions for the work and for yourself as a worker.
- Take notes or keep a journal on your experience. Reflect on the place of prayer in your work. How did you experience work differently because of prayer? What were the outcomes of paying attention to God in your work?

PRAYER JOURNEY

Alicia Wheelock

I've had my own business as an esthetician for over twenty years. I go to people's homes primarily to do manicures, pedicures and facials. Since I was young, I liked to make people beautiful. I started in Nicaragua doing people's nails. When I came to America I worked hard and studied to get my license. I started in salons and then began my own business. I wanted to help people feel good about themselves by beautifying their hair and feet and nails.

Many people can't get to a salon because they are older or not well. I like going to their homes. I've helped families with special occasions like weddings. Sometimes after a client has passed away, the family will thank me for bringing joy into their loved one's life. I've been a Christian for many years and connecting my faith with my work matters to me. God touched me when he changed my life. Now I'm changing people's lives by touching their hands and feet. Something about a touch brings healing.

Before I go to a client's house, I pray. I ask God to bless and prepare my hands. I work with older clients who often have illnesses, so I ask God to use my hands to bring comfort and release from their pain. Some of my clients I've had for many, many years. Sometimes I arrive at a client's house and they want to cancel. They say they don't feel well; they are in a bad mood. I ask them what's going on? Many times they say they don't feel good, so I ask permission to massage their shoulders and then I pray silently for them. I encourage them to talk. I put hand warmers on their back to help them feel relaxed. By the time I leave they say, "I feel so much better. I was cranky, but now I feel good again." I believe my work is my ministry, my way to give back to God for what God has done for me. I love helping people feel better. I love the beauty of God's touch.

Jason Quiring

After an amazingly wet winter, the roads turned complete mud. One of the things we do during the winter is haul hundreds of loads of grain from our farm to the place we sell it. So that means hundreds of trips in our semis on mud roads—resulting in about two thousand pounds of gravel and dirt stuck up under the trailer and tractor.

It was my job to crawl under and up into the rigs to power wash the mud off. Much of it was so solidly caked on that it took repeated soaking and blasting to get it off. It was one of the messiest things I've ever done. Drenched, covered with rocks and mud, the thought that this could be my prayer time almost made me laugh. I started to talk—and listen— to God about how he cleans us. Not just the shiny outer parts, but the disgusting inner parts that most people just skip. It sounds a bit cliché now that I'm warm, clean, dry and in the comfort of my home, but as mud, rocks, steam and road grime were flying all over me, I was struck about the cost and effort this cleaning process means for God. He's covered with our grime. It has to be humiliating.

Thank you, God, for loving me enough to cover yourself with my mess. Help me to never take it for granted. God, I don't want to keep caking myself with grime and then flippantly expecting you to rush in and "do your thing." I love you and thank you!

Jane VanderPloeg

In 2005 our small communications company successfully won a one-million-dollar federal contract to supply the USA Air Force with noise-canceling headsets. Then in 2008 we tried again, at great up-front expense, to get another federal contract for $800,000. Because of personnel transitions in government offices, the headset order wasn't moving forward. Finally, the money was released for purchasing headsets, but to each Air Force base instead of a centralized purchase with our company. Because we didn't have the capacity to have sales people in touch with each purchasing agent at the different Air Force bases, most of the orders went to a competitor in a matter of days.

Many conversations and meetings were taking place, but on the side a small group of us began praying. Initially two employees were praying. They were like watchmen, observant and proactive. They targeted that product and asked God for the sales to come in some other way and to direct traffic to our website. Then we, as owners, joined them in that specific prayer. We didn't say anything to anyone about it. We just prayed. To our delight, new customers, including international ones, started to order the headsets from our website in unusually large numbers. By December 2009, more than the budgeted revenue amounts had been supplied through customers directed to our website! The following years, more sets of large orders came in, unsolicited. Our sales team couldn't figure it out, but those of us that prayed knew.

FURTHER READING

Beckett, John D. *Mastering Monday: A Guide to Integrating Faith and Work.* Downers Grove, IL: InterVarsity Press, 2006.

Copeland, Germaine. *Prayers That Avail Much for the Workplace: The Business Handbook of Scriptural Prayer.* Tulsa, OK: Harrison House, 2001.

Thompson, William. *On-the-Job Prayers.* Chicago: ACTA Publications, 2006.

4

Contemplative-Rest Prayer

Peace is a deep disposition of the heart.
It is an ability to let go of the need to be right, an ability based on
the knowledge that our rightness or wrongness in any issue is
totally irrelevant to God's love for us or for our neighbor.

ROBERTI BONDI

In Centering Prayer we go beyond thought and image,
beyond the senses and the rational mind, to that center of our being
where God is working a wonderful work. There God our Father
is not only bringing us forth in his creative love . . .
he is indeed making us sons and daughters.

BASIL PENNINGTON

GOD AS REST

After our work, we rest—on our porches, around meals with friends, watching sports, walking our pets and ultimately in our beds. We need rest. We physically have difficulty functioning when we lack sleep. We are grumpy, make bad decisions and have more accidents. God designed us for rest. In Genesis 1 and 2, there emerges yet another picture of the core nature of God. *God also rests.* The rhythm between work and rest is established from the very beginning. As people made in the image of God, we too are most human in community, when we create, when we work and *when we rest.* The balance of resting and working is fundamental to our well-being.

God rested on the seventh day. God worked and then stepped back from the work and rested. God enjoyed the fruit of labor by creating space for non-doing. This rest was so essential to God's design, that as God himself rested (Gen 2:1-3), he also gave his people a commandment to rest.[1]

> Remember the sabbath day, and keep it holy. Six days you shall labor and do all your work. But the seventh day is a sabbath to the LORD your God; you shall not do any work—you, your son or your daughter, your male or female slave, your livestock, or the alien resident in your towns. For in six days the LORD made heaven and earth, the sea, and all that is in them, but *rested* the seventh day; therefore the LORD blessed the sabbath day and consecrated it. (Ex 20:8-11)

One of humanity's great temptations is to equate our value with our accomplishments. Activity can become a great distraction. If we accomplish much and are recognized widely, we assume we matter and are significant. If we are unemployed or underemployed, disabled, or working as a homemaker or in the service industry, we consider ourselves dispensable. We don't matter as much. In rest, we all stop and before God we are all equal. God blesses and consecrates the rest, not the work.

In the Exodus passage above, the slave and the owner and the animals rest. Natural rest happens every night when we sleep, which is necessary for life. A person becomes physically dysfunctional without sleep. The physical body requires rest. The rest required is not just for bodily strength. The physical body includes the thinking, feeling, relating and doing processes, all of which need rest to function optimally. Rest is necessary not only during sleep but during the rhythms of our day and week. God consecrates rest and calls it holy. Rest is for wholeness.

One of the great killers of our day is stress. Stress is the social product of relentless doing and relentless worry about what we cannot control. One of the primary contributors to physical disease is the great onslaught of stress. If we are stressed, we cannot rest. Stress is a physical response triggered when a body's alarm system goes off. Adrenaline is released, which increases heart rate, blood supply and energy. Cortisol, the stress hormone, focuses the body on essential behaviors for survival and reduces the nonessential ones such as the digestive and immune systems, and the reproductive and growth systems. When the threat is over, the body returns to normal conditions.

The less control we feel over our situation the longer and more intense the stress cycle lasts. Eventually, prolonged stress leads to multiple health problems including memory difficulties, sleep and weight difficulties, heart disease, and digestive problems. Depression, anger, addictions and social isolation are all emotional responses to prolonged stress. Resting draws the heart and body back to God's overarching love and sovereign will. Rest recalibrates us and brings us back to the center. Rest is a trust response to God's love. Rest reminds us that ultimately our true significance is in our love relationship with God and not in our productivity.

Activity and work is a way to define ourselves and to measure our success. Activity is part of God's design for us but *rest* is also part of the design. We are designed to be still and listen. In our prayer lives we also need to rest from the activity of praying. We do that by taking a sabbath of words and action. When we rest in God, his quiet presence can reset our perspectives and reorient our desires. When we physically sleep, our minds sift through all the activity of the day and prioritize what is remembered and what is forgotten. When we sleep, connections are made and creative ideas surface.

CONTEMPLATIVE PRAYER—PRAYER OF REST

Contemplative prayer, a prayer of rest, is a way to "sleep" in God for his provision of perspective, direction or simple connection. Contemplative prayer is the absence of conversation and control. Contemplative prayer releases us from constant stress and self-judgment.

Contemplative prayer is a prayer without words or activity. Instead of asking for things or saying things or doing things, we are simply silent. We believe God is present and God invites us to rest in him. It's as if we are sitting on the porch after a busy day just to be with God. Usually a specific amount of time is set so that we are not always wondering if we are done. We still our thoughts to be more aware of God with us. We put God at the center and we rest on the side.

Thomas Merton, a Trappist monk and writer, defined contemplative prayer as "simply the preference for the desert, for emptiness, for poverty."[2] The challenge is the exploration of the human spirit when faced with its own smallness and God's infiniteness obvious in the silence. Contemplative prayer requires an excruciatingly honest courage to abandon the comfort of known self and the limits we impose on God. Do we have the courage to do this? Would we pay the price? The price is radical commitment to and a trust in God's fullness. The believer who says, "Here you may enter or here, but not in this corner room of moving shadows," keeps God at a distance.

> **Contemplation has** proved a healing rest for my soul. To be, without effort, in the presence of God has been a newly opened gift, and oh, the sound of that ripping paper. "Be still *neurosis,* be still *perfectionism,* be still *appetites,* be still *noise,* be still *graspers,* and know that I am God. I will be honored in every nation. I will be honored throughout the world, *even in you, Jason"* (Ps 46:10, italics mine). Contemplative prayer has been the steady affirmation I am lovable and loved with a crazy kind of love. So much un-love I took in without question makes love questionable for me now. Contemplation is my time to be loved by my Creator.
>
> —Jason Minnix

Contemplative prayer, the prayer of rest, is not usually natural for busy people. Therefore, we begin by taking a little time, anywhere from five to fifteen minutes, to sit quietly and resist the temptation to do. Instead we embrace the quiet presence of God. The prayer of rest happens when we focus on nothing but God. The Quakers call it centering, and Thomas Keating called the experience centering prayer. Whatever it is called, it is a prayer experience that requires some training. Like exercising, one begins simply, so as not to strain the body and discourage the spirit. Sometimes walking a familiar route and getting away from activity and people helps you experience a prayer of rest. The basic requirements are no words, a relaxed body and a focus on God's presence.

CONTEMPLATIVE PRAYER GUIDELINES

- Physical comfort—find a comfortable physical posture such as lying down or sitting in a comfortable chair with legs uncrossed and hands loose on one's lap. Take slow even breaths to help relax your body.

- Mental focus—though this is a prayer of rest, it helps if the mind is focused on a simple thought or picture.

  - Words—focus on a few words from Scripture such as, "The Lord is my Shepherd," "The Lord abounds in loving kindness" or "The Lord is good; for his steadfast love endures forever." Don't analyze them but simply repeat them to bring you back to center.

  - Pictures—imagine you are either floating in a river or sitting along a river bank. Other possibilities are sitting in a field or on a porch or going down an elevator. Allow yourself to simply be in the environment. If thoughts or feelings come up, let them float by and return to the simple scene.

Contemplative prayer reminds me of a highly discussed piece of music by composer John Cage, titled *4'33"* (4 minutes and 33 seconds of silence). The score instructs the performer not to play the instrument throughout the entire three movements. Instead of the sound of music you hear the sounds of the environment. This is what happens at first when you sit in a room that is "silent" and listen for God's voice. It's uncomfortable. You squirm. You wonder when the "performance" is going to begin. Then you realize the sound of your breathing, the ticking of the clock, the sound of crossing and uncrossing your legs, the bird outside singing. I often find that it's these smaller sounds that help me realize the vastness of God's creations and help me focus on him and hear his still, small voice within.

—Sandra Klemm

- Practical concerns—set a timer to go off after your set amount of time. Keep note-taking elements close by so if a persistent thought such as "pick up the dry cleaning" or "call Jeff" continue, just write them down and then return to the quiet.

- Traps—avoid analyzing or evaluating your experience by asking, "Am I doing this right?" or "I don't feel anything." These are the distractions of a busy mind that place value on effectiveness rather than on God's presence. Choose a time during the day when you are most alert and have the physical resources to focus. If you fall asleep, your body needs rest. Invite God into the sleep.

- Spiritual safety—some are concerned with the possibility of evil influences while the mind is in a state of rest. Richard Foster suggests beginning with a prayer, "I surround myself with the light of Christ, I cover myself with his blood, and I seal myself with the cross."[3]

CONTEMPLATIVE PRAYER EXPERIENCE

Group Experience

- Choose a guide for the group contemplative experience. This person should be comfortable leading the group and willing to pay attention to the time and the comfort of the group.

- Have everyone find a comfortable position either lying down on the floor or sitting comfortably in a chair. If possible, dim the lights and choose an environment where distractions would be at a minimum.

- Depending on the age and experience of the group, decide ahead of time whether the silence will be for ten, fifteen, twenty or thirty minutes. If this is a first time experience, ten minutes is long enough.

- Have everyone close their eyes.

- The guide begins helping everyone get comfortable by telling them to relax the body and focus on slow even breaths. Loosen the shoulders. Roll your head. Shake out the arms and hands. If sitting, put both feet evenly on the floor. Relax the hands. Breathe in God's presence and exhale slowly distractions.

- The guide prays aloud that God would bless the prayer time and the Holy Spirit would watch over the group and help each one to trust God.

- The guide then tells everyone to see themselves floating on water, sitting by a river, or any of the other possible pictures named above. Remind them to let distractions float by.

- The guide moves into complete silence all the while paying attention to the time and the comfort of the group. If the majority of the group becomes fidgety before the time is over, the guide can bring the time to a close.

- At the conclusion of the agreed upon time, the guide prays aloud a prayer of thanksgiving for the God of rest and grace.

  - Have people pair up or get into small groups and share about their experience. Invite individuals to ask questions of the group about contemplative prayer. If someone wishes to share in front of the whole group, let them.

Partner Experience

- Choose a time and place when you can be together for uninterrupted prayer.

- Make sure that you both understand the purpose and guidelines for contemplative prayer.

- Decide not to discuss prayer needs or concerns or catch up on life before the centering prayer experience.

- Set a timer for the agreed upon time—ten, fifteen or twenty minutes. Begin with a simple prayer to center on the God of rest. Move into silence.

- Discuss your experience afterward. What was difficult? Did you notice anything different about yourself? What persistent thoughts or feelings continued to arise? How might the prayer of rest be part of your daily life?

Individual Experience

- Find a time when you are most alert and relaxed. If you can, do contemplative prayer for a few minutes at the beginning and end of your day.

- Begin with a small amount of time such as five minutes. Then slowly increase by three minutes each time until you get to twenty minutes or to a time that is beneficial for you. Some people will want to be still for ten minutes, others for thirty. Try to stretch yourself without making the experience trying.

- Follow the guidelines for contemplative prayer. At the end of your prayer time, journal about your experience. How did it impact your body, thoughts, emotions or perspectives? If you felt guided to respond some way, such as to call someone or complete some task, follow through on the guidance. Often, contemplative prayer rests and reorients the mind so that the capacity for creativity and generosity is increased.

- Repeat this experience three to four times this week.

THE PRAYER JOURNEY

David Stewart

Taking time to contemplate Jesus' presence with me was very special. I took the advice of just imagining Jesus with me on a porch pretty literally, and before I left the office to go home for the day I went over and just sat on the church steps imagining Jesus there sitting with me. We people-watched together, watching dog walkers, joggers, cars passing by . . . as I did that I had a deep peace that Jesus was indeed with me and delighted in my curiosity and imagination of what and who all the people we were watching were up to. I thought about how he knew all of the details I did not and yet was very present and interested in me—just me.

Dan Ward

I didn't think much about the challenges of contemplative prayer, until I tried to do it. Simultaneously I wrestled with what Jesus looked like and what he was wearing, and what could it possibly feel like to have twenty minutes of one-on-one time with JESUS. However, when I think about *sitting* next to Jesus, that's a whole different thing. Sitting there I had a powerful feeling of peace, love and acceptance with no real anticipation or agenda. I'm struck that Jesus who is so busy listening to endless prayers beyond number and constantly sustaining all creation has time to sit quietly with me and accomplish nothing more than being. I just don't have the words for it.

Three or four times I started to talk: "Jesus?"

"Yes."

And that's as far as it got, and as far as it needed to go.

Lynn Gill

One Monday morning after getting my children off to school, I looked at my calendar for the week and was overwhelmed with all the tasks and deadlines. I had reports to complete, coaching calls to make, a coffee appointment for fundraising, preparation for a presentation I was to give the following week in Chicago and several major meetings, and all that on top of the kids' music and gymnastics lessons and church activities. I was already tired just looking at all the decisions, conversations and work that needed to be done. I knew I did not have the resources—emotional, physical or spiritual—for the week ahead. I sat there for a while. Then I knew what I needed to do. I needed to spend the morning in reflective prayer. I needed to sit with Jesus and listen to him. I needed him to order my priorities for the week. I did just that. Made myself a cup of tea, took out my Bible and journal and sat with Jesus. I don't remember much about the morning except a deep

Ryan Hee

Contemplative prayer is a bit of a struggle. It could be the openness of it, that nothing can be measured. This week was rough and I felt out of sorts. I saw that I have these cans stuck deep down in the mud of my life, just like trash settles in a body of water. The water can look clear but if one takes out the stuff stuck on the bottom, mud and debris are stirred up, dirtying the water.

feeling of refreshment. The rest of the week went surprisingly well and I felt Jesus with me.

I felt like that this week. Even though I may not be asking for anything, I sometimes feel God goes to work healing and transforming me. Though it is not without some discomfort and unsettled feelings, I believe that in the long term, God is clearing out some long buried stuff that needs to be taken out of my life. Then the water in my life may be clean, clear and a source of blessing.

FURTHER READING

Johnson, Jan. *When the Soul Listens: Finding Rest and Direction in Contemplative Prayer.* Colorado Springs: NavPress, 1999.

Keating, Thomas. *Intimacy with God: An Introduction to Centering Prayer*, 3rd ed. New York: Crossroad, 2009.

Thibodeaux, Mark. *Armchair Mystic: Easing into Contemplative Prayer.* Cincinnati: St. Anthony Messenger, 2001.

5

Prayer of Confession

A monk was once asked, "What do you do up there in the monastery?"
He replied, "We fall and get up, fall and get up,
fall and get up again."

ESTHER DE WAAL

Despite my struggles, brokenness, imperfection, and sin,
prayer is the redemptive gift of God that presents the greatest gift of all
—the chance to connect and commune with God.

JIM MCLAUGHLIN

GOD AS HOLY

A newborn baby is so innocent, yet as the child grows so does her willfulness and so does his frustration. Parents remember the first times their sweet baby threw a temper tantrum. We are flawed human beings. We make mistakes, sometimes big ones. We are mean and judgmental to each other. We over- or underestimate our "quality." God, on the other hand, is perfect. God is a holy God. Holiness is fundamental to God's nature. Because God is holy, God is also perfectly just, distinguishing good from evil.

The first time *holy* is used in the Old Testament is in Exodus 3:5 when Moses saw the burning bush: "Come no closer! Remove the sandals from your feet, for the place on which you are standing is holy ground." God's holiness covers and makes holy whatever or whomever God touches. In Moses' "Song of Deliverance" from the Egyptian army, Moses sings about God's holiness being majestic and God guiding the people to his holy dwelling. God set his people aside to be holy and to establish holy places. The Lord God is holy, so we are to be holy.

The LORD spoke to Moses, saying: Speak to all the congregation of the people of Israel and say to them: *You shall be holy, for I the LORD your God am holy.* You shall each revere your mother and father, and you shall keep my sabbaths: I am the LORD your God. Do not turn to idols or make cast images for yourselves: I am the LORD your God. (Lev 19:1-4)

In the Garden of Eden God created Adam and Eve to be his holy partners in work and rest. Holiness came through the integrity of their daily relationship with God. The primary means of experiencing holiness is in right relationships to God and others. The commandments in Leviticus are about maintaining right relationships with God by not turning to idols, with creation by resting, with family by honoring our father and mother, and with neighbors by not hurting or cheating them.

When Adam and Eve chose to sin in Genesis 3, they were no longer single-minded, seeking to be with God. They became divided and self-focused. With their sin came guilt and they hid. They knew they had disobeyed God's command not to eat from the Tree of Knowledge. Prior to eating the fruit, knowledge came through their intimate relationship with God. It was what they shared together. Knowledge was discerned and shared in community with a holy God. Knowledge was not decided by independent interpretations.

By choosing to eat the fruit, they chose to stand alone. Adam and Eve separated themselves from God and hid; they knew they were naked and exposed. They felt ashamed. Shame results in feelings of ostracism and blame. The woman blamed the serpent. The man blamed the woman. They no longer knew themselves through their close relationship. Now they knew each other as sinners. They no longer walked and talked with God in the Garden.

God created us to be a holy people, a nation of priests, but our tendency to want to be a god and do our own thing separates us from God. Holiness comes primarily from staying connected to a holy God. It is not about behavior—doing the right things—but about being in right relationship with a holy God. When we are in a right relationship, we seek to honor God with our lives.

There are several ways in which we sin and separate from God:

- *It's wrong:* We know it is wrong, and we do it anyway. We know we shouldn't yell at our kids when we're tired. We know we shouldn't gossip about the obnoxious coworker. In the Old Testament God's provision was for a guilt offering (Lev 5). Guilt is the result of breaking a known law or rule of behavior. When we commit an intentional sin, we confess to God and to witnesses that we are guilty, offer atonement, and then we are forgiven.

- *Oops:* In life we all make unintentional mistakes. A comment we made in a meeting hurt a coworker. We forgot to follow through on an assignment from school or missed meeting a friend for lunch. In the Old Testament these required sin offerings (Lev 4). These are still wrongs because others are hurt by our thoughtlessness. We confess and apologize.

- *It's complicated*: Sometimes people are slowly caught in addictive behaviors that begin as small dangerous choices and then become completely overwhelming physical addictions. Smoking, drugs, pornography, overuse of social media, overexercising or overeating, any compulsion that fills our thoughts, isolates us and separates us from others and God is an addiction. The Twelve Steps of Alcoholics Anonymous follow a similar pattern as the Old Testament sacrifice for sin. Admit your powerlessness and your need for God. Trust God. Admit wrongs and make restitution.

- *It's not my problem*: Sometimes people take responsibility for another's behavior. If I were kinder, he wouldn't yell at me. If I work harder, my boss won't cheat his customers. If I don't study and get As, then the other kids won't bully me. Whenever we take the sin or guilt or shame of another's bad behavior upon ourselves, we take away the opportunity for others to mature. There is nothing to confess.

> **I have learned** through many hours of speaking plainly to God that confession is my honesty before God. But it isn't just honesty about the bad stuff, about me or others; it is also about good stuff. For me, confession, honesty, humility and thankfulness are tied together. Confession allows me to hear from God the totality of my life. Releasing the bile of my guilt allows me to receive the joy of God's grace, which eventually leads to thanksgiving. Then I am able to see the totality of myself: strengths and weaknesses through the grace of God. In shame, I found fear and hiding. In confession, I found relief and integrity.
>
> —Larry Williams

When we choose our own way out of pride, rebellion, fear, brokenness or addiction, we separate ourselves from the love of God and thus God's holiness. Holiness is not something we earn but something that God sees when he looks at us. We are covered by God's gaze. We are on holy ground with God. When we sin, the way to restore the relationship is to recognize our sin, feel remorse and confess. This is the central tension of our faith. God is holy and just and yet God is also love. Our sinfulness and self-involvement separates us from the love of God. Turning to God and confessing reestablishes us with God. Confession returns us to being with God and not against God. Confession is a prayer of return.

PRAYER OF CONFESSION

God created all things and God is perfect. We are imperfect, yet God loves us. So God designed a way for us to come close to God through the prayer of confession. From the Old Testament through the New, God is a holy God. When we are made new in Christ, we can approach God's throne as holy, blameless and without accusation. When we slip up, our responsi-

Every single day I am reminded of what a loser I am. I have this image of an angry God constantly telling me that I have wasted my life. It's funny how much God is like my own father. Every time I feel stressed I pull out that candy or bag of chips. I can't stop eating. I tried prayer but it didn't work. One evening I was desperate. I started yelling at God at the top of my lungs. I screamed and shouted and kicked cushions around. After a couple of hours I fell to the floor, sobbing and spent. I cried out, "Lord, Lord, help me. I am so miserable." Then I heard God say, "You are my beloved son." I could hardly take it in.

—Jeff Reynolds

bility is to confess our faults and God is just to forgive them. Confession is part of the daily rhythm of prayer. It reminds us that love and wholeness is in God and not in our efforts.

Some neglect prayer because they feel they are sinners and can never be safe with a God who is holy. They believe there is no hope. They have tried to live better lives, and it doesn't work. Others are angry with a God who would create us and then judge us for misbehaving. To them God is the unyielding parent ready to punish whenever we stray. Some are ashamed and don't want to be reminded that they don't measure up. Others just don't care. Life is tough. Everyone makes mistakes. All these reasons for neglecting prayer are rooted in a behavior theology rather than a relationship theology. God is inviting us into a loving relationship. The apathy, blame or fear we feel is a result of our separation from God, ourselves or others.

In the Old Testament when people felt deep penitence, they used their body to make a statement of their sincerity. They would lie on the ground or kneel. The body, as well as the mouth, confesses a desire to be restored. Saying a quick prayer on Sunday or a simple "forgive us

Once as a new Christian in college, I backslid in a most terrible way. For a few days I tried to hide from God by not acknowledging what I had done until I couldn't stand it anymore. After a Sunday service, I returned to my room and began to plead for God's forgiveness. I was kneeling beside my bed, and then I was flat on the floor beside my bed. And then out of incredible shame for what I had done, I stuck my head under my bed and shimmied as much of me as I could fit, all the while confessing and pleading for release of the guilt and shame, not only for what I had done, but for destroying Christ's integrity in me to those who witnessed my sin. It was an occasion of extreme sincerity, and God's grace covered my sin.

—David Manning

our debts" is not enough. A Band-Aid is not enough. The wound needs to be exposed, cleaned, attended to and cared for in order for healing to be complete.

Confessional prayer is both individual and communal.[1] We sin in our personal lives and we sin as groups: churches, communities, institutions, schools and businesses all sin intentionally or unintentionally.

> Corporate sin is so disconnected from the reality of our typical American Christian life that we are shocked when it actually enters our world. Rather than confront sin, we begin to look for ways to categorize it as a theologically liberal agenda—thereby stripping corporate confession and repentance of its prophetic power.[2]

Thinking together about how we might have sinned as a group and then confessing the sin, receiving God's forgiveness and asking for guidance for restitution are all elements of community confession.

CONFESSION PRAYER GUIDELINES

- *Remember God's goodness*: Begin in a place of love and grace by reflecting on God's goodness.

- *Honest reflection*: In prayer, return to the specific event. Reflect on it. Take responsibility for the part you played, even if someone else was responsible for initiating it or for being more hurtful than you. What part did you play?

- *Specific confession*: General confessions, such as "Forgive me for being angry," are not helpful. Specific confessions are: "Forgive me, Lord, for yelling at my son and calling him 'hopeless,'" "Forgive me, Lord, for being impatient with my coworker when she asked me for the third time to help her."

- *Tell someone*: Confessions are told first to oneself and God, and then to a trusted friend or a spiritually mature Christian. Have an accountability partner, someone who loves you and believes in you but who will walk with you in Christ.

- *Make amends*: Sin is not a personal affair. Someone is always hurt. Apologies are often needed. "Son, Daddy is sorry for yelling at you and calling you 'hopeless.' I love you more than anything and I was wrong. I'm very proud of you. Please forgive me."

- *Remember God's goodness*: Finish by thanking God for his goodness.

PRAYER OF CONFESSION EXPERIENCE

Group Experience

- If in your context it is not appropriate to do a group confession experience, pair people up and do the partner experience explained below.

- For a group confession read aloud together Psalm 32, "Blessedness of Forgiveness and Trust in God."

- Group reflection:
  - Is there something that the group as a whole has done either intentionally or unintentionally that has hurt others?
  - Have we made fun of someone or of a group of people?
  - Have we neglected to do something that we should do? Have we neglected the community or the environment?
  - Is there something for which we feel arrogant or prideful?
  - Is there a group we hate or feel jealousy toward?
  - Is there idolatry, something more important to us than God?
- As a group write a prayer of confession. It should include
  - Contrition—sadness for the sin
  - Disclosure—confession of the sin
- Kneel or lie flat on the floor, if you are able, and pray together the prayer you wrote.
- Discuss how you might make amends and follow through on some specific action.
- Receive God's blessing. "If we confess our sins, he who is faithful and just will forgive us our sins and cleanse us from all unrighteousness" (1 Jn 1:9).

Partner Experience

- During your prayer time together, share one specific event during the past week of a hurt you caused either intentionally or unintentionally. Be clear about the event.
- Following the pattern in the guidelines section, confess your sin to one another (be specific) and pray for each other. "Lord, I confess I sinned by X. Forgive me."
- Receive God's blessing and forgiveness (1 Jn 1:9).
- Discuss how you might make amends and how you might hold each other accountable. Confession is possible because forgiveness is free. Hold each other accountable to follow through with the amends.

Individual Experience

- You can daily reflect on your life and bring to prayer some hurt you incurred on yourself or others following the above pattern in the prayer partner section. Write your confession in your journal. Pray it out loud. Receive God's forgiveness and reflect on how you might make amends.
- Or you can follow a daily routine of confession from Psalm 139.[3] Leighton Ford created this pattern for himself:

- *Morning*: "Lord, search me and know my heart." Is my heart centered rightly as I begin today?

- *Noon*: "Test me and know my restless thoughts." Recognize and rest from thoughts that you cannot let go.

- *Evening*: "See if there is any hurtful way in me." What hurts have I caused that need confessing?

- *Bedtime*: "Lead me in the way everlasting." As I sleep, I rest in God's hands.

PRAYER JOURNEY

Pamela Gifford

I had asked my husband daily for the past three weeks to check with his boss about a meeting with Human Resources. He had been at his new job for over six months, and the HR manual said that he would be reviewed and could get a raise at that time. We talked about it after work each day, very low-key and amicably. He agreed and sometimes would even ask me to write a note to remind him, which I did. Then he would come home and say he forgot or was too busy or didn't feel like it that day. We were really hurting financially and could use the raise.

After many weeks, I couldn't take it anymore. One night I couldn't sleep and was getting angrier and angrier that he hadn't done this simple thing for us. Around midnight, I jumped up and yelled, "I can't take this anymore!" He was trying to wake up. "What? What? Was I snoring?" I stormed out in the dark, but came back shortly, yelling, "Why don't you make an appointment with HR? I don't understand it!" We didn't speak to each other the next morning. I felt terrible. During my prayer time I prayed and asked God to help me. I was wrong to get so angry, but I was really mad. I called my best friend and she laughed when I told her what happened. Then I realized how ridiculous it was to burst out in the middle of the night. No matter what, I still hurt him. When he got home I said I was sorry for being so angry. He said he was sorry for not taking care of this sooner and he had done it that day. We prayed and confessed to each other and asked God to restore our relationship.

MaryKate Morse

Several years ago I met with a group of women leaders from around the world in Berlin, Germany. The purpose of the gathering was to encourage one another and to learn together about leading like Christ in difficult places. Most of the leaders were young entrepreneurs who were doing front-line work with the very poor and marginalized. It was moving for me to be in a city known for its brutal division between East and West Germany and now united again. One afternoon we visited the Reichstag Building, the parliament building that held in its chambers the history of the German people from its opening in 1894 to its present-day use. Across the face of the building were the words "For the German People." At the top of the building a huge glass cupola gave a 360-degree view of Berlin.

When we had finished walking the glass structure, one of the German women began to weep. She said that she had felt impressed for some time and it was now confirmed that she needed to ask forgiveness for herself and her nation for the sin of the Holocaust. Some of the other women tried to stop her, saying that she was not responsible and she was a good person. However, she said she felt deeply the guilt for herself and her people and she wanted to confess the sin of the darkest kind of racism. She believed the Holy Spirit was calling her to stand and confess this sin in this place with us women. We made a circle around her on the roof of the Reichstag Building and moved into a deep silence. She prayed a prayer of confession for herself and the German people, asking for God's forgiveness. She also prayed for God's revival among the German people. Then we each prayed for God to pour out blessing and spiritual renewal on Germany. We went up the roof as tourists and we came down hopeful and touched by God's grace even for the darkest of sins.

FURTHER READING

Carter, Kenneth H., Jr. *Prayers and Liturgies of Confession and Assurance.* Nashville: Abingdon, 2009.

Renner, Rick. *365 Days of Power: Personalized Prayers and Confessions to Build Your Faith and Strengthen Your Spirit.* Tulsa, OK: Harrison House, 2004.

6

Blessing Prayer

God is love.
Therefore love.
Without distinction,
without calculation,
without procrastination,
love.

HENRY DRUMMOND

The concrete manifestation of love often comes
in acts of helpfulness to one another.

DALE A. ZEIMER

GOD AS LOVING-KINDNESS

When we hold our first child we fall immediately in love. We are bound in heart to the little bundle. The love of a parent or caregiver is the most shaping force in every child's life and in every caregiver's life. Growing up loved and cherished is a fundamental need for all of us. God designed us to love, because God is love. Our God is a God of *hesed*, loving-kindness. The Hebrew word *hesed* is difficult to translate into English. It can mean grace, loyalty, faithfulness and kindness. The word suggests generosity, commitment and love. God's love is bountiful and is experienced in a committed relationship characterized by tenderness. "[Solomon] said, "O LORD, God of Israel, there is no God like you in heaven above or on earth beneath, keeping covenant and steadfast love for your servants who walk before you with all their heart" (1 Kings 8:23).

God's love is like that of a parent. God creates us, nurtures us, protects us, guides us and sets healthy boundaries for us. God is our Father, and God loves us as a Mother. God's love is not romantic and variable, but deep and everlasting.

> As a father has compassion for his children,
>> so the LORD has compassion for those who fear him. (Ps 103:13)

> Listen to me, O house of Jacob, all the remnant of the house of Israel, who have been borne by me from your birth, carried from the womb; even to your old age I am he, even when you turn gray I will carry you. I have made, and I will bear; I will carry and will save. (Is 46:3-4)

Our response to God's loving-kindness is trust. We commit to God and to imitating God's nature. The response isn't about "behaving well," though God, as a good parent, teaches us how to live according to his heart. When we embrace God's love we experience peace and have access to God's wisdom; we see the world as God sees the world. This is not a naive childish love, but a mature one born out of faithfulness and often suffering. Our response to God's love is to be true to all the ideals of a holy partnership. We trust God to be God. Because of God's generous love, God sets us apart, God rescues us, God gives us guidelines for a mutually satisfying love relationship and God expects us to be generous in our love of others.

When God chose Abraham to be a great nation, he established a covenant with him. An Old Testament covenant is a sacred agreement between God and individuals or nations. God made a covenant with Abraham in Genesis 12–17 to make him a great nation and bless him. Circumcision of every male was the sign of the covenant. The covenant passed from Isaac to Jacob and then to Moses when the Ten Commandments were received. The sign for the Mosaic covenant was the sabbath. When God made a covenant with David in 2 Samuel 7, God promised to bless David and through his descendants would come the Messiah and a new covenant for all people. The requirements of the covenant are faithfulness

I felt truly abandoned by God. I had rescued and loved a little boy, and now he was going to someone else. He had filled a deep place in my heart for four months. Now he was gone. Did God really love me? Did God really know me? After long walks in the night I concluded that God was God and that God was good, but I didn't think he knew or loved me specifically. The next day someone I barely knew called to say, "Janey, I was praying and saw a vision of you with your head down in church. God gave me this prayer to sing over you and I did again and again. The song is, 'When I am thankful, when I am thankful, when I am thankful, I am thankful for thee.'"

—Janey Williams

to live and love as God does in God's holiness and *hesed*.

God made a covenant with his chosen people and tasked them with becoming a kingdom of priests to the nations. God promised loving-kindness forever. God would be their God, and they would be his people. They in turn would be the priests and blessers of nations around the world: "you shall be called priests of the LORD, you shall be named ministers of our God" (Is 61:6).

In the Old Testament the word for priest, *kohen*, is used about eight hundred times. A priest was responsible for serving in the temple, teaching the law and praying. When God said that his chosen people would be a kingdom of priests to the nations, he expected that they would be God's holy representatives through their witness and through their kindness and prayers. The Old Testament had a formal priesthood; those priests were located in the temple. Larry Shelton, a theologian and pastor, wrote in his book *Cross and Covenant*, "the priestly responsibilities in the Old Testament were broader than just the offering of sacrifice and intercession. The priest served as a mediator, 'a bridge-builder who effects the bringing together of two parties.'"[1]

> **I prayed for** a week for the neighborhood I've lived in for thirty years. The first day I prayed for my neighbors: the one who hardly comes out of her house; the skateboarders who skate down the middle of the street; the scowling old lady that walks her little white dog; and the Hindu lady, who wants to talk about my God. The second day I visited places where I have been able to help people, like the lady who had a seizure in the park. I stopped at each place and prayed. The third day I spent remembering people from high school. I prayed in front of their old houses, places we played baseball and picnic tables we hung out at. The fourth day I prayed for the people I see regularly in town, the bank teller and the grocery clerk. This week my prayer world grew.
>
> —Jennifer Riggs

BLESSING PRAYER

Today believers are priests who are the bridge-builders in their neighborhoods. Believers are priests not as arbitrators, people who stand between God and the sinner, but as people who connect them with God through compassionate prayer and blessing. A person who accepts God's covenant of love embodies it as a generous priest to his or her community. The Jewish people considered *hesed* a core value linked to compassion. The love was observed in service to those in need such as the poor, the orphan and the stranger. It was believed that this value alone could heal the world. We are extensions of God's love through service and blessing.

Out of the security of our love in God, we pray for others without any thought of gain. Blessing prayers are priestly prayers. Priestly prayers are not just formal prayers prayed by pastors and spiritual leaders in the church. Priestly prayers are prayed generously and with loving-kindness for the nations and peoples of the world by all of us. By blessing with our prayers we give witness to the faithfulness and goodness of God. We trust God to be God in his purposes throughout time and place. The only judge is God. Our role as God's children is to bless and love. We incarnate the love of God.

Blessing prayers give us opportunities to love others and hold them before God in prayer. Anyone from the small child to the bed-bound invalid can love others through blessing prayers. There are no fancy words or rituals. Blessings are affirmations of God's loving-kindness toward the world God created.

BLESSING PRAYER GUIDELINES

- We are all called to be God's priests, God's blessers, to a suffering world. Therefore, one of our duties is to pray for and bless others wherever we go and among whomever we meet.

- Blessing prayer is characterized by compassion, grace and kindness.

- Blessing prayers are generous and intended for everyone, not just people we like or with whom we agree.

- To pray a blessing as a priest is to pray for an experience of God's favor.

- If you feel judgment, fear or anger, take time in prayer to process your feelings. Though the feelings may seem justifiable, ask for God's perspective. God yearns for everyone's redemption and healing.

- Blessing prayers begin with recognizing God's loving-kindness, move to particular prayers for God's intervention or favor, and close with a blessing.

- Blessing prayers are every believer's ministry and calling. They are prayers of loving-kindness.

- Blessing prayers prayed in local community are part of our incarnational presence to the concerns and needs of others. We don't pray and run. We pray and work to restore.

BLESSING PRAYER EXPERIENCES

Group Experience

- Using a local newspaper, Twitter or newsfeed, agree on a nation, people group or event to pray for and bless. Ask God to lead you to something about which you all feel strongly. This may include a country experiencing war, such as Afghanistan, human trafficking victims in India, AIDS orphans in Kenya, a tragedy or challenge in your local community such as a fire, shooting, accident, unemployment or homelessness.

- Learn as much as you can about the group or event. If you can, locate the place on a map and share pictures and information. Be as concrete as possible. This can be done using the Internet in a short amount of time.

- Talk together about what the needs might be and what blessings might be expressed.

- You can either write these on Post-It notes or paper and tape them all around the room at a level where everyone can read them, or you can list them on a sheet of paper that all can see.

- For the prayer time begin by reading Psalm 36:5-9 together.

- Walk individually around the room and pray on your own aloud for each written request. As a blesser you can place your hand on the request.

- When everyone has finished, say together the blessing in Numbers 6:24-26.

- Share about your experience as "priests" praying for this concern. What was most meaningful? What was challenging? How might you serve as priests in your individual lives? Is there some follow-up for this prayer experience?

Partner Experience

- During your regular time together choose a concern, either local or international. If the concern is local, you can go to that location for the prayer time, if feasible. If it is national or international, find out what you can about it.

- Pray for the person, community, event or concern in this manner:

  - *Adore God.* Begin by reminding yourselves of God's attributes and promises such as in Psalm 9:1-2.

  - *Bless others.* Pray specific prayers for God's favor and help.

  - *Close.* Say the blessing together from Numbers 6:24-26.

- If you can walk and pray in the area, follow the same pattern. You can pray aloud together as you walk, but if it is too disruptive, then pray silently as you walk.

- Talk together about the experience. How might you continually serve as priests in your neighborhood and town? Is there a country or international concern that God is inviting you to pray for and bless on a regular basis? What was it like to pray in this manner? How did you experience God?

Individual Experience

- For three days one week pray a blessing prayer in this manner:

  - *Day One*: Walk through your immediate community or visualize your neighbors during your prayer time and pray for God's blessing and help. Be as specific as possible.

- *Day Two*: Walk through a part of your larger community (downtown, mall or business area) and pray for blessing.

- *Day Three*: Using a local newspaper or news event, pray for God's blessing on a national or international concern or event.

- Begin each prayer period with reading aloud Psalm 145:1-10 and end each prayer with the blessing in Numbers 6:24-26.

- Journal on your experience: Did you learn anything about yourself, others or God? What was the most meaningful part of the experience? What are the challenges? How might you continue to pray for others around you?

PRAYER JOURNEY

Miriam Mendez[2]

Esperanza Church is a new church plant about a year old with a vision to follow the life of Jesus and empower with prayer, service and compassionate witness the Portland Latino community. One Sunday in April, we had two guest speakers, one from the New Oregon Sanctuary Movement and one from the Voz Workers Rights Education Project for day laborers. The latter speaker had been a day laborer himself and he talked about how he had been cheated and abused. We realized how we all felt uncomfortable with driving by areas where day laborers were waiting for work, and we felt convicted by his words. The speakers invited us to attend a rally on May 1, The International Workers' Day rally. The rally involved a walk and then speeches about workers' rights.

After the speakers left, we all agreed that we wanted to pray for the rally and the people impacted by these issues. However, we couldn't see how we would attend because it was held during our scheduled worship time on Sunday afternoon. As we talked more about it, we thought, "What would it look like if, instead of being a church praying for the rally, we were a church walking in the rally and praying?"

On May 1 we met at the rally early. We prayed to be mindful of the people around us and why they're walking. Some didn't have a job and some were treated unfairly. For some the walk was very risky because they were undocumented. After the rally we gathered and prayed again, thanking God for the experience.

Some shared they saw that these issues affected not just adults but children. During the rally the people chanting and marching were families with children of all ages. One Esperanza member shared, "I've been here for many years, but I'm not part of this struggle. As I kept walking I started joining in the chant, and I was saying it louder and louder. I realized, I am part of these people and I am part of the struggle." He later told me, "This was transformative for me. Thank you for exposing us to experiences that challenge what it means to follow the life of Jesus." We agreed we wanted to be a part of this next year. We want to pray and bless what God is doing with the communities in Portland.

Paul Lyda

As I prayer-walked my neighborhood this week, I was reminded of an especially sad time in my life. My dad was diagnosed with stage four lung cancer in June of 2000. He died January 10, 2001. It was a hard journey to take; one filled with anguish, prayers and tears. In the weeks leading up to my dad's last Christmas, there was a family near my parents' home that had started prayer-walking the neighborhood, asking God to reveal which homes might need extra encouragement and hope for the coming holidays. After several nights of walking block after block and praying outside home after home, everyone in the family got to pick one house that they wanted to secretly deliver a special gift and note to before Christmas.

Days before Christmas, my mom found a beautiful wooden snowflake with a small inset mirror and a personalized letter from a man letting us know that our house—our family!—had been chosen by their child to be lifted up in extra prayer during the holiday season. The letter went on to say that his family did not know what our situation was, but that they would love to offer up specific prayers on our behalf if we wanted to respond to this outreach of love and faith. My mom did follow up and shared the life struggle that my dad was in with cancer. Although a little over two weeks later he died, we were still deeply blessed by this family that prayerfully joined us to ask God for comfort, peace and even joy in those last days we spent on earth with my dad, George.

As we walk together, my wife and I have always wondered about what goes on behind so many closed doors and drawn drapes. What challenge is that family wrestling with at this time? Although we may never know, we can offer faithful prayers that the people and families represented by those homes will know Jesus who stands and knocks at the doors of their hearts. In remembering this experience that once blessed my family, I'm prompted to start a similar tradition with my family. I believe that prayer matters.

FURTHER READING

Mandryk, Jason. *Operation World: The Definitive Prayer Guide to Every Nation*, 7th ed. Downers Grove, IL: InterVarsity Press, 2012. www.operationworld.org.

Omartian, Stormie. *Powerful Prayers for Troubled Times: Praying for the Country We Love*, reprint edition. Eugene, OR: Harvest House, 2011.

7

Worship Prayer

A man can no more diminish God's glory
by refusing to worship Him
than a lunatic can put out the sun
by scribbling the words "darkness" on the walls of his cell.

C. S. Lewis

The sun shall no longer be
   your light by day
nor for brightness shall the moon
   give light to you by night;
but the LORD will be your everlasting light,
   and your God will be your glory.

Isaiah 60:19

GOD AS WORTHY

If you were away from city lights some evening and looked up to the skies, even with the naked eye, you would see millions of lights flickering in the dark. Those lights represent solar systems, planets, stars, comets and sometimes a plane or two. Nothing can make you seem so small and the universe so big, than watching the heavens in the dark. The wonder of the vastness of space and the immensity of God in comparison to our frail littleness evokes worship in us. Without the light we would see nothing but pitch blackness. Without God we would not exist. In response we are filled with a sense of God's glory and sovereign presence.

God is the God of light and glory. God is light because of God's just and perfect goodness. God is glory because of God's holiness and majesty. God is so magnificent that no one can look upon God and live (Ex 33:18-23). The Hebrew word for "glory," *kavod*, poetically means distinction, honor, splendor, magnificence, authority and power. Its original concrete meaning was "heavy" and was used to refer to battle armaments. Glory, *kavod*, is something that can be seen and experienced and is powerful like weaponry. Light has the same qualities. It makes seeing possible and has power to sustain life. In fact, the root of the word translated "glory" is *kaved*, meaning liver, which was the seat of the emotions in the Ancient Near East. Jewish people equate honor with something seen and felt. It has a visceral energy.

Our response to God's glory is also visceral and has energy. The nature of God compels us to worship. It is our felt response. In Deuteronomy 10:20-21 we read, "You shall fear the LORD your God; him alone you shall worship; to him you shall hold fast, and by his name you shall swear. He is your praise; he is your God." The first mention of worship is in Genesis 22:5 when Abraham took Isaac his son to sacrifice as God commanded. Abraham told his servants that he was going to worship God. Abraham was confident in God's promise that from his son would come a great nation. Just as he began to sacrifice Isaac, God called him to stop. God said that he now knew that Abraham was completely devoted and would withhold nothing, not even his beloved son. Abraham's obedience foreshadows Jesus' obedience to sacrifice himself for our salvation.

However, in our human weakness many of us are less clear about our devotion than Abraham. We sometimes choose God because of the benefits package and not simply because God is God. We like the assurances, eternal life, protection and hope for a good life. We confuse being part of God's sovereign plan for the world with being the recipients of special benefits. If our relationship to God is about what we can get, our worship will be weak. The first commandment is to worship only God and to have no other substitute (Ex 20:2-6); only God is worthy of our devotion.

The Hebrew word for worship, *hishtaphel*, means to "bow down deeply, to declare, to obey." The meaning is to show complete service and devotion to whatever or whoever is bowed down to. Therefore our complete devotion and worship is directed toward God, not idols. Today we are too sophisticated to bow down to wooden idols, but we do bow down to other things: wealth, status,

> **I've wanted to** follow and serve God ever since I accepted Christ in college. But whenever I focus on simply worshiping God, my prayer is quickly over. I can't think of anything to say after a few minutes. I've tried it in groups too. We've agreed to only praise God, and within a couple of minutes there is no more praise and we are on to requests. I am humbled that God has done so much for me, and I can only praise him back for a few minutes. I'm trying to make life turn out a certain way. I need to stay in worship until I am centered in God alone.
>
> —Peter Vaughan

power, money, success, self-righteousness, academic, athletic or artistic achievements, personal looks, food, anything that we think more immediately meets our needs than God. We wouldn't call them "idols" but they are pursuits and things that separate us from a core devotion to God. When we worship these "idols," we don't trust God. God is not visceral in our lives, not real. We need the comfort or control of other things in order to feel safe and valued. When we worship God with a humble heart and a faithful trust in God's worthiness, we don't need other gods to save us.

In the early Christian church all believers gathered together on the sabbath to celebrate the resurrection of Jesus. The tone of worship was joyful. The main event was the Lord's Supper, which reminded all of the liberating sacrifice of Jesus' death on the cross. Before Jesus Christ, God was worshiped for delivering the Jews out of slavery and for being in a covenantal relationship of love and protection with the Jewish people. Worship's primary purpose was to glorify God. Worship reminded believers of God's greatness, and the gathered believers remembered the joy of their redemption. Worship in the early church was also the great leveling place where all classes of people were one before God. In worship we are reminded of God as One in community and we the believers are one together before the throne of grace.

WORSHIP PRAYER

Graybeal and Roller, in their book *Prayer and Worship*, wrote, "Prayer and worship are inextricably intertwined. When we come into the presence of God in prayer, something leads us to worship, and it seems worshipping God automatically moves us to pray."[1] Worship prayer does three primary things for us.

1. Worship prayer reminds us that God is preeminent in us, our world and the universe.

2. Worship prayer reminds us that God is good and just and holy.

3. In worship prayer we connect relationally with our God.

These are things that lift us to hope, not despair. The psalmists again and again lamented difficulties in their lives. But at the end of their laments they remembered God as the Deliverer and as sovereign. David and other psalm writers came back to hope in God.

Scientists have discovered that the brain is changed, even into old age, by love and by hope. The brain is plastic, able to develop new neuron connections and thus new ways of thinking and behaving throughout one's life. This can be positive or negative. On the negative end, for example, addiction is the slow rewiring of the brain as it adapts to needing some particular fix. On the positive end, having a narrative of hope can rewire the brain to be more optimistic and creative. Scientists have discovered that changing a person's behavior is more likely to happen through hope than through fear.[2] Hope comes from a picture of future possibilities. If a man is addicted to cigarettes, he will have more motivation to change if he thinks about playing with his future grandchildren rather than fearing lung cancer.[3]

Scientists have also discovered that we are changed by loving relationships. "Love alters the structure of our brains."[4] We are wired for connection and our bodies are constantly seeking to stabilize ourselves by being in loving relationships with others. With the right relationships anyone from a child to an elderly adult learns that love is visceral and active. It translates into "protection, caretaking, loyalty and sacrifice."[5] With a feeling of being loved the brain resurrects memories of past experiences of love. Fear, anxiety and depression lessen. Love generates hope and hope generates love. Therefore,

> **I found that** when I was singing worship songs, I would sometimes think, "Am I singing that on key? Is that the right harmony?" And if I weren't singing, my mind wandered to things like, "What should I cook for dinner? I wonder if that birthday gift idea will come together." I was appalled at how quickly my mind was distracted. Then I started to focus better. At first I only gave thanks to the Lord for the things he's done in my life and the things he's blessed me with. But when I looked deeper I thanked the Lord for who he is in my life, as Father, Redeemer, Comforter, Husband, King, etc. Each way of viewing who God is to me has a story and is a relationship.
>
> —Heidi Elliott

> **My daughter's first** cries this week were infinitely sweeter than any worship song I had ever heard. There was no greater thankfulness and praise that I have had for a long time than in that moment. It reminded me of how fragile life is and that if I value this child with my all, then how much more does God value us all?
>
> —Mathew Panattoni

worship is an incredibly important part of our physiology and health as well as a natural response to a loving God who promises humanity a future in a new heaven and a new earth.

Worship is a response on which we dwell on a good and glorious God. We remember all God's attributes, promises and past experiences of God's grace. Remembering who God is instills in us again God's perspective. We hope again by knitting ourselves to a God of glory. We remember that we are chosen, redeemed, made holy and glorified with him who sacrificed for us. We are wired into a deep connection with God.

Worship is prayer. It is individual and communal. It renews our bond and gives us hope. Many times we think of prayer as a time to ask for things or to pray for others. Prayer is first and foremost a visceral, active response to a loving, holy and glorious God. Worship reminds us of God's love and draws us back into the Father's arms. We are renewed in worship.

WORSHIP PRAYER GUIDELINES

- Worship prayer is both an individual experience and an experience done in community.

- The focus of worship prayer is God and God's glory and light. The focus is not our needs, though after worship we often pray for our needs. The primary purpose is to glorify God and to remember God's promises.

- Worship prayer involves *praise*, giving glory to God for who God is, and *thanksgiving*, giving glory to God for what God has done. Praise reminds us of the character of God. Thanksgiving reminds us of what God has done.

- Worship prayers orient us toward God.

- Worship prayer can use music, dance, art, silence, words and any medium that helps draw us to God with a visceral active expression of thanks.

- The result of worship prayer is a reorientation of love both toward God and others.

- Worship prayer is not for revving up our emotions. Being emotional does not mean we have worshiped. True worship prayer changes our thoughts and behavior after worship. We are more hopeful and kind. Less anxious and angry. Emotionalism is about us feeling great. Worship is about humility and lifting up God.

- Worship prayer sometimes takes practice. We are used to singing praise but not always used to saying prayers of adoration and thanksgiving.

- Some people are helped by following a guideline for worship prayer and others need more spontaneity. Pay attention to what draws you to God in worship.

> Worship prayer was harder than anticipated. Time was costly this week, and it was never more apparent than when I was trying to take fifteen minutes for daily prayer. Music helped my emotions and thoughts center on the task of prayer. In the midst of stress, short praises resulted in a cathartic transition. I would begin begrudgingly and as I relaxed, my worship prayers praised God for his existence. With the thanksgiving prayers my reference point shifted. I was not focused on me in a selfish way but I shifted to being aligned with God.
>
> —Roger Kellers

WORSHIP PRAYER EXPERIENCE

Group Experience

- For worship prayer have a 10-10-10 experience—ten minutes for music and singing, ten for adoration and ten for thanksgiving. Designate someone to keep track of time.

- *Ten minutes of worship music*: Begin with worship music for the group to sing or listen to. If singing, choose songs that focus on God. If listening to music, have the group close their eyes. If you want to use movement, you can.
  - *Ten minutes to praise God*: Pray aloud together words of praise for God. We remind ourselves of God's character and greatness. Prayers begin with "God, you are X." Don't try to be original. Listen to your heart. Don't worry about repeating yourself or repeating what others say.
  - *Ten minutes to thank God*: Take turns thanking God aloud for what God has done in your life, in Scripture and in the world. Do these prayers one at a time as short simple statements—"God, thank you for X."
- To close, say together Psalm 100:1-5.
- Talk about your experience. How did worship prayer feel physically, emotionally and intellectually? What is your experience of doing this as a group? Do you have any questions or concerns? What would enhance a worship prayer experience for you? What would honor God?

Partner Experience

- Follow the same guidelines as above.
- What was it like for you to pray in this manner? Was it natural or difficult? How might it impact your time together as prayer partners? In the following days, share with each other how the experience continues to impact you.

Individual Experience

- Follow the guidelines above. I encourage you to use movement if you are by yourself and you are physically able. As you hear the music, how might your body express praise to God?
- If you prefer a more spontaneous prayer time, set the time for 15 minutes and allow yourself to follow your heart as you praise and thank God.
- If you like structure, use a 5-5-5 time frame—five minutes for music, five for adoration and five for thanksgiving.
- Journal about your experience. Did it impact your spiritual life or your relationship with God? Sometimes people have difficulty relating to God because of an abusive or difficult relationship with a father figure or significant male. This type of prayer helps the brain replace the negative memories with redemptive memories.

PRAYER JOURNEY

James Palmer

When I first started praying, I did the typical letter prayer, asking God for world peace and Snickers bars. Finally I thought to myself, "Wow, this is a real lame way to pray," so I changed. I sat in a field near my house and thought, "Why pray?" My answer was to get closer to God. So I said a few names for God (Jesus, Lord, Father, Abba, etc.) and waited. It took over two hours of dwelling on God to come up with something to pray for. After I stopped worrying over trivial things, I focused on God and said, "God, you are really big, and I am really small. I need you." A wave of peace swept over me that I had never felt before. After that large amount of time and that small prayer, it felt like the floodgates opened and I just started praying for everything and everyone I could think of. Not letter-type prayers of "Dear God, be with Jimmy," but a passionate prayer of "God, Jimmy really needs you and tell me where I can help and how."

Scott Whaley

I began praying the 5-5-5 worship prayer on the Monday I left for Africa. The first time I did it was on a plane heading for NYC. Every time since then, I was in Africa. I mention that because Africa exasperated the problem I had with this prayer experience. The people I'm with here are a very expressive people. They are a praising people, a worshipful people. It is nothing for them to go on and on about how good God is. That's the problem. I discovered that I'm not at all good at it.

The music time at the beginning was very good. I was able to surrender to the music and allow it to lift my heart toward praise for God. As long as the song provided the words, I was good. However, with great shame, I must confess that five minutes is a very long time for me to verbally lift God up! Two minutes in, I find myself faltering. By three minutes in, I'm repeating myself and starting to hear the warning of Jesus about the babbling pagans in Matthew 6:7. Before I get anywhere near the four-minute mark, I'm wishing I was doing some other prayer experience!

The thanksgiving part came easier —I was in Africa! I had plenty to be thankful for. But that middle part was a chore. Struggling for words took my mind off of God. Instead, the words were center. I guess I will continue to wrestle with that and perhaps build my vocabulary to match my heart's desire to adore God.

FURTHER READING

Graybeal, Lynda L., and Julia L. Roller. *Prayer and Worship: A Spiritual Formation Guide.* New York: HarperOne, 2007.

Hays, Edward. *Prayers for the Domestic Church: A Handbook for Worship in the Home.* Notre Dame, IN: Forest of Peace Books/Ave Maria Press, 2007.

Holtam, Nicholas. *The Art of Worship: Paintings, Prayers, and Readings for Meditation.* London: National Gallery London, 2011.

PART TWO

God the Son

8

Daily Reflection Prayer—The Examen

As a child I received instruction both in the Bible and in the Talmud.
I am a Jew, but I am enthralled by the luminous figure of the Nazarene. . . .
No one can read the Gospels without feeling the actual presence of Jesus.
His personality pulsates in every word.

ALBERT EINSTEIN

In the beginning was the Word, and the Word was with God, and the Word was God. . . .
And the Word became flesh and lived among us, and we have seen his glory,
the glory as of a father's only son, full of grace and truth.

JOHN 1:1, 14

JESUS AS HUMAN

When we experience a disappointment or loss, it's very difficult to hear words from people who are clueless about our experience. When they say things like, "God is teaching you something," or "Jesus wanted your child to be one of his angels," or "Just stop eating—what's wrong with you?" they betray in hurtful ways their lack of understanding. What is so remarkable about our God is that he came in the flesh to be with us and to be as us in our life experiences.

Jesus, God's Son, came in the flesh, a mystery of divinity and humanity. He was a rabbi/teacher, prophet, healer and also our Savior and Lord. Jesus subsisted as both fully human and fully divine during his earthly life in first-century Palestine. He was the incarnational presence of God among humankind and in his own creation. "In the beginning was the Word, and the Word was with God, and the Word was God. . . . And the Word became flesh and lived among us, and we have seen his glory, the glory as of a father's only son, full of grace and truth" (Jn 1:1, 14).

After Jesus' resurrection and ascension there were conflicting views of his nature. The difficulty for some early Gentile believers was accepting a "savior" who had died as a criminal on a cross. In Greek thought the divine and the flesh were impossibly separated and distinct. Someone divine could not suffer or change; he would only "seem" to change. Therefore, Jesus didn't really die on the cross. For the Jewish believers the problem was the fundamental belief in one God. Jesus was a remarkable prophet, rabbi and healer, but Jesus in his humanity was not "God."

To the apostles it was clear that Jesus was both divine and human. Paul summarized the teaching in 1 Corinthians 15:3-4 and Ephesians 4:4-6. Early church hymns such as Colossians 1:15-20 and 1 Timothy 3:16 also celebrated the mystery of Jesus as both human and divine. Jesus' physical suffering and historical resurrection became the fundamental belief for Christians. At the Council of Chalcedon in A.D. 451 the church fathers settled the matter, concluding that Jesus Christ was truly God and truly man.[1]

As Christians we sometimes drift in how we perceive the nature of Jesus Christ. We sometimes make Jesus our buddy. He becomes an extension of our personal needs and perspectives. We sometimes overemphasize his divinity, so that our call to be "Christlike" is not really possible. Jesus emptied himself of what he could gain as God and became like us (Phil 2:6-8). He limited himself and identified with us so that through him we might find true life.

As a human Jesus had limitations just as we do. Jesus was born and grew up in a family in the town of Nazareth. He learned carpentry from his father. He was involved in a trade to make a living. In Scripture we discover that Jesus got tired, thirsty and hungry, angry and sad, and jubilant. He was honored, betrayed, ridiculed and loved. He suffered horrifically on the cross. Jesus was like us in the limitations of his flesh and in the experiences of his life. Despite these limitations, Jesus regularly communed with the Father and reflected on his earthly life in prayer. In the Gospels we see that Jesus prayed traditionally like a pious adult Jew, and he also went beyond praying regularly. He was a man who brought prayer into all of his life experiences. He is a model for us as we seek a close and thoughtful relationship with God.

If we go through the Gospels and notice every time Jesus prayed, we find:

- Jesus prayed in all sorts of ways—alone (Mt 4:1-11); with small groups (Lk 9:28-36); and in large crowds (Lk 10:17-24).

- He used all types of gestures—quoted Scripture (Mt 4:1-11); touched (Mk 1:30-31); looked up to heaven (Mk 6:41-46; Jn 11:41; 17:1); spoke aloud (Lk 10:21-22; Jn 11:42); laid hands on (Mt 19:13); and broke bread (Lk 24:30).

- He expressed different emotions—jubilation (Lk 10:17-23); great distress (Jn 11:38-44); grief (Mt 14:6-14); and deep agitation (Lk 22:40-44).

- Jesus prayed in all sorts of places—in the wilderness (Mt 4:1-11); in the mountains (Lk 6:12-15); in houses (Lk 24:30); in a boat (Mt 8:26); in a garden (Mt 26:36-45); in public areas (Mt 19:13-15); and on a cross (Mt 27:45-46).

- He prayed at different times—early in the morning (Mk 1:35); over several days (Mt 4:1-11); all night (Lk 6:12-15); during meals (Jn 17:1-23); after teaching (Mt 19:13); after his baptism (Lk 3:21-22); before healings and miracles (Jn 11:41-

42); after successful events (Lk 10:17-23); and during times of distress (Mt 26:36-45; 27:45-49; Jn 11:38-44).

- Jesus prayed for all sorts of reasons—to overcome temptation (Mt 4:1-11); refocus (Mk 1:35-39); make decisions (Lk 6:12-15); receive God's blessing (Lk 3:21-22); perform miracles from multiplying food to raising the dead (Mk 6:41-44; Jn 11:41-44); receive ecstatic vision (Lk 9:28-36); praise God for good things (Lk 10:17-23); bless children (Mt 19:13-15); intercede for his disciples (Lk 22:31-32); receive God's comfort (Mt 14:6-14); prophetic intercession (Jn 17:1-23); relinquishment (Mt 26:36-45); and search for God's presence (Mt 27:45-49).

From Jesus' life we see how prayer encompassed all that he did. Jesus said, "The Father and I are one" (Jn 10:30). He didn't just say it; he lived it. Jesus in his humanity shows us how prayer is not a discipline but a lifestyle of faith. Prayer is an ongoing relationship that involves every aspect of our bodies, our time and our lives.

DAILY REFLECTION PRAYER— THE EXAMEN

Jesus, though in very nature God, in his humanity still made connecting with God a priority. At the end of his earthly life, Jesus left two commands: (1) Go and make disciples (Mt 28:18-20), and (2) Abide in me and I in you (Jn 15:4-5). We as Christians often give most of our energy and time to the first command and less to the second. Both are necessary. The two commands are a perfect polarity.[2] A polarity occurs when two opposite ideas can't function well independently. A Christ follower needs to both go and abide. Jesus was active and stayed connected to his Father. If you mainly go and pray little, or mainly pray and act little, your relationship to Jesus becomes skewed. Jesus was active and prayed.

> What struck me about the daily prayer of reflection is that it is essentially about the incredible love and grace of God. Sometimes when I examine myself before the Lord, it is to point out all the ways I've fallen short of him. But the bigger part is the sheer abundance and availability of God's grace to wash over us.
>
> —Bob Hudson

Jesus prayed three times a day, but he also would go off by himself in the morning or in the evening to pray. Jesus took time in private to reflect on his day and on his tomorrow. This is the practice of daily reflective prayer. Reflection refers to "bending back" as light reflects off surfaces. Reflecting is an act of "bending back" on a day and giving it careful consideration. A reflection gives an image, a bending back from the original. In reflective prayer, we invite God to give us God's image of our day. We invite God to review our day, thoughts, actions and encounters for God's wisdom and insights.

I loved the idea of replaying my day like a movie and seeing where God showed up. During the prayer I saw and felt things about God that I had not noticed during the day. Certain events plainly had his hand in them, and yet I had been too busy to notice. The Lord was extremely gentle with me in the review of my own weaknesses and struggles— showing them to me in a very loving way, yet giving me the assurance that I could learn from them rather than feel guilty. I think God encouraged me by helping me feel how much he cared that I was talking to him.

—Ruthann Rini

This type of daily reflection prayer is commonly known today as the prayer of Examen. St. Ignatius of Loyola (1491–1556) developed the prayer for the Jesuits, a Catholic male religious order. He taught that God was in all things and so we want to listen for God in our day. He suggested the daily exercise occur twice, once in the afternoon and once in the evening. John Wesley (1703–1791), founder of the Methodist movement along with his brother Charles, also developed a list of reflective questions to review the day. He believed holiness was possible because the love of God could reign in our lives. However, we needed the grace of prayer and accountability. Wesley believed that accountability in small groups was essential for discipleship, and he developed a list of reflective questions. The first question was "How is it with your soul?" Daily reflection in prayer connects our humanity to our spiritual desires in the same way that Jesus' daily prayers of reflection connected his earthly life to his divine nature by communing with the Father.

DAILY REFLECTION PRAYER—THE EXAMEN GUIDELINES

- Reflection prayer is based on the truth that God is in all things and the Lord is near.
- The purpose of reflection prayer is to deepen our life in Christ by discerning God's movement throughout our day and aligning ourselves with God's purposes.
- Jesus called us to love, and reflective prayer allows us to "see" how we are or are not loving as Jesus loves. The prayer reminds us that Christ first loved us and always does.
- The prayer helps develop in us a realization that we are not alone and God is ever with us and active.
- The prayer is not about judgment but grace. We see more of God's goodness in us and in our days.
- The prayer is a daily reflection usually twice a day, afternoon and evening. Once in the evening also works well.

- The prayer takes at least fifteen minutes and can be done anywhere.

- There are traditionally five steps to the prayer, though you will find many variations:

    - Step One: Quiet yourself and remember you are in God's presence.

    - Step Two: Ask God the Holy Spirit to help you review your day.

    - Step Three: Reflect with gratitude on the good gifts of the day, the people, places, events.

    - Step Four: Review your day asking yourself (1) when did I love and (2) when did I not love? Or (1) when did I experience God and (2) when did I not?

    - Step Five: Resolve with Jesus any pattern or concern that arose from the examination. Pray for your needs for tomorrow.

> **What a process** it has been to intentionally examine my day and the impact it has on my life and soul. I sleep better. I wake up more refreshed. I feel a more clear sense of my calling. I am more self-aware. Amazing! Very rarely am I intentional about discerning and reconciling my day or week. I find my naiveté to be astounding and I even feel a bit silly about how undisciplined I am in this regard. After just four days of practicing this, I want to take advantage of this prayer and intentionally build a discernment process into my evening rhythm.
>
> —Ben Sand

DAILY REFLECTION PRAYER EXPERIENCE

Group Experience

- Have enough paper and writing utensils for the group or have them use their tablets, smart phones or laptops.

- Plan for fifteen to thirty minutes depending on how much sharing you'd like to do at the conclusion of the reflection prayer.

- Prepare either as a handout, on a large paper or electronically these prayer of reflection steps:

    - *Step One—Preparation*: Prepare yourself by focusing on God's presence. Jesus said to his disciples, "I have said these things to you while I am still with you" (Jn 14:25).

    - *Step Two—Invitation*: Invite the Holy Spirit to help you review the day. Jesus then said, "But the Advocate, the Holy Spirit, whom the Father will send in my name, will teach you everything, and remind you of all that I have said to you" (Jn 14:26).

- *Step Three—Thanksgiving*: Think back over the day and give thanks for all the gifts in the day. Jesus assured his disciples, "Peace I leave with you; my peace I give to you. I do not give to you as the world gives. Do not let your hearts be troubled, and do not let them be afraid" (Jn 14:27).
    - *Step Four—Reflection*: Review your day. Jesus said to his disciples, "I am the true vine, and my Father is the vinegrower. He removes every branch in me that bears no fruit. Every branch that bears fruit he prunes to make it bear more fruit. You have already been cleansed by the word that I have spoken to you. Abide in me as I abide in you" (Jn 15:1-4). Ask yourself these questions:
        - When did I love as Jesus loved today?
        - When did I not love as Jesus loved today?
    - *Step Five—Resolution*: Ask God to guide and take care of any concerns that rose up during the examination. Pray for God's help for tomorrow. Jesus at his last gathering with his disciples told them, "My Father is glorified by this, that you bear much fruit and become my disciples. As the Father has loved me, so I have loved you; abide in my love" (Jn 15:8-9).
- A leader guides the process. The first two steps are done together with the leader inviting everyone to be quiet and reflective. The leader can say a short prayer for the first two steps: "Lord, you are here with us. Help us to be mindful of your presence." Leave a couple of minutes for quiet and then pray, "Holy Spirit, watch over us and guide our reflection." Leave a minute for silence.
- For steps three to five allow each person to process at their own pace and to take simple notes or make simple lists. For step five have each person pray their own prayer.
- Come back together at the end of the agreed upon time and partner up with another person. Share about your experience. What surprised you about your day? Did you notice any patterns? Where did you most experience God?

Partner Experience

- Use the same steps as are detailed above in the group experience. Plan on fifteen to thirty minutes for the prayer experience.
- Do steps one and two together, praying prayers as the ones above or similar ones.
- For step three, reflect alone and then share together all the good gifts in the day.
- For step four, reflect alone and then share together the answers to the questions in step four.
- For step five, pray for each other.
- Talk about your experience. How did it help you see God more in your day? How did it help you feel connected to Jesus' life? What did you learn about yourself?

Individual Experience

- This prayer is most helpful when it is done regularly. Decide whether you will do this prayer twice or once a day and for which days of your week.

- Follow the steps above in the group experience section and use your journal or note-paper or an electronic device to complete steps three and four. Steps one, two and five can be done quietly, though sometimes writing out your final prayer is helpful.

- As you do this more regularly, you begin to notice more things about yourself and God. What comes up for you? How are you a blessing to God? Where is God inviting you to more freedom in your life?

PRAYER JOURNEY

Michael Souza

I love the daily reflection prayer, the prayer of Examen. I've been practicing it now for many years. It always takes my awareness of self, others and God during the course of everyday experiences to a deeper level. That was true in three ways this week. First, the prayer of Examen kept my daily life grounded in God. I have recently begun helping my dad try to better manage his diabetes. This week, I had a distinct sense of God's presence as I took the bandage off Dad's ankle sore, cleaned it and re-dressed it. I felt compassion for him, not criticism, and he was not embarrassed but appreciative. I also sensed he is grateful for the time we're spending together. I'm sad for all the lost years. Jesus indicated that being here now will gradually restore those lost years. Another way was that I found it very satisfying to reflect on where I gave gifts to people today and that I was also able to receive gifts as well. When I gave my dad the gift of taking care of his feet, I found it a modern-day version of Christ washing his disciples' feet. I feel not only connected to God, but also connected to Dad. Finally, knowing that I would be practicing the Examen at the end of the day has made me more attentive to God's presence during the day. I noticed God's presence most when I became aware of my limitations in a situation and that it would be with God's help to carry it out.

Eric Lindquist

The prayer of Examen was challenging for me. I saw the value in this prayer as it really helped me to become more sensitive to the way that I loved (or didn't love) throughout the day. The challenge for me was the realization of what my day actually consists of. I was reminded of a *Seinfeld* episode, where they explained the inspiration for the show.

The show was going to be about "nothing." I have to admit that in reviewing my day it occurred to me that it is pretty uneventful. There were times where I loved and times where I failed to love, but most of the time it was just the ordinary day-to-day activities of life. Get up, get dressed, go to work, come home, have dinner, put the kids to bed, do my homework. I know that there is value in all these things and the challenge is how to live a life that honors God in the ordinary, but I was a little shocked in how ordinary my life has become. The exercise was valuable, but it has raised a lot of questions for me about the meaning and purpose of my daily life, and I know I will have to wait on God for the answers.

Matt Conniry

The prayer of Examen did not feel much different than solitude. Settling down, getting comfortable and inviting the Holy Spirit to enter in are all aspects of solitude. The prayer of Examen differs, of course, in the most important way—it asks me to examine my day. It's probably the most I've ever smiled during prayer. These smiles were not because I found something humorous but because I was surprised at how much I could learn about myself through such a method of examination. I also at times felt ashamed; mostly at the way I missed opportunities to shine. During my prayers I remember thanking God for all the small gifts (e.g., getting to spend an additional hour with my wife in the morning, my mother taking my dog on runs in the morning, extra sleep, lunch with my father). Too often I neglect giving praise for these small gifts and, more often than not, never even notice them as gifts. I also remember going through my day and remembering all the times I lacked love (e.g., passive aggressive to customers, lazy with my chores, quick to anger when talking with my wife). Just as I neglect these small gifts I also neglect my smaller sins. This sort of prayer brings a profound sense of self-awareness. Every time I finished my prayer I felt like I had completely new insight into myself and how I operate. I was able to catch myself before I made the same mistakes or had the same bad thoughts. I felt like I could do this prayer while lying down in bed for the night.

FURTHER READING

Manney, Jim. *The Prayer That Changes Everything: Discovering the Power of St. Ignatius of Loyola's Examen.* Chicago: Loyola Press, 2011.

Warner, Larry. *Journey with Jesus: Discovering the Spiritual Exercises of St. Ignatius.* Downers Grove, IL: InterVarsity Press, 2011.

9

The Lord's Prayer

People talk about imitating Christ, and imitate Him in the little trifling formal things, such as washing the feet, saying His prayer, and so on; but if anyone attempts the real imitation of Him, there are no bounds to the outcry with which the presumption of that person is condemned.

FLORENCE NIGHTINGALE

Not everyone who says to me, "Lord, Lord," will enter the kingdom of heaven, but only the one who does the will of my Father in heaven.

MATTHEW 7:21

JESUS AS LORD

We know how difficult it is to be two things at the same time. It's hard to be a parent and a friend to a child. It's problematic to be a boss and a close friend to an employee. If you are in authority over someone either because you pay them, evaluate them or have influence on their future, it's difficult, and probably unhealthy, to make that person also a confidant. Jesus was two things. Jesus was unique in that he was both human and divine. He was like us and the "judge and lover" of us.

Jesus' divine nature is expressed in the titles of Lord, *Kyrios,* and Christ, *Christos.* The title "Lord" signifies his absolute authority and oneness with God throughout all time. The title "Christ" signifies his messianic mission to reconcile the world to himself and to save us from anything that would separate us from a holy God, whether sin or death. Jesus preexisted with God and all things were created through him.

He is the image of the invisible God, the firstborn of all creation; for in him all things in heaven and on earth were created, things visible and invisible, whether thrones or dominions or rulers or powers—all things have been created through him and for him. He himself is before all things, and in him all things hold together. He is the head of the body, the church; he is the beginning, the firstborn from the dead, so that he might come to have first place in everything. (Col 1:15-18)

The Pauline epistles refer to Jesus as Lord over 230 times. Paul had no difficulty understanding Jesus as both human and divine. He adapted the Jewish prayer, *Shema* ("Hear, O Israel: The LORD our God, the LORD is one," Deut 6:4 NIV), to encompass Jesus: "Yet for us there is one God, the Father, from whom are all things and for whom we exist, and one Lord, Jesus Christ, through whom are all things and through whom we exist" (1 Cor 8:6).[1] Becoming a Christian, a follower of the Christ, means to confess and live the lordship of Jesus Christ (Rom 10:8-9).

> The first memory I have of prayer is watching my mother stand in the living room at four in the morning, her arms stretched out and her face toward the sky. Hearing her hum and pray about the problems of being a single mother with eight children has pushed me to look for the best in the heart of God. I can understand why she was so stern and tough on all of us. But to remember how serene she was at that moment shows me that she was my example of Christ and I did not realize it until now. I am hoping that my example is greater to my girls— so that they can imitate Christ in me.
>
> —Kevin Wade

Jesus came as a prophet, a priest and a king. Either of these roles was conferred with anointing the head with oil. Thus the title *messiah* means "the anointed one." *Mashiach*, translated "messiah," is the Hebrew word for anointed one. Jesus proclaims the word and will of God, heals us of our sins and diseases, and leads us to a better world. His title "Christ Jesus" means "The Messiah Jesus." When Jesus asked his disciples, "Who do you say that I am?" Peter replied, "You are the Messiah" (Mk 8:27-29).

As the Messiah, Jesus' earthly words teach us about God and God's mission in the world. In particular, the Lord's Prayer is a synopsis of his message. During Jesus' time, rabbis would teach their disciples a prayer. The rabbi's prayer would "brand" the key messages of that rabbi to distinguish him from other teachers. Jesus' disciples asked him to "teach us to pray, as John taught his disciples," not because they didn't know how to pray, but because they wanted that mission understanding that set them apart from all other discipleship groups. The Lord's Prayer, then, contains in it all the important fundamentals of Jesus' proclamation. When we pray the Lord's Prayer we affirm Jesus Christ's priorities and we join with the catholic (meaning all-embracing or universal) church throughout time and place, proclaiming our united calling.

THE LORD'S PRAYER

The Lord's Prayer follows the pattern of early Jewish prayers. There is an opening focus on God and then a series of petitions. Jesus' prayer is found in two places, Luke 11:1-4, when the disciples ask Jesus to teach them how to pray, and in Matthew 6:9-13, given during the Sermon on the Mount after Jesus says, "Pray then in this way." Luke is the shorter version. The prayer has two parts. In Matthew there are three God affirmations and then three (some scholars say four) community petitions.

"YOU" AFFIRMATIONS

Our Father in heaven,

- "Our"—The "our" and "we" emphasize our identity as a community. We are the children of God.

- "Father"—is used fifteen times in the Old Testament signifying God's authority and God's compassion, both the fatherly and the motherly attributes of God. Jesus referred to God as "father" 170 times, most often in Matthew and John.[2] He used the term to emphasize the fatherliness of God to forgive and to be compassionate.[3]

- "in heaven"—a phrase used most often in Matthew to emphasize God's transcendence and to equate God to light.[4]

Hallowed be your name.

- "hallowed"—"Holiness" is a primary attribute of God. This was a common phrase in Jewish prayers. To ask that God's name be made holy is a declaration that God be glorified through God's work in us (Lev 11:44 and Mt 5:48).

- "your name"—In first-century culture a name encompassed one's character, authority and role.

Your kingdom come.

- "kingdom come"—The theme of the coming of God's kingdom is fundamental to Jesus' message. He spoke of the kingdom 148 times. God's *basileia* (Greek for kingdom) means the beginning of something sacred under the rule of God. Praying for God's kingdom to come is to align with God's rule in the world.[5]

> There is something timeless about praying the Lord's Prayer. As I pray this model I am almost always overcome with a sense of connection with God—his purposes to my purposes. I can't help but want to be a part of what he is doing. I know that as his kingdom comes and his will is done on earth, it includes my life too. When I pray for his kingdom and will to come on earth and in me, I get a sense for the ways that my life connects with the bigger picture of his will.
>
> —Ed Pagh

Your will be done, on earth as it is in heaven.

- "your will be done"—This phrase is not found in Luke's version. Most scholars believe it is a parallel phrase to "your kingdom come," which is typical of Hebrew poetic parallelism. The prayer is for the consummation of God's kingdom (Rev 22:20).

- "on earth as in heaven"—God reigns supreme in the universe. God's kingdom on earth will be restored (Eph 1:9-10).

"WE" PETITIONS

Give us this day our daily bread.

- "give us this day"—The use of "this day" and "daily" highlights the fundamental necessity of bread for our existence. Our daily food is the one thing we are most able to get by our own efforts.[6] The phrase reminded the Jewish people of God's provision of manna in the desert.

- "daily bread"—Jesus was called the bread of life (Jn 6:48). Daily bread is both physical and spiritual.

And forgive us our debts, as we also have forgiven our debtors.

- "forgive us our debts"—Jesus' free offer of forgiveness is central to understanding the nature of God's kingdom. The Aramaic word for sin, *hobha*, is "debts." The Luke version uses the Greek word for "sin," meaning to miss the mark.

> **I have a hard time** trusting God to provide my family's "daily bread," and I end up placing my trust in financial security rather than God's hand of provision. I don't want to have to rely on God's hand of blessing; I want to be the one to provide for my family and remain in control of my life. I thus relive the self-deception of Adam and Eve by seeking the knowledge of good and evil to make my own decisions and be the master of my own destiny. By relying on God for my family's "daily bread," I remind myself that God is our Father.
>
> —Brad Rohr

- "as we forgive others"—Receiving forgiveness without temple sacrifice or acts of good behavior and then reciprocating by freely offering it to others is the most radical idea in God's kingdom. Forgiveness is not just a right. It is a responsibility.

And do not bring us to the time of trial, but rescue us from the evil one.

- "do not bring us to the time of trial"—God does not tempt us as this line is often translated, "and do not lead us into temptation." The word sometimes translated "lead" actually means to bring or bear. The phrase "do not bring us" alludes to the Exodus experience when the people of Israel would doubt God's faithfulness and then turn again and again to their own devices.

- "rescue us from the evil one"—The "evil one" refers to Satan, the great adversary of humanity. We are reminded that Evil is ever ready to corrupt and defeat God's kingdom vision of eternal love and justice (Mt 16:18).

The ending to the prayer, "For thine is the kingdom, and the power, and the glory forever and ever," is a doxology added around the late first and second centuries. It is found in the *Didache, The Teaching of the Twelve Apostles.* The *Didache* explains the early church's teaching on Christian ethics, baptism and the Lord's Supper, and church organization. In the early church, the Lord's Prayer took the place of the usual Jewish prayers. The church continued the practice of praying three times a day—at sunrise, three o'clock in the afternoon and at sunset—but replaced the Jewish prayers with the Lord's Prayer and other mealtime prayers.

THE LORD'S PRAYER GUIDELINES

- The prayer is an affirmation of the nature of God and the nature of our relationship with God. Jesus understood his mission as participation in the mission of God—God's kingdom come.

- The prayer begins with naming and praising the primary attributes of God. These attributes contextualize our focus. God is presented as sovereign, holy and purposeful in God's vision for the kingdom.

- Jesus gives us three primary requests. These requests are for our physical, relational and spiritual needs. At the center of Christ's requirement of us is to trust God.

- The tone of the prayer is familial. We have an intimate close relationship with God. God cares for our physical, relational and spiritual needs. God provides for our daily necessities, wholeness in our relationships and life eternal with God separate from evil and sin.

I was familiar with The Lord's Prayer prior to knowing Jesus, whom I accepted when I was well into adulthood. It was a prayer that I more or less knew from attending weddings or funerals. I did not grow up in a Christian home, and church attendance was limited to the times I went with my great grandmother. To first understand this prayer as Jesus' model for prayer and now to pray it as an affirmation of Jesus' priorities makes it a sweet, personal and intense poem of reflection and honor. It is no longer a rote recitation, but an invitation to align my life and priorities with those of Christ.

—Kathy Pride

- The prayer is not a ritual but a reminder of the distinctiveness of our faith in Jesus Christ.

- The prayer can be used privately but more often it is said together in community.

- The prayer also mimics Jesus' temptations in the wilderness: turn stones into bread, test God's special love by casting himself down and assume power with the evil one.

LORD'S PRAYER EXPERIENCE
Group Experience

- As a large group or in small groups of four or five pray the Lord's Prayer together aloud, phrase by phrase and add prayers as suggested below.

- The rhythm involves saying together a line of the Lord's Prayer, waiting a few seconds in silence to reflect on the words, and then adding small additional prayers around the suggested themes.

- Lord's Prayer Experience

  - *Our Father in Heaven, hallowed be thy name.*

    - Ten seconds of silence.

    - Thank God for his Father Love, affirm God's holiness and ask to be imitators, children called to live holy lives.

  - *Your kingdom come. Your will be done, on earth as it is in heaven.*

    - Ten seconds of silence.

    - Ask to align yourselves with God's kingdom purposes. Pray for those endeavors of your group reaching out to the local and global community.

  - *Give us this day our daily bread.*

    - Ten seconds of silence.

    - Pray for all your physical needs, whatever they might be: food, work, health, living situation, job, studies and so on.

  - *And forgive us our debts, as we also have forgiven our debtors.*

    - Ten seconds of silence.

    - Pray for God to forgive your own sins. Ask God to help and guide us to forgive those who have sinned against us, not in a general way but in a specific manner.

  - *And do not bring us to the time of trial, but rescue us from the evil one.*

    - Ten seconds of silence.

- Pray for God's protection over ourselves and our communities. Pray especially for those places or for those persons who are experiencing darkness either because of war, famine, addiction, temptations and so on.

- Close by singing the doxology "Praise God from whom all blessings flow." Or say together, "For thine is the kingdom, and the power, and the glory forever and ever."

- Discuss together your experience with the Lord's Prayer. What part of the prayer was most meaningful for you? Did you feel God speaking to you or guiding you in any special way? What questions do you have?

Partner Experience

- With your partner or small group, pray the Lord's Prayer as explained in the group experience section.

- At the conclusion, talk together about your experience using the questions above.

Individual Experience

- As an individual this experience can be even more meaningful if you can go through it standing up and speaking the prayer phrases and suggested prayers out loud.

- You might also consider journaling the prayer experience.

- Another experience might be to say the Lord's Prayer out loud over a period of prayer times during the day while standing and consciously reflecting on each word.

- Did you experience any particular place where God felt more near? Did you sense God leading you to address anything more closely in the Lord's Prayer?

PRAYER JOURNEY

Seth Henderson

While praying the Lord's Prayer, the phrase "Your kingdom come, your will be done" struck me. It is an easy phrase to say, but the reality of this statement is powerful. It's about complete submission to a God who is sovereign and is not shaken or surprised by any circumstances.

I sensed this question back to me: "Are you really okay with my kingdom coming if it is different than what you want it to be or doesn't look like what you think it should look like?"

As I thought about the question, I didn't even want to answer because I knew the answer and was convicted. I wasn't okay with it. I wanted to be, but I wasn't. My limited understanding of God had created a view of what I thought was permissible and it may have been contrary to what God wanted. So my desire that I want to be okay with is "God, let your kingdom come in whatever way you see fit, even if I don't like it."

Dan Ward

Building personal meaning into the Lord's Prayer provided an interesting, perhaps formative experience. I entered into the prayer experience with great optimism anticipating a conceptually comprehensive and satisfying experience since the Lord's Prayer covers all the bases and brands me as Jesus' follower. I'm an analytical, structure-friendly kind of guy, and I figured this would start my days on the right foot and pay off with increased balance.

It turned out that the prayer felt a lot like work. I counted this prayer experience as a poor fit for me until I sat down to journal about it. "Prayer is the work." I've heard it, and said it, dozens of times. If that's true, why shouldn't prayer feel like work? I didn't receive a sense of flowing blessings, inner peace or greater balance, but in retrospect the days I prayed my way through in line with the process turned out to be solid and effective days serving God's purpose evenly in the small and mundane things of life. I've talked often about the beauty and necessity of living these days, but I hadn't stopped to notice what they feel like until this week.

Danny Coleman

Many years ago I attended a prayer seminar, at the end of which we were given an 8x5 laminated card with instructions on praying through the Lord's Prayer. Using the prayer card as a guide, it was easy to spend two hours in prayer—all built upon the framework of the Lord's Prayer. This provided me with quite a sense of accomplishment, since prayer had never been my strong suit. But after a few weeks I became tired of the sound of my own voice (both internal and audible). The problem was that I was spending hours talking *at* God. Rather than bringing me a sense of closeness, I felt like I was sending my prayers out as a message—a stream of words like data packets—to some distant place where God would (hopefully) receive them.

When I first became a Christian, I would lie in bed at night and God would talk to me in the way that a loving father talks to a child. I realized that I need to have quiet and have a listening closeness when I say the Lord's Prayer, not just throw words at God.

FURTHER READING

Mulholland, James. *Praying Like Jesus: The Lord's Prayer in a Culture of Prosperity.* New York: HarperOne, 2001.

Packer, J. I. *Praying the Lord's Prayer.* Wheaton, IL: Crossway, 2007.

Towns, Elmer. *Praying the Lord's Prayer: Prayer for Spiritual Breakthrough.* Ventura, CA: Regal, 2012.

10

The Servant Prayer

Humility is the foundation of all the other virtues
hence, in the soul in which this virtue does not exist
there cannot be any other virtue except in mere appearance.

AUGUSTINE OF HIPPO

He who is not a good servant will not be a good master.

PLATO

JESUS AS SERVANT

When the bathroom needs cleaning in a home, we don't jump up and down saying, "Pick me! Pick me! I want to clean the bathroom!" Some work is hard dirty work that few enjoy. In the past and in some cultures servants do this type of work. Being a servant is not something anyone would normally choose as a profession. Servants keep quiet and do whatever they are told to do. Their sole purpose is to meet the needs of their masters and employers. Those of us who have served tables in a restaurant know how humbling the position can be. You are not often seen or valued. Therefore, it is all the more astonishing that Jesus came to serve us.

Jesus is the Son of God and the Son of Man. He was God and he was a human being who lived among us and redeemed us. Despite his incredible capacities—to heal, raise the dead, multiply food, still storms, ignite hope by his prophetic words, challenge minds with his teaching—his most paradoxical role was to be the Son of God and yet also humbly serving us broken, incomplete individuals. Peter's horror at having Jesus wash his feet would be no less our horror for God to kneel down and wash ours. It doesn't make sense. He has all authority and status above all and yet he chooses to wander the countryside with us and kneel and wash our feet.

From the very beginning of the church, believers understood that Jesus came as Lord and Servant. One of the first church hymns celebrates Jesus' divinity and humanity, but more importantly his willingness to be a slave to accomplish the will of God.

> Let the same mind be in you that was in Christ Jesus, "who, though he was in the form of God, did not regard equality with God as something to be exploited, but emptied himself, taking the form of a slave, being born in human likeness. And being found in human form, he humbled himself and became obedient to the point of death—even death on a cross. (Phil 2:5-8)

During the time of Christ, status came primarily through the acquisition of honor. In Greek and Roman societies, competing for civic honor was normal. For Jewish believers honor came through their piety by observing God's commands, the Torah, and the interpretation of them in the Talmud, rabbinic discussions on the law. Honor set one apart and gave one opportunities for influence as nothing else would. Honor was more important than wealth, though wealth made it far easier to practice and attain honor.

Class consciousness was also in the fabric of all relationships. Therefore, Jesus' choosing downward mobility from being in the form of God to being in the form of a slave made no sense. It was unnatural. Jesus, who is the Creator and King, chose the position of "slave." The Greek word for slave, *doulos*, comes from an adjective meaning unfree. A slave legally belongs to another. He or she has a master, who can buy and sell the slave at will.[1]

A slave had no choice but complete obedience and service to the owner. Jesus freely chose to be a slave for the love of us. Not a slave to us, but a slave for us. He did not use his position as God to impose his will or force his way on us. Jesus also made clear that he completely obeyed God. Because he humbled himself, God then exalted him as the name above all names.

If we are to have the same mind, then we too do not use our special place as God's children as an opportunity to gain honor, status or favor for ourselves. In the same way, we humble ourselves to serve others, even to the point of suffering and personal cost. And in the same manner, we are then glorified with Christ; "When Christ who is your life is revealed, then you also will be revealed with him in glory" (Col 3:4).

Jesus not only chose the role of "slave," he lived it. There was no doubt that he was Lord to his disciples and followers; however, like no other lord before, he used his position to lift others up. He chose and mentored his disciples.

> **I work in the** architecture/developer field and have met people who use their Christianity as a calling card. For some reason they feel it gives them status. My boss, unfortunately, cites it as part of why he doesn't like Christians. He says he has been burned by Christians more than any others.
>
> —Matt Wimer

He mingled with sinners, especially those without hope of social or spiritual re-demption. He spoke with women, the blind, lepers and children. He honored a Samaritan in a parable as one who put aside his personal honor, unlike the religious leaders, in order to help someone in distress. This is not easy, and in prayer we find a place to reflect on Jesus' life and our own call to imitate him.

Some believers confuse servanthood with complete submission to a human or human institution. Jesus was not a doormat to any human or to any institution. There are churches that enforce radical submission of vulnerable people such as women and children, but do not hold people in power accountable to the same standards. Therefore, physical and emotional abuses can occur. Jesus' call to servant-hood was to those in positions of authority.

Another misunderstanding of servanthood is to make radical lifestyle changes without the wisdom of prayer and guidance from friends and church community. Jesus' service did not involve him giving up who he was but his need for gain and recognition. He is still our Lord. In the same way, we don't give up our personalities or privileges unless called to do so, but we give up the need to be honored and rec-ognized. We freely submit to a God who loves us above all, and thus we are also able to freely love others.

SERVANT PRAYER

Even writing this I shudder knowing how deeply ingrained it is in us to want our own glory. For this reason prayer is an important part of living as humble servants of Jesus Christ. In prayer we ex-amine our own places of hubris, or pride, and ask for Jesus to replace pride with acts of service. Hubris can come in many subtle forms. Some are obvious such as when a person constantly references his or her own accomplishments in a con-versation. Some are not, such as when a person takes pride in not being prideful. In this state a person is often judgmental of others. They hold themselves apart as more righteous in thought and deed than others. When a person is judg-mental there is no room for compassion. When there is no room for compassion there is no imagination for service.

> **When I began** the servant's prayer experience, I was apprehensive. I did not want to feel convicted by God to *do* something and change the way I serve him. However, neither of these fears materialized. Instead, he wanted to work on my pride. I rejected this notion outright: "What pride?" I asked. I could not see what God was getting at, but decided to be open to his voice. I was shocked to see so many layers: pride in myself resulting in gossip about a new ministry, pride with my relationship with money and giving, pride in my intentions for service. The list goes on and on. My time with God helped me realign my path.
>
> —Michael Mahon

In Jesus' final hours, before his feet and hands were nailed to the cross, he used his hands to wash the feet of the disciples. Jesus lived service to the disciples to the end. Later after he washed their feet, he prayed for them. The practice of service prayer is a combination of service acts and prayer. Service prayer is visible and tangible. It is small acts of love coming out of discernment and prayer. For instance, during the Lausanne Conference in 2004, the group who worked on reconciliation was asked to give a five-minute report to the Assembly on their findings. Instead of giving a verbal report, this is what they did:

> On the platform, a Hutu sat next to a Tutsi, a man next to a woman, a Black person next to a White person and an Asian person, a Palestinian next to an Israeli, an Orthodox priest next to a Catholic priest and a Protestant pastor. Then they all proceeded to wash each other's feet. They were living out their covenant to break dividing walls of hostility. . . . The call: go and do the same![2]

I meditated on emptying myself like Jesus did so that he would fill me with his fullness. I thought about what I would need to empty myself of. The Holy Spirit gave me surprising insights—empty myself of preconceived ideas about how to serve God and of my desire to stay in my comfort zone.

The Spirit nudged me one morning to call an elderly woman I visit almost weekly to truly care for her with God's heart. Another day he asked me to talk to two people at my office and encourage them— they were pleasantly surprised when I told them what I felt the Lord wanted me to tell them.

—Eunice Oyungu

Psychologists have discovered that it is not often the big differences that create hostility between people, but small gestures of exclusion. If a person tries to connect with another and they are rebuffed or ignored, then a little rift is created between the two. This can be easily forgiven if the individual were having a bad day and this wasn't typical. But constant gestures of exclusion eventually create a huge chasm of hurt and/or hostility.[3] The true measure of service is not in the public gestures, but in the private acts in one's most intimate relationships.

When Jesus washed the disciples' feet, it was an intimate gesture not executed on a grand stage. When you sat at a meal table in Jesus' time, the feet were always washed first. Today we ask our kids when they come to the table, "Did you wash your hands?" Foot washing also established status in relationships. Usually, you would wash your own feet, or a servant would wash your feet, if the host wanted to honor you. However, the greatest honor of all was to have the host wash your feet, indicating his deep love and respect for you. When Jesus washed his disciples' feet, he set a permanent example that we use our status as the children of God to show love and hospitality through everyday gestures. These are done in our homes and communities.

Jesus called us to serve others and to care about bringing his kingdom into the everyday and into every community. We are Jesus' sisters and brothers. We are his family. Therefore, our mission is to serve as he did by blessing, encouraging and reminding others that they are noticed and they matter. Jesus said we are his sheep when we attend to the needs of the hungry, the thirsty, the stranger, the naked, the sick and the prisoner. These needs are physical realities and internal realities. Prayer is a discipline of hospitality when we meet with blessing and physical presence a need in the community or with our neighbor.

SERVANT PRAYER GUIDELINES

- Servant prayer reminds us to imitate Jesus' obedience and service.

- Servant prayer leads us to acts of service.

- In prayer we examine places of pride, reflect on its origins, confess our sin and ask Jesus for guidance in responding in service.

- Servant prayer results in small acts of generosity and kindness directed toward specific people or groups. Servant prayer is a combination of prayer and prayerful service.

- The servant prayer is not a one-time prayer experience but a prayer lifestyle.

- By reminding ourselves of our status in Christ, we are set free from the world's definition of success and our need for status. In prayer our honor comes in humble gratitude for a Savior who gave his all for us.

SERVANT PRAYER EXPERIENCE

Group Experience

- Make sure each person has paper and pencil or some way to journal their leadings.

- As a group, pray Philippians 2:5-11. You can say it together out loud, have each person sing the hymn in their own way, or put the passage to music and sing it together as a prayer.

- Spend ten minutes in silence. Each person asks God to reveal someone or some group they might serve with a specific gesture of kindness and generosity. Write down any impressions. This might be something as small as talking with someone you are uncomfortable with, doing yard work for someone unable to do it or spending time with someone who is alone. A one-time gesture does not a servant make. Think of things that will change how you behave toward someone.

- During the silence pray for the person and for God to use your service to form you as a servant.

- At the end of the silence, again sing or say together Philippians 2:5-11.

- Discuss the experience. Share what impressions and leadings you had. Talk about any questions. Discern together as a group if you want to do individual acts of service or if the group wants to do something together. You are trying to change how you behave toward others, not how others might benefit from your kindness. You want to have the mind of Christ.

- Agree on how you will follow up on your servant actions and prayer. Hold yourselves accountable. When you follow up the next time you are together, divide into groups and share your servant prayer experiences. What was the experience like? How did it remind you of Jesus' service? What was easy and what was hard? How did it impact you spiritually?

Partner Experience

- With your partner or small group pray Philippians 2:5-11 together.

- In silence for ten minutes reflect on places of pride or judgment in you or in your community. If it helps to journal, write down your impressions.

- Ask Jesus to reveal to you something you might do as a gesture of kindness. After the silence confess in prayer where you yourself or your community have not been humble or kind in attitudes or actions.

- Next, ask Jesus for guidance in how to imitate him in responding in service.

- Close the prayer with praying Philippians 2:5-11 again.

- Discuss your experience. What do you believe God is asking you to do as an act of service and kindness? Which of the actions would be most difficult for you to do? Why is that? Which one would most change you or your community? How might you hold each other accountable to follow through? Next time you are together, share about your experience.

Individual Experience

- Sing or pray Philippians 2:5-11 each day for four days.

- Sit in silence to reflect on the words.

- Journal your impressions and leadings.

- Confess any hindrance to being a servant, any place of pride.

- Ask for guidance for which servant behavior you should do.

- Close the prayer time with singing or praying Philippians 2:5-11 again.

- Follow up right away on the servant behavior. Servant behaviors that will most change you or an important relationship are especially valuable.

- The next day journal on your experience. How is Jesus shaping you into a humble servant? What are your challenges?

PRAYER JOURNEY

Lorraine Wilson

All I do is serve others. I cart my family around, clean the house, shop, prepare meals and take the kids to their activities and appointments. I'm not serving. I'm slaving. Just once I'd like someone to say, "Thanks, Mom," and mean it. Just once it would be nice to have someone do something special for me. Not only do I work all the time, we don't have two nickels to rub together. The constant stress of doing with little resources is wearing me down. Even if I wanted to do something for myself, I couldn't.

I was praying this morning after the kids left and grousing to God about my invisible life. I wrote in my journal, "Lord, you don't even care. At church all I do is the same serving of others that I do at home. Every-where I go, it's all about others. I feel like I'm slowly disappearing and no one cares." Then that afternoon—it's even hard for me to write this—I received a card in the mail from a woman in the church. She was a drug addict and homeless woman who came to Christ and is recovering in our church. She doesn't have much, but we've been family to her as she gets stronger. I was surprised to receive a card from her. I opened the card and out dropped $5.00. She had written a little note, "Lorraine, I was praying for you this week and God told me to send you $5.00 and to write 'This is for you.'" I sat down and wept that Jesus would speak to me through the generosity and faithfulness of the least of these. Thank you, Lord, for loving me.

Carol McLaughlin

I have recently joined with those in my church family to provide weekly soup and conversation for our neighbors—those without homes and those struggling with life's hardships. I am learning from these weekly experiences especially when I reflect on them in prayer. Servant prayer helped me to see Jesus' interactions and posture with others in a fresh light. Christ not only heard those in his company but saw those excluded within society. Christ heard them even when others had not. Sometimes I can go about doing something for another without really seeing them. I think most of my serving had been through the lens of meeting needs rather than "seeing" a real person. One thing I am learning as I come alongside these neighbors is the positive difference of making eye contact, of knowing their name and of saying thank you. This isn't always as easy as it sounds. Life's hardships are worn on their faces. I know it is not always possible to know someone's story. However, my growing edge is being present—to listen, observe and be willing to come alongside. I am learning that serving has a human face that I love in simple, tangible ways.

FURTHER READING[4]

Mother Teresa. *In the Heart of the World: Thoughts, Stories, and Prayers.* Novato, CA: New World Library, 1997.

Starr, Mirabai, ed. *Saint Francis of Assisi: Devotions, Prayers, & Living Wisdom.* Boulder, CO: Sounds True, 2007.

Woolman, John. *The Journal of John Woolman.* 1873 (various editions, available free in many online archives).

11

Simplicity Prayer

Our Christian obedience demands a simple lifestyle, irrespective of the needs of others.
Nevertheless, the facts that 800 million people are destitute and that 10,000 die of
starvation every day make any other lifestyle indefensible.

JOHN STOTT

To reduce one's life to essentials, to ask merely for daily bread, forgiveness of others,
and denial of self is, in many ways, a form of madness. It is also a form of liberation.
It lets go of complexity and focuses on simplicity.

ANDREW SULLIVAN

JESUS AS RECONCILER

Our world is rife with divisions and troubling trends. The divisions and hatred we
have always had. The rift between ourselves and our world is growing. We live
mostly indoors requiring huge demands for energy and products in our everyday
lives. Our world is paying a price for our consumer requirements with changing
weather patterns and disappearing species. These requirements are far detached
from the physical world where living things are in a balance with air, water and
earth to survive.

Jesus came into the world he had created and to the people he had chosen.
During his human lifetime he was intimately connected to the created world and
the Jewish people. When he spoke, he referred to such things as wheat, water,
bread, planting, sheep, fish, trees and fruit. Wherever he went, he intimately engaged with the crowds around him teaching, blessing and healing. He came to be
our Peace in his flesh by breaking down the dividing wall and reconciling a hostile
and broken world to his perfect self (Eph 2:14). Jesus brought near all those who

were far. By the blood of the cross he reconciled all things on earth and on heaven (Col 1:20). He made possible a vision for the restoration of the world and its people to a pre-fall condition. Paul writes about the scope of Jesus' reconciling role:

> So if anyone is in Christ, there is a new creation: everything old has passed away; see, everything has become new! All this is from God, who *reconciled us* to himself through Christ, and has given us the ministry of reconciliation; that is, in Christ God *was reconciling the world* to himself, not counting their trespasses against them, and entrusting *the message of reconciliation* to us. (2 Cor 5:17-19, emphasis added)

Being "in Christ" is a mystery meaning Jesus lives in and through us. We are changed internally and it is lived out externally. This is not magic; it is our inheritance as the children of God to have within us Jesus. Jesus reconciled the world, the *kosmos*, meaning the orderly universe in all its senses. He restored it back to himself. Reconciliation is the act of bringing back together things that were meant to be together. The term could refer to married couples whose relationship had broken down. The Greek word for reconciliation, *katalasso*, has a preposition prefix implying a complete change back to the original intimate relationship. We are restored to our pre-fall state before the very holy eyes of God.

Jesus' act of reconciliation impacts individuals, nature and communities. The purpose was to bring back to its natural order and harmony things that had been divided through sin and hostility. Because of this great gift our responsibility is to teach and proclaim the message of reconciliation. Preaching the message means living the message in ourselves and with our world. Life in this new creation illustrates God's activity in the world and hints at the final cosmic renewal.[1]

Reconciliation to others is our fundamental calling and it will be addressed in the chapter on forgiveness. In this chapter we focus on reconciliation with our environments. Randy Woodley, a Cherokee scholar, author and activist writes:

> As people of Faith, we should view every drop of oil, every diamond, every lump of coal, and every source of water with a theological eye. We should try seeing our world through the eyes of the One who created it. All the earth

> The supreme injustice of the killing of Jesus at the hands of humans is overcome by the resurrection—life eclipses death; reconciliation trumps alienation; mercy triumphs over judgment; love conquers all. We are invited to join in this ongoing and expanding process of redemption. It begins within us and then flows out from us to our surroundings: relationships, systems, the world. I think of reconciliation as a deep work of the Spirit—a process— which gradually becomes externally evident as a lifestyle.
>
> —Danny Coleman

is sacred. It seems quite foolish that only after we have gone too far will we realize that no amount of capital gains, no particular economic system or no modern convenience will be worth the price that we will be forced to pay. . . . I sometimes wonder if modern humanity will drive itself to extinction over greed.[2]

Things have been so cluttered in my life lately, I can almost taste it. My house is cluttered. My work is cluttered. My relationships seem cluttered. I feel if I continue, I will suffocate. Galatians 5:1 says, "For freedom Christ has set us free. Stand firm, therefore, and do not submit again to a yoke of slavery." This is the recipe for true simplicity. I don't desire to be enslaved by the clutter. I believe that the only way that I can be proactive in simplifying my life is pursuing the understanding of Christ's freedom. I pray to develop in that quickly.

—David Huffman

Shopping is the great pastime of industrialized nations. We equate our right to shop with our right to freedom. All advertising implies that if you purchased a particular product you would be happier and have fewer troubles. Many studies do demonstrate that there is a bond between wealth and happiness. However, the bond completely disappears after a certain level of economic development in a country. The United States passed the mark years ago.[3]

Consumerism is the compulsion to buy more. The issue for us as people of faith is the destructiveness of constant spending and accumulation on our identities and on our world. Stuff is our modern-day idol. The desire for stuff can separate us from God, and ballooning consumption is slowly destroying our world. Simplicity is a lifestyle of constant reconciliation with ourselves, the poor and the land.

Globally speaking, I belong to the 20 percent of the world's population—and chances are you do, too—that uses 67 percent of the planet's resources and generates 75 percent of its pollution and waste. This doesn't make me proud. U.S. citizens by ourselves, comprising just 5 percent of the world's people, use a quarter of its fuels. An average American gobbles up the goods that would support thirty citizens in India. Much of the money we pay for our fuels goes to support regimes that treat their people—particularly their women—in ways that make me shudder. I'm a critic of this shameful contract, and of wasteful consumption, on general principles. Since it's nonsensical, plus embarrassing, to be an outspoken critic of things you do yourself, I set myself long ago to the task of consuming less.[4]

Our relationship to earth and resources mimics our trust and faith in God. When we clutter, hoard, shop too much or worry about our houses and lives, we are taking responsibility for them. God told the Israelites that they were strangers in the land.

They were to always remember that the world and all its goodness was God's. They were also always to remember that their purpose was to be as God's ambassadors and reconcilers in the world.

SIMPLICITY PRAYER

Simplicity prayer brings the physical world and the spiritual world together and addresses the disparity between Jesus' love of the world as a reconciler and our mission to follow his steps. Simplicity prayer is a combination of discernment and action through a listening conversation with Jesus. Jesus led a simple life and called his disciples to do the same. The purpose was to live honestly and clearly in a world that needs healing.

When we begin a simplicity prayer, we ask Jesus to reveal to us, "What interferes with our living simpler lifestyles?" and "How might I live my calling as an ambassador of reconciliation in my physical world?" Then in silence we listen for Jesus to help us see what he sees. When we are made aware of some action to simplify our lives or to be reconcilers in our communities, then we are obedient to complete the action.

Simplicity prayer unites us to God's heart and helps us to let go. It is a reminder of our call to be ambassadors of reconciliation. We sometimes reduce our ambassadorship to telling others the Good News. Telling is vitally important, but the power of telling comes from a deep connection with the heart and purpose of God. Much of our busyness comes out of our pursuit of success. Through the simplicity prayer we are reminded of Christ's sacrificial gift of reconciliation and our responsibility as ambassadors. Through simplicity prayer we listen for Jesus' direction. We receive his courage and perspective.

> **Simplicity prayer** revealed a lot of feelings in me of being overloaded, obligated and indebted to others' expectations. This prayer also caused me to examine some of the ways that my choices are consuming me and helping me avoid pain, stress and discomfort, like buying coffee or a meal rather than preparing either at home. Buying them is an escape from my life and a way to avoid the distractions and demands of home. Simplifying my life impacts others in ways that often raises questions. When I took my lunch to work, it dramatically impacted who I ate lunch with and resulted in two others joining me.
>
> —Patrick Miller

The simplicity prayer also involves an action of reconciliation, which is often sacrificial. Instead of buying another cup of coffee out, we prepare coffee at home and use the grounds to fertilize our plants. Instead of shopping, we spend time volunteering in a local community garden. Instead of driving, we walk to the neighborhood grocery store. Instead of watching TV, we clean out a closet and give the unused clothes to Goodwill or Salvation Army. In prayer we ask Jesus to see the world as he sees it and to be faithful stewards of its care.

SIMPLICITY PRAYER GUIDELINES

- Solitude and simplicity go together.[5] Solitude is an experience of the heart. Solitude creates the space to detach from the power of things. In solitude we see the dividing wall constructed by the accumulation of things and the drive of consumption.

- Prayer of simplicity is based on complete trust in the reconciling power of God. We do not need to strive. The world provides enough resources if we live simply with what is enough.

- Prayer of simplicity frees us from conformity to this world. It develops in us a capacity for generosity toward others. We are more able to be new creations.

- Prayer of simplicity impacts individuals, relationships and communities. Our social settings drive the compulsion to accumulate. It is easier to see when we discuss it in community.

- Simplicity prayer reminds us of our responsibility to the poor and holds us accountable to caring for the earth.

- Simplicity prayer involves *silence, listening* and *a responsive act* of reconciliation either through simplifying one's life or making a choice to live sustainably.

- Responsive acts are very specific choices to act in reconciling ways in one's personal life, home or environment. The act can be as small as cleaning out a closet or as large as starting a recycling project in your church or community.

SIMPLICITY PRAYER EXPERIENCE

Group Experience

- Pray together aloud:

  "Lord Jesus,
  In you we are a new creation.
  Everything old has passed away;
  see, everything has become new!
  Teach us the ministry of reconciliation.
  Give us courage and wisdom as your ambassadors,
  that your kingdom come and your will be done on earth as in heaven.
  Amen."

- *Silence.* In quiet, perhaps with music in the background, invite everyone to imagine themselves sitting around Jesus. The prayer leader prays, "Jesus, show us how we might live more simply as your ambassadors of reconciliation."

- *Listen*. After five to ten minutes, depending on the capacity of the group to be still, close the time with a few words such as, "Jesus, thank you for your gift of reconciling us to you. Guide now our conversation." Then have everyone get into groups of three to four and share their ideas that came up in prayer. Take ten to fifteen minutes.

- *Respond*. When people have finished sharing in groups, come together and have the groups share their ideas. From these, discuss what the group feels led to do together. It might be to reduce waste or clutter in your church or ministry, or learn how to be less consumer-oriented and live simpler lives. It might be to do something for the environment, such as keep a section of highway or a local park clear of trash or turn a vacant lot into a community garden.

- When the group has decided what it wants to do, discuss the details of how it will be accomplished.

- Close with a prayer such as: "Help us, Lord, to be your ambassadors in this world you love. Help us to be people of simplicity and peace. Amen."

- After you complete the activity and are together again discuss your experience of prayer and action. How did you experience Jesus? Do you have any personal leadings about how you might live a simpler lifestyle? How might this become a regular prayer discipline for the group?

Partner Experience

- This experience requires you to spend time in each of your houses. This doesn't have to be on the same day. If this is not possible, do the group experience instead, but focus on your homes rather than on your faith communities. Also, if you are not comfortable with others helping you simplify your home or garage, do the group experience.

- Plan for at least a thirty-five- to forty-five-minute prayer time. Begin by saying together the opening prayer above in the group experience.

- Sit in silence for five minutes with the desire for Jesus to help you simplify your home, office, garage, workshop, any space you use.

- After the time, with your partner(s), clean out a closet, kitchen, drawers, storage area or garage for thirty minutes. Consider giving what you don't need or use to an organization that recycles used items such as Goodwill or Salvation Army.

- At the end of thirty minutes, talk together about your experience. What was your silent time like with Jesus? What feelings or thoughts came up for you during the simplifying phase of the prayer? What is difficult about simplifying? Consider repeating the experience on your own perhaps once a week.

- Close with closing prayer above.

Individual Experience

- Begin with the opening prayer.

- Then in your journal make a list of what creates clutter in your life and the difficulties for living a simpler lifestyle.

- Move into a period of silence, imagining you are sitting with Jesus, and listen to how he might guide you concerning your list.

- After ten minutes of silence, choose something to do to begin simplifying your life. Before you do it, whether it is getting rid of clutter or not buying something you usually buy, pray the prayer, "For freedom Christ has set me free. Stand firm, therefore, and do not submit again to a yoke of slavery" (Gal 5:1). Pray this prayer each time to create a place of prayerfulness around these acts of reconciliation.

- Consider doing this prayer several times during a week or once a week for at least a month.

PRAYER JOURNEY

Julia Serrano

I've pastored a Latino congregation in Connecticut for several years. At this point in my life my kids were grown and gone, so I wanted to get a different car. I had a van that I'd driven for over sixteen years. I kept it for so long because the van was full of memories. My husband, who had passed away several years earlier, had bought this van for us. Our family grew up with that van. It was still in great condition interior and exterior, but I needed to let go of it and get a smaller, more economical car. I decided to place the van on Craigslist, but when I went to do it, I felt God say to me, "No, just wait."

A week later I went to visit a family who recently began attending the church. The family had four little children and they'd been through a hard time. Though both were college grads, the father had lost his job, and things went from bad to worse. They were homeless for a year, first living out of their car, and then after losing that, living with relatives. Eventually, he got a new job and they were getting their lives back together.

They came to church by bus every week with the four little kids. To go grocery shopping the mom would take the baby carriage to use as a grocery cart and a cold pack to keep food cold. She would walk to the store and back, taking two hours for the journey. While I was visiting with them, they never complained about riding the bus or their difficult situation. Instead, they shared about how much they loved the church and were committed to the church. For them that meant to start tithing, so while I was there, they handed me a check.

As I left and began driving home, I heard God say to me, "Give them the van." I was surprised. The extra cash would help with buying a new car and I realized it was still hard to let go. So, I called my kids and my dad and told them what I was thinking and feeling and they were in agreement. My daughter said, "You are blessed, so do this."

The next morning I called the couple and told them about the van. I said it was old and might need some work, but it was in great con-dition. I said, "If you want it, let me know." The wife replied, "Yes, yes we do want it. Just this week we were starting to make preparations to move our son to a different school because of transportation problems." They were very happy.

In the end, it wasn't about the money but how grateful I feel for what I do have. I realized it was more about what God was doing in me. By being obedient and letting go of the van, I felt more generous and free. I had been praying to God previously about how to be more grateful, and I discovered that being grateful means being more generous.

Hunter Williams

My church gave me the gift of a three-month sabbatical, and one of my goals was to *simplify* my life. This had many layers, but one very practical one was to reduce the number of things I owned. I wanted to go through every drawer and closet and clean out anything I wasn't using and didn't need. I decided to begin with my home office, which I thought would be the easiest. Before I began I sat in prayer and asked God to help me let go of what I needed to let go. My office had shelves of books and notebooks and file drawers full of speaking materials from seminars and workshops, presentations, sermons, retreats, along with information I thought I might want to use someday.

After prayer I began with gusto and found the decision-making fairly easy. Soon I had a huge pile of books to give away. When I began to go through the file folders, a level of self-reflection began to happen. I file chronologically, so I walked through the past fifteen ministry years of my life. All my sermons from two pas-torates were there. For a few minutes with each sermon I relived what was going on in my life, some of which was wonderful and some very dark and hard. With the dark I heard the Lord saying to me, "Hunter, you did well. Trust in me." Experiencing the Lord's favor released me from a lin-gering sense of failure. I began to cel-ebrate what God had accomplished through me, a simple, imperfect man.

FURTHER READING

Andrews, Cecile, and Wanda Urbanska. *Less Is More: Embracing Simplicity for a Healthy Planet, a Caring Economy, and Lasting Happiness.* Gabriola Island, Canada: New Society, 2009.

Foster, Richard. *Freedom of Simplicity.* New York: Harper & Row, 1981.

Hartman, Laura M. *The Christian Consumer: Living Faithfully in a Fragile World.* New York: Oxford University Press, 2011.

12

Prayer in Play

You can learn more from a person in an hour of play,
than a year of conversation.

PLATO

Seriousness is an orientation embedded in constant, chronic anxiety.
The antidote is playfulness.

EDWIN FRIEDMAN

JESUS AS LOVE

Sometimes we adults sit around in a circle and the sole source of entertainment is a child or a puppy. These innocent creatures discovering their world for the first time are an endless source of amusement and interest. If the child is trying to get up on the couch for the first time or the dog is chewing on a toy, we are mesmerized. It feels ridiculous, but we are made to play and we often don't give ourselves permission. Watching children and animals play gives us a vicarious experience of new discoveries and joy. Children are supposed to play.

Jesus loved children. He noticed them, blessed them and said theirs is the kingdom of God. Jesus also referred to those he loved as children. There is a deep connection between following Jesus and children. The story of Jesus blessing the children is found in all three Synoptic Gospels: Matthew, Mark and Luke.

> People were bringing little children to him in order that he might touch them; and the disciples spoke sternly to them. But when Jesus saw this, he was indignant and said to them, "Let the little children come to me; do not stop them; for it is to such as these that the kingdom of God belongs. Truly I tell you, whoever does not receive the

kingdom of God as a little child will never enter it." And he took them up in his arms, laid his hands on them, and blessed them. (Mk 10:13-16)

In Jesus' time children were loved, but they were also the most vulnerable human beings. Child mortality rates were estimated at an excess of 60 percent by age sixteen.[1] Though loved, children didn't have any status until they had survived to adulthood. They were on the same par as a slave in the household. Since children led fragile lives during this time, parents were eager for a holy man to bless them with a prayer of protection. To the disciples this was a waste of time, but for Jesus the innocence and vulnerability of the children modeled how followers were to enter God's kingdom. To enter into the kingdom is to accept God's patronage, which means to fully accept and trust God's care and protection.

Jesus refers to his followers as children, as in John 13:33, "Little children, I am with you only a little longer." The Greek word for "little child" is *teknia*. Later in John 21:5 he calls to his disciples from the shore after his resurrection, "Children, you have no fish, have you?" He uses the Greek word *paidia*, meaning infant or very young child. Even though the disciples didn't recognize him at first, he still referred to them with love. Jesus' affection for his followers is the same as a loving parent for his or her children.

As adults, being the *children of God* is a hard notion to fathom and therefore, we can struggle with understanding Jesus' love for us. We know it, but we sometimes don't live as if it were true. As a grown-up, we become responsible and busy. Others depend on us. If we want to live, we must eat and have shelter and most adults provide and care for others. Most of our time is spent in serious pursuits.

We also lose our innocence, because we are more and more aware of our shortcomings and life's complexities. Life's disappointments stack up like pancakes. Life is not simple. We can drift further and further away from a trusting, loving relationship with our Lord. We understand what it means in our heads to be children in the kingdom of God, but our lives are filled with our work. With the focus on our work we strive for greatness, some way to distinguish ourselves and assure ourselves of our value so we can protect our own.

> I realized how I have conditioned myself not to play—for I have embraced the burden of meeting everyone else's needs at the price of my depletion. Every time I play, I realize the blessing I am denying myself. Praying in play comes naturally as gratitude fills the experience and thanks for the blessing comes to mind over and over again.
>
> —Teresa Heesacker

PRAYER IN PLAY

Jesus' definition of greatness was very different: "Truly I tell you, unless you change and become like children, you will never enter the kingdom of heaven. Whoever becomes humble like this child is the greatest in the kingdom of heaven" (Mt 18:3-4). The term for child is again a reference to a very young infant. A young infant is completely dependent on his or her protector. A very young child's only role is to play, eat and sleep. As adults we need to eat and sleep, but play is optional. I believe play can draw us back into Jesus' love. Combining prayer with play reminds us of our status as Jesus' little children and helps us remember and know his love.

Children in healthy environments are not cluttered with presuppositions or insecurities. They are the most open. Play mirrors their ability to create and experiment with life. Children play to learn and socialize and explore, yet play is not just for children. Play is important throughout life because it is generative and creative. Play for adults helps us shed inhibitions and allows us to transcend ourselves. Play builds community and releases stress. Adults who are unable to play often lack imagination and are anxious. These adults are usually very unhappy or controlling. Play gets rid of the scaffolding of success and achievement. It requires us to be in the present moment with the simplest of things. Play is free from judgment and enhances the development of the whole person: physical, emotional, mental and spiritual.

Love is intimately connected to play. People who cannot love are unable to freely play. Prayer reminds us that the world is good and God is in the world. Play is also a form of prayer when God is invited into the experience prior, during and after play. In play we see ourselves in the image of God and we develop compassion. It is almost impossible to despise someone with whom you have happily played. Play helps us develop a more accurate self-image and God image. Play is not possible if we are afraid or sad. Through play we are renewed and brought together with each other and Jesus.

Prayer and play experiences combine *Praying + Playing + Reflecting*. First, we

Ever give a cat a paper ball? My cats go nuts when I give them one. All of a sudden, their entire world is that scrap of crumpled paper, until it gets swiped under the couch, then they are lost in a well of despair. I laugh and give them another world to play with. My dog is the same way with his ball. When I throw this ball, his entire world is flying over his head as he runs to catch it. Sometimes he loses his world in the tall grass, but it always comes back. We are not so far from our pets in how play affects us. This world seems so big and overwhelming sometimes. When we play and the world gets smaller, God seems to get bigger, more beautiful and comforting.

—Erik Free

pray either silently or together to be aware of Jesus' love and delight in us and to ask his blessing as we play. Then we play, mindful that Jesus is with us during the play time as well as our serious times. At the end of play, we reflect on the experience. How did we experience Jesus in our play? What did we learn about ourselves and others? How did our perspectives change? Jesus was the Messiah blessing the little child just as much as he was the Messiah forgiving the thief on the cross. Prayer and play bring balance to our lives.

PRAYER IN PLAY GUIDELINES

- Human experiences are platforms for prayer, and play is a basic human experience anywhere in the world.

- Giving ourselves permission to play is often the first step toward incorporating an experience of God in our play.

- To be mindful of Jesus in play, we *pray* asking for his presence in our play, we *play* and then we *reflect* on it afterward. Often talking with someone else about your experience helps you see what you might normally have missed.

As a class we experienced play and prayer in a way I never imagined. On the surface it was a crazy stunt when the students tricked the professor into leg-wrestling with another student. But looking deeper into the liminal space, every person in the room will remember that labels, positions, maturity, age, sex, race or any other divisive element in the world can't separate us from the joy and love we receive from God. There was the professor leg-wrestling with Tracie on the floor during a seminary class on prayer. We were no longer a class of students and professor. We were not even a class anymore. We were children of God who grew together while also growing closer to God—and that was the value of surrounding play with prayer. It blew me away.

—Jason Roberts

- Wholesome play and prayer is not outcome based. Playing to win that tramples kindness and fun is no longer play and no longer prayer. It has become a drive for status.

- Competition and play can go together. Paul says to run the race so as to win. Athletes who run competitively love the joy of the challenge. The prize for Paul was doing your best for God's kingdom. It wasn't about greatness but the thrill of God's purposes.

- Prayer and play is very close to how children play and pray. It is immediate, spontaneous and generous with time. There is no drive to achieve or get it right.

- Play and prayer is a simple experience. It can be time with a pet, a table game with friends, flying a kite, racing bikes or playing nonviolent electronic games together.

PRAYER IN PLAY EXPERIENCE

Group Experience

- *Active prayer and play experience*: Any type of group play activity can work as a prayer in play experience. From group games to athletic games to table or electronic games, any type of fun game works.[2] The games should be interactive and nonviolent and not so competitive that some people feel marginalized or left out.

- *Less active prayer and play experience*: If the group doesn't want to be or is unable to be active, you can use the following activity after the opening time of prayer and silence. Have the instructions on a paper and make sure the groups have writing implements.
    - Get into small groups of four or five.
    - Go somewhere close by together in the building or area.
    - Share with each other:
        - An unknown, quirky, unusual thing about yourself or some funny thing that happened to you.
        - A character trait of Jesus that means a lot to you.
        - Create on the front of the paper a representation of the group's quirks or stories and on the back a collage of Jesus' character.
        - Allow twenty to thirty minutes for the time in groups.
        - When you come back together, have a person from the group briefly share.

- *Opening instructions*: Begin the time with a few minutes of silence to draw yourselves into God's presence. Then the leader *prays*, "Jesus, we are your children. Be in our play. Help us to know you in this time."

- *Play* together, some activity that involves everyone present.

- *Closing instructions*: At the end of the play time, talk in small groups and *reflect* together: What was the best part of the play experience? Was there a difficult part? What did you learn about yourself? What did you learn about Jesus and your spiritual walk?

- Close the discussion time with another few minutes of silence. The leader can either close the time with a short prayer or ask the group to offer sentence prayers to Jesus thanking him for his love.

Partner Experience

- Set aside time to pray and play together. You can go somewhere, such as to walk your pets or sit in a coffee shop, or do some fun activity together like shoot hoops, bake or fix a car.

- Begin the time with silence and the opening prayer above in the group experience.

- Play for at least thirty minutes.

- At the end reflect on what you learned about yourself and what you learned about your prayer partner. Share how you experienced Jesus in your play time and the impact on your faith journey.

- Close with prayer especially thanking Jesus for his love.

Individual Experience

- For three or four days one week, choose a play experience that takes fifteen to thirty minutes.

- As you begin the time, remind yourself that Jesus is present in all aspects of our lives and is eager to be with us.

- At the end of the time, journal about your experience. How was Christ present to you? What insights or nudgings did you get about your spiritual life?

- Write or say a prayer of thanks.

PRAYER JOURNEY

Alec Sandu

While I was still thinking on what prayerful play to do, my three-year-old son came and asked me if he could play with me. He took his foot scooter and we went to the park. He said, "Dad, let's race." I was running and he was on his foot scooter. It became an entertainment for the people who were at the park. He liked to win and was excited as he won every time. My son noticed that I was growing tired and he asked me to ride his foot scooter. I had never ridden a scooter before. He taught me how to ride it and how to brake. This was a good experience for me to play with my child. As we were racing I remembered the apostle Paul's words to the Corinthians, "Run in such a way as to get the prize" (1 Cor 9:24 NIV). My racing with my child had spiritual significance. As he taught me to ride, I realized that no one is useless in the world. You can always learn from someone whether young or old.

Ben Sand

My wife usually gets home before I do on work nights. Her rhythm is to quickly get changed, grab a cup of tea and sit on the couch with a book or a television show and wait.

This rhythm has also built a

rhythm for our dog. When my wife sits down, he stops pestering her for attention and begins to whine until I get home. He will stand at the front door and wait for me to get home, sometimes for hours on end. He waits because he knows that when dad gets home, we wrestle.

This week, my assignment for "play" was to spiritually wrestle with my dog. Every night, the first thing I've done when I walk in the door after a long day is explode all of my spiritual energy on my Australian Shepherd. I pin him, pet him and pester him. He plays at first with reckless abandon.

When he gets tired, he loses spunk and begins to flop over and give in instead of putting up a fight. He will lie on his back and pretend to "give up" when I really know he has lost persistence for the cause. What a metaphor for my spiritual life! I start new practices, new methods or new relationships with gusto, only to fizzle on my own. When I depend on myself, I end up flopping over in surrender. Lord, teach me how to play in you.

Chris Black

My wife has had a stressful week. The job she really wanted did not come together and she has been struggling with her boss at her current work. We have been trying to buy a house and now I'm in my last two weeks of graduate school. It has been a very stressful time, but on Saturday night we invited some of my wife's family over to eat pizza. There was some sorrow over the fact that the job had not worked out, but there was such a spirit of encouragement in our home. As we conversed we dreamed about different possibilities and job opportunities that my wife could have. We laughed and enjoyed each other greatly. As I reflected on God's presence in the midst of our fun, it became clear that God had encouraged her heart. The next day she was filled with new ideas and motivations and her spirit was being lifted from the earlier letdown. God was present in our conversation and pizza.

FURTHER READING

Berrymore, Jerome. *Children and the Theologians: Clearing the Way for Grace*. New York: Morehouse, 2009.

Peterson, Eugene H. *Christ Plays in Ten Thousand Places: A Conversation in Spiritual Theology*. Grand Rapids: Eerdmans, 2005.

Ragsdale, Susan, and Ann Saylor. *Great Group Games: 175 Boredom-Busting, Zero-Prep Team Builders for All Ages*. Minneapolis: Search Institute, 2007.

13

Scripture Prayer—*Lectio Divina*

To memorize the Bible, we have to pray the Bible first.

JOSHUA KANG

We do not see things as they are. We see them as we are.

TALMUD

The eye is the lamp of the body. So, if your eye is healthy,
your whole body will be full of light; but if your eye is unhealthy,
your whole body will be full of darkness.
If then the light in you is darkness, how great is the darkness!

MATTHEW 6:22-23

JESUS AS TEACHER

Books and media and teachers have changed our lives. Who hasn't read something or heard a presentation or watched a documentary or film on some topic and not felt internally shifted? Our minds are opened and clear. Our hearts are filled with passion. We see. We are hungry to understand and know.

Jesus was a first-century wisdom teacher and a prophet. Most holy people lived one of the roles. Jesus lived both. He was *the* prophetic sage, the Wisdom of God in the flesh.[1] A prophetic sage knew the purposes of God. In the Gospels Jesus is addressed as *didaskalos* (Greek for teacher) or *rabbi* (Hebrew for teacher) forty-five times. When proclaiming the gospel, Jesus called people to *metanoite*, "change your mind."[2] As a wisdom teacher Jesus helps change our minds in study and learning and prayer. As the Messiah, his grace enables our ongoing transformation into the image of Christ.

Sages, wisdom teachers, are part of the biblical tradition from the Old Testament through the New Testament. The biblical wisdom tradition was grounded in a reverence for Yahweh, God, who was Redeemer and Creator. Wisdom has a concern for the truth, with an orientation toward ethics, how we live well and right before God. Wisdom is the experience of God in the everyday.[3] Two biblical wisdom traditions coexisted throughout Scripture, conventional wisdom and critical wisdom.

Conventional wisdom sages were concerned with a paradigm of social order that focused on correctness, righteousness and conformity. God in his goodness created a just and orderly world. Conventional wisdom sayings are concerned with practical guidance in a paradigm of order.[4] These sayings are similar to our common-sense sayings such as "an apple a day keeps the doctor away" or "haste makes waste." Common-sense sayings represent a group's shared beliefs about the nature of life. Proverbs is a book of conventional wisdom sayings. A classic example is Proverbs 22:6, "Train children in the right way, and when old, they will not stray."

Critical wisdom sages, on the other hand, were concerned with the struggle between order and chaos. To them order was not static, but was a process forever evolving. Human nature and institutions instead of bending toward righteousness were bent toward selfish desires. Critical wisdom sayings dealt with the contradictions in life and were focused on self-understanding rather than well-being.[5] Critical wisdom pondered the deepest questions of human experience: why the good suffer, why evil triumphs, why children stray, why humility does not equal wealth. Ecclesiastes is an example of critical wisdom in the Old Testament, such as Ecclesiastes 7:15, "There are righteous people who perish in their righteousness, and there are wicked people who prolong their life in their evildoing."

Both wisdom and common sense are necessary. The Bible preserved the tradition of order and well-being and the tradition of conflict and self-understanding. They balance each other. On the other hand, Jesus falls into the critical wisdom tradition. His teachings provoked the ruling order's understanding of God's purpose and God's teaching. The Pharisees and ruling religious leaders were trying to cope with a difficult situation, the occupation of the Holy Land and Jerusalem by the Roman Empire. They did this by becoming strict adherents of the conventional wisdom of their faith.

Jesus' using parables and aphorisms challenged the naiveté and optimism of traditional wisdom. *Aphorisms* are individual statements reflecting the conflict between reality and order. An aphorism provokes the hearer to ask questions and have further discussion. The sayings upset one's assumptions. Parables are stories that do the same. Jesus' stories and sayings created disorder, and they would surprise and shock the hearer. These stories are vehicles for thinking, not for abstract representations. Jesus used aphoristic sayings and parables to challenge the first-century conventional wisdom and values toward a more accurate and prophetic understanding of God's kingdom.[6]

> I became aware of the power
> of meditating on Scripture after
> having walked away from God
> for several years. I had had a bad
> experience with a cult-like church,
> so I immersed myself in Scripture to
> understand God's truth for myself.
> I was struggling with forgiveness
> of sin and the perfectionism that
> caused me to recount every act so
> that I would have a clean slate with
> God. God led me to Scriptures that
> proclaimed the truth about God's
> complete forgiveness of sin through
> Jesus before I had even entered the
> world. It was the most freedom-
> filled months of my life as I learned
> that I was completely righteous
> before God because of Jesus' once
> and forever sacrifice.
>
> —Ruthann Rini

God sent Jesus Christ to invite everyone, even the marginalized and sinners, into his kingdom. Birthright came not through blood but through relationship. Jesus proposed an economic system based on generosity and hospitality rather than honor, which no one could really gain through right behavior. It was this bold worldview that caused the religious leaders to fear and despise him. Jesus was undermining their authority as he challenged their dependence on legal behaviors rather than on God's love. Order and being right had replaced radical dependence on God for holiness. Jesus' well-being came through a lifestyle of hospitality and grace. Examples of Jesus' critical wisdom teaching abound in the Sermon on the Mount. One of the most radical and most representative of Jesus' wisdom is found in Matthew 5:43-48, the passage calling us to love our enemies.

Teachings such as these take a lifetime of walking in faith to understand and to live out. We are much more comfortable with order, safety and success than the disorder of constantly trying to live out this teaching. Who are our enemies? How do we love them? Do we really pray sincerely for their well-being? Responses to questions like these also change. Our enemies change. Our world changes. We change. Understanding and truth become more closely aligned with the heart of God over time and with experience. The wisdom tradition allows us to continue to seek insight and to know God's truth.

SCRIPTURE PRAYER

Bringing our questions and biblical passages to Jesus in prayer helps us pay attention to what Jesus is doing in our world and not what we think he is doing. This means in prayer we are constantly seeking to understand and know the heart and mind of Christ. When we stop seeking insight and guidance from Christ we begin to shape our own social order and our own perceptions about how things work.

> **The rush of my life**—cell phones, email, YouTube, the news—creates so much noise that I miss the voice of God in his Word. How wonderful the thought that God could speak to me personally and intimately if I can slow down long enough to hear him. To allow God to speak to me through Scripture, not just to my congregation, is the desire of my heart. I pray that the words of Scripture would cease to be a quotation dictionary and become instead words of life that lead me to Christ and to my God-intended self.
>
> **—James Pagels**

Stanford University psychologist Carol Dweck wrote that researchers have determined that the view a person adopts about themselves will determine their success in life. People who have a fixed mindset believe their abilities and their world are fixed. They focus on getting things right, being accepted and looking smart or put together. Fixed mindset people are more likely to be unhappy with their life and less likely to receive input from outside sources. People with a growth mindset focus on learning from mistakes, growing their skills and relationships, and finding fresh ways to overcome obstacles.[7] The same insights apply to our faith development. If we have it all figured out, we are less likely to experience the full flowering of God's presence in our lives. Our minds are fixed. If we are open to hearing fresh from God, we are more likely to expe-

rience the vital presence of God in our everyday lives.

We have the Bible, a wealth of truth, to guide us, but our humanity and our time and circumstances can hinder our full understanding of God's truth. The living Word Jesus Christ lives in us and continues to teach us and fill us with his grace and truth (Jn 1:14). Therefore, in prayer we come to Jesus to see his mind. Study is important. Discussion with others is helpful. Scholars, teachers and pastors guide us. The Lord is light in others and in history. However, we also need a prayer style for reflecting on truth in our lived experiences.

Historically, this prayer style is called *lectio divina*, Latin for spiritual

> **Scripture and love** are two parts of the same equation. Through the Scriptures we see love in action and by praying the Scriptures we are able to express that in a real way. Learning to truly meditate on Scripture and letting it transform us is the difficult part. We want so badly to make Scripture into what we want it to mean. By meditating on the Scriptures we are able to immerse ourselves in God in a new and awesome way.
>
> **—Andrew Baird**

reading. *Lectio divina* invites us to listen to the living Word for perspective and teaching as we reflect on the written Word. It requires a rhythm of spoken word and silence for reflection.

SCRIPTURE PRAYER (*LECTIO DIVINA*) GUIDELINES

- Any Scripture passage can work for a *lectio divina* prayer, though some more easily lend themselves to the experience than others. For this chapter we are focusing on Jesus' parables and teachings. The passage ideally should be two to ten verses.

- Scripture prayer (*lectio divina*) is based on a pattern of silence, reading, silence and reflection. The spiritual premise is that when we listen, the Lord will instruct us in his ways.

- Silence is used to center on Christ before the passage is read. Silence after the reading is for listening to Christ. There are no expectations. Sometimes we receive insights. Sometimes we are comforted. Sometimes we have more questions.

> Too often when I open the Bible my first thought is, "Okay, what is God trying to teach me?" I rush to try and find the new insight, the lesson for the day so I can feel accomplished and then move on. Actually sitting with the text, imagining myself as part of it, hearing it firsthand or being part of the greater scope of Scripture seldom occurs to me.
> As I was reading the parable of the prodigal son, a story I can't begin to tell you how many times I've heard, I just sat and thought of how I want to be seen, how I think I'm valued by God. It resonated with me so deeply.
>
> —Jacob Garrett Foster

- Even if you are alone, read out loud. The Bible was written for an audience that would hear the Word. Very few people had access to the written text at that time. By hearing the Word, we receive the Word as the writers intended the experience for the original hearers.

- Scripture prayer is not a substitute for Bible study. The Word of God is worthy of careful study. In the act of study, God also can and does speak. Scripture prayer is a way to allow God access to our inner being and thus instruct us in ways we might not have considered.

- Scripture prayer is especially helpful during holy days of the Christian year such as Advent or Lent. The prayer can help us enter into the historical experience of Jesus' birth and journey to the cross.

- Formal *lectio divina* traditionally has four steps and works best with a group. There is a designated reader and the rest are listening, reflecting and sometimes responding aloud. The steps are:

- *Reading God's Word* (Lectio). The passage is read aloud slowly two times. The listeners close their eyes in order to focus on the hearing. Listen for a word or phrase that is highlighted for you. Sit in silence for a couple of minutes.

- *Reflecting on God's Word* (Meditatio). The passage is read again. During the silence reflect on how the passage speaks to your life today.

- *Responding to God* (Oratio). Read the passage again. During the few minutes of silence, consider how God is calling you to respond. Pray and tell Jesus your intended response to what you've heard. It might be praise, some action, something to think about more and so on.

- *Resting in God* (Contemplatio). Read the passage again. Rest in the words in silence for a few minutes. Close with your own prayer or the Lord's Prayer.

- After your prayer, journal about your experience or talk with a spiritual friend. The value of wisdom prayer is to keep ourselves open to the teaching of Christ.

- Informal *lectio divina* is often the individual experience of hearing the Word as you speak it aloud, reflecting in silence and responding. Journaling helps to process the experience.

SCRIPTURE PRAYER EXPERIENCE

Group Experience

- A leader guides the process. This experience takes twenty to thirty minutes.

- Have everyone get comfortable sitting where they can hear and in positions that allow them to relax and focus on the passage.

- Any passage works, but here is an experience using Matthew 5:43-48.

- Begin by praying and having the group repeat after you:
  Leader: *Lord, how can we know the way?*
  Group: *Lord, how can we know the way?*
  Leader: *Jesus answers, "I am the way, the truth and the life" (Jn 14:5-6).*
  Group: *Jesus answers, "I am the way, the truth and the life" (Jn 14:5-6).*
  Leader: *Lord, teach us to see.*
  Group: *Lord, teach us to see.*

- *Reading*: Have everyone close their eyes. Say, "Listen for a word or phrase that you particularly notice as I read the passage aloud two times." Then read Matthew 5:43-48 or some other passage of your choosing.

- After the reading, have everyone sit in silence for two to three minutes. Then say, "With your eyes closed, speak out the word or phrase you noticed. Don't worry about others speaking at the same time."

- *Reflecting*: The leader says, "As I read the passage again, listen for what Jesus might be teaching or saying to you." Read the passage. Sit again in silence for two to three minutes.

- *Responding*: The leader says, "As I read the passage again, listen to how you might respond to the teaching." Read the passage. Sit in silence for two to three minutes.

- Have the group get into pairs and share what reflection and response they might have heard. Sometimes people will hear profound life-changing things and other times people might be challenged, affirmed or even stimulated to ask more questions. Then at times nothing happens. All of the above are normal.

- *Resting*: Have everyone close their eyes again and listen while you read the passage for the final time. Say, "Receive the words and rest in Jesus' truth."

- Close the prayer time by saying the Lord's Prayer together or by the leader saying a closing prayer.

- At the conclusion, have the group talk together about their experience. What are some questions or insights? How does listening help us to see and hear the Word differently than from a Bible study? How might the group respond to these words from Jesus?

Partner Experience

- With your prayer partner or small group of prayer partners, follow the same guidelines as given above in the group experience.

- If there are only two of you, instead of having a leader, either take turns reading the passage or read the passage of choice aloud together.

Individual Experience

- To really experience the wisdom benefit of *lectio divina*, practice the prayer experience over three to four days. Use the same passage each day and have a less structured format.

- Ask Jesus to give you eyes to see and ears to hear.

- Read the passage aloud a couple of times. Then sit in silence reflecting on the words. Consider the words or phrases that seem particularly relevant to your life. Listen for how Jesus might be teaching you or leading you to respond.

- Journal your prayer experience. Do you notice any patterns after reflecting on the same passage for a week? How might you move from noticing things to really changing a behavior? What specific thing might you do?

PRAYER JOURNEY

Scott Whaley

This is a prayer exercise that I am very familiar with and one I have enjoyed very much in the past. I was concerned, however, about reading the same passage throughout the week. My concern was that, once the passage spoke to me the first day, each subsequent day I would find myself with the same message. I was wrong. It was stunning to me how each day a different part of Scripture stood out. The passage that had jumped out one day was completely overshadowed by a different part of Scripture the next day.

One day, it was "You may be children of your Father in heaven." I was convicted that to love like a child was to love with trust, with innocence and without fear. I tend to love cautiously and with self-protection. Later that day, we unexpectedly had to put one of our dogs down because she was extremely sick. I didn't want to go in the back of the vet's office with her because I didn't want to start crying and look foolish. I've got three grown daughters—I'm not the guy who treats my dogs like one of the kids. Still, it was sad and I didn't want to be the guy crying over his dog in PetSmart. Then I remembered the commitment I had made that morning to love without fear. I was not expecting the challenge to love bravely to come from a situation with a non-human. But there it was.

That evening, my wife, my daughters and I said our goodbyes to our ten-year-old, brown, black and white, overweight beagle, Maggie. I didn't cry . . . much.

Simone Weil (French philosopher, 1909–1943)

[Memorizing Scripture as a prayer is another way to have the Word change us as this example from the past shows.]

Until last September, I had never once prayed in all my life, at least not in the literal sense of the word. I had never said any words to God, either out loud or mentally. Last summer, doing Greek with T___, I went through Our Father word for word in Greek. We promised each other to learn it by heart. I do not think he ever did so, but some weeks later, as I was turning over the pages of the Gospel, I said to myself that since I had promised to do this thing and it was good, I ought to do it.

I did it. The infinite sweetness of the Greek text so took hold of me that for several days I could not stop myself from saying it over all the time. A week afterward I began the vine harvest I recited the Our Father in Greek every day before work, and I repeated it very often in the vineyard. Since that time, I have made a practice of saying it through once each morning with absolute attention. If during the recitation my attention wanders or goes to sleep, in the minutest degree, I begin again until I have once succeeded in going through it with absolutely pure attention.

Sometimes it comes about that I say it again out of sheer pleasure, but I only do it if I really feel the impulse. The effect of this practice is extraordinary and surprises me every time, for, although I experience it each day, it exceeds my expectation at each repetition. At times the very first words tear my thoughts from my body and transport it to a place outside space where there is neither perspective nor point of view. The infinity of the ordinary expanses of perception is replaced by an infinity to the second or sometimes the third degrees. At that same time, filling every part of this infinity of infinity, there is silence, a silence which is not an absence of sound but which is the object of a positive sensation, more positive than that of sound. Noises, if there are any, only reach me after crossing the silence. Sometimes, also, during this recitation or at other moments, Christ is present with me in person, but his presence is infinitely more real, more moving, more clear than on that first occasion when he took possession of me.[8]

FURTHER READING

Benner, David G. *Opening to God: Lectio Divina and Life as Prayer.* Downers Grove, IL: InterVarsity Press, 2010.

Collins, Thomas. *Pathway to Our Hearts: A Simple Approach to Lectio Divina with the Sermon on the Mount.* Notre Dame, IN: Ave Maria, 2011.

Foster, Richard, with Kathryn Helmers. *Life with God: Reading the Bible for Spiritual Transformation.* New York: HarperCollins, 2010.

Kang, Joshua Choonmin. *Scripture by Heart: Devotional Practices for Memorizing God's Word.* Downers Grove, IL: InterVarsity Press, 2010.

14

Relinquishment Prayer

By refusing to share our . . . worries,
we limit God's lordship over our life and make clear that there are parts of us
that we do not want to submit to a divine conversation.

BRENNAN MANNING

Usually prayer is a question of groaning rather than speaking,
tears rather than words. For He sets our tears in His sight,
and our groaning is not hidden from Him who made all things
by His Word and does not ask for words of man.

AUGUSTINE OF HIPPO

JESUS AS SUFFERING SON OF GOD

Throughout time humans have experienced deep disappointment, betrayal, evil and pain as the fabric of our lives. Suffering takes air from our souls and innocence from our hearts. Jesus, a God above all other gods, is acquainted with our sorrows and our grief. He sits with us in the dark. He has been there and has shown us a way up from the grave. Our God knows the twisted nature of evil and has overcome the dark. Jesus Christ embraced the sufferings of humanity.

The beginning of Jesus' victory was in the Garden of Gethsemane. There he accepted the Father's will and submitted to his fate. He accepted the path to his suffering, death, burial and resurrection. We often go to the cross to remember our salvation, but without the Garden the cross might have been a defeat and not a victory. Jesus' radical obedience in the Garden reminds us to relinquish to God our need to control, be safe and have the outcomes we want or to relinquish to God sinful behavior and relationships. The road to the open tomb began in the Garden of Gethsemane.

One of the most painted pictures of Jesus, after the crucifixion and resurrection, is his prayer in the Garden of Gethsemane. After his final meal Jesus prays in John 17 for his disciples that God will protect and sustain them. He also prays for those of us who would come to believe in him. Before Jesus entered his suffering he prayed for us. Then in the Garden, Jesus prays for himself. Jesus understood that a difficult journey of suffering would soon begin, and it would begin by the betrayal of one of his own. All three Synoptic Gospels—Matthew, Mark and Luke—tell the story of his prayer in the Garden of Gethsemane on the Mount of Olives. John mentions the prayer in one verse.

This prayer is different from the Lord's Prayer though there are similarities. In both Jesus prays to the Father. Jesus asks that God's will be done, and he prays that his disciples not be led into temptation. However, the poetic beauty of the Lord's Prayer is a stark contrast to the intensity, emotion and desperation of the Garden prayer. Phrases such as "began to be grieved and agitated," and "deeply grieved unto death" and "threw himself on the ground" express the intense physical and emotional experience that it was for Jesus. Jesus suffered so much that in Luke 22:44 there is the sentence, "In his anguish he prayed more earnestly, and his sweat became like great drops of blood falling down on the ground." Luke as a physician recognized the significance of this rare phenomenon. People can, under extreme duress and agony such as when facing death, have blood in their sweat. Jesus was suffering.

When Jesus prays, he calls God "my Father," and in Mark he uses the intimate term, "Abba." He went to his Father with his pain and his questions and his requests. In Genesis Adam and Eve ran away from God and hid when they encountered their temptation in the Garden. When Jesus entered the Garden, he asked his disciples to stay awake, alert, so they would not fall into temptation. Jesus ran toward God. He brings to his Father a raw, disturbed and honest self.

He prays three times for deliverance. Making the same request three times is a biblical literary device to signify completeness. Jesus praying three times means that he prayed until he felt he had resolved the issue within himself and with God. Relinquishment is physiological and emotionally difficult. Therefore, we come to our Father over and over again like Jesus until we experience release.

Each time Jesus asked, "If it is possible, let this cup pass from me." The "if" does not mean that Jesus doubted whether God could make a different choice or not. The "if" means that "since" God can make a different choice, would he do it for him. Jesus accepted the utter sovereignty and power of God to make happen whatever God wanted to make happen. He also knew God to be holy and good. He came to his Father asking for another way.

Asking for "this cup to pass" has significance. The word cup, *poterion* in Greek, is an everyday drinking cup, and the word also describes the cup used in giving offerings in the temple.[1] Paul uses the "cup of offering" to describe the Last Supper to the Corinthians (1 Cor 11:25). The cup represented to the early Christians the suffering they experienced because of the persecution. They took great comfort in Jesus' ability to face his own suffering. We each have our cups of suffering. No one wants to suffer. Jesus brought his suffering to God and asked for another way, but with each request he added, "Yet not what I want but what you want" and "your will be done." He trusted in God's absolute goodness and love despite the personal experience of suffering and pain.

RELINQUISHMENT PRAYER

Jesus trusted himself to God. He trusted God's plan to redeem the world, its inhabitants and creatures because of God's great love. Suffering is everywhere because of evil and a broken world. No one escapes it. We can follow in Jesus' steps when we enter into our own cup of pain. We do this in prayer in an intimate relationship with God. In all honesty and with exposure of the deepest fears and traumas living in us whether from the evil of others or our own sin, we come to God. We continue in prayer until we experience release.

At the end of Jesus' prayer he willingly began his journey to the cross. This acceptance and this kind of love are a great mystery, and not one that is easily understood with theological insights or well-phrased answers. We see Jesus' journey, but when it is our own, it becomes terrifyingly personal. The mystery is that only in prayer, persistence in prayer, and raw, naked honesty can we experience the same victory of the open tomb, the end journey of suffering.

We often limit prayer to our requests and concerns. Jesus brought to God times of extreme distress and confusion. Prayer is a place where the most difficult personal issues of suffering, betrayal and the world's evil are brought to God. In the Garden Jesus' prayer was not answered but his assertion of trust in God was declared. In prayer we face the world's evil and accept the power of grace to overcome. The brilliance of grace is its capacity to convert evil to something holy and redemptive.

When Margaret Duggan's twenty-three-year-old niece died of cancer, she wrote telling me of her struggles with this horrific pain and loss:

> Just a couple of days before Jenny's funeral, I sat in the car in the driveway at home—I'd been so angry at God, threatening and scornful of Jesus' physical suffering compared with what Jenny went through. I spent days "letting rip" and then this moment in the car, I thought, "There is no way out of this, there is only a way through it. I can either go through this with God—the God who I am so angry with right now—or I can go through it alone. Whichever way, I *will* have to go through this." In that moment in the car, I let go; I let go of blaming God for how Jenny died, let go of blaming him for not answering so many prayers, let go of his having to "work this together for good" for my family in order for Jenny's death to have any dignity or purpose—basically I let go of God needing to be anything other than what I've come to know him to be over these many years, my Friend and my Father of the good times and the bad. Over the course of those few moments, with my head on the steering wheel, I let go. No big sparks or whooshes of joy, but a sense of a deal done, a laying down of demands and a tremulous picking up of the hope of peace and the dream that one day the tears will stop.

Entering deeply into our pain is sometimes difficult. We don't like to give up control and we are afraid of our emotions. Emotions are thought to be a sign of weakness. So often we compartmentalize our suffering. Sometimes we simply say, "your will be done," without struggle, as a Band-Aid, and it does little to inspire or comfort others. True relinquishment requires honest emotion.

When we cry, tears originate in all parts of our brain. Tears are connected to our emotions in the limbic area of the brain, to our thinking such as reflective crying in the neocortex area of the brain, and to our survival in the brain stem where tears register fear for safety and pain. Tears reflect the entire human gamut of life experiences: grief, connection, despair, joy, frustration, anger and even physical stress. Crying is a significant human function. Jeffrey Kottler, in one of the few books written about crying, stated, "Tears are an authentication of meaning. They communicate powerfully, forcefully, honestly what you are feeling inside."[2]

Tears cannot be ignored. If someone is crying, everyone notices. Crying is an expression of powerlessness, if it is authentic and not manipulative. When we cry, it is a defining moment. We remember those times. Frederick Buechner, a pastor, writer and theologian, wrote, "Whenever you find tears in your eyes, especially unexpected tears, it is well to pay the closest attention. . . . More often than not God is speaking to you through them of the mystery of where you have come from and is summoning you to where, if your soul is to be saved, you should go to next."[3]

Tears also symbolize surrender. When a person cries they are the most vulnerable. Alan W. Jones, in *Soul Making: The Desert Way of Spirituality*, explained, "Tears are the means by which we have the chance to *see* things differently and be rescued from whatever little hell we may have chosen for ourselves."[4] Tears uncover our life. Pretense is not possible. Masks fall off. Tears connect with the most primal part of our lives and tears connect us with others. Tears soften our hearts and open our minds.

> **I am a control freak.** I attempt to subdue every force, to slay every dragon that seeks to uproot me from my peace. Paradoxically, it does little to give me peace. I had an experience ten years ago where I broke down in tears while I was alone in my apartment. I didn't know why. I thought I was having a nervous breakdown and began leafing through the phone book for the number of a local psych unit. About an hour later, as quickly as it began, the crying stopped and I shrugged it off. On the following Sunday, I was at church and while we were singing, I closed my eyes and when I opened them, I was on my knees. I don't remember kneeling down yet there I was, and I felt God say to me, "I am in control."
>
> —Erik Young

In order to pray a prayer of relinquishment, we surrender control. We cling to the Father in the Garden until we are released by God. It requires a radical trust and a profound obedience that isn't based on a naive, simplistic understanding of faith, but on a raw, distress-filled, emotional encounter with God. Our true selves touch the true nature of God. We find our peace, though the finding isn't pretty. Alan Jones wrote, "When do tears come for the attentive believer? They begin to flow at the moment we see the contradiction between what we hope for and what we actually are; when we see the deep gulf between the Love that calls us and our response to it."[5]

PRAYER OF RELINQUISHMENT GUIDELINES

- The prayer of relinquishment is needed when we feel stuck or disconnected from ourselves because of some life struggle or distress.

- The prayer might involve the need for surrender, such as Jesus in the Garden, or for release from some desire that occupies your thoughts, such as an addiction, disappointment or betrayal, or from a relationship that overwhelms us.

- The release from relinquishment cannot be forced. The timing is always God's.

- The purpose of the prayer is many things: a new joy and freedom, transformation of the personality, attachment to God in a deeper way, a sincere desire to love others, a reordering of our priorities, purification of our motives and a commitment to trust God completely.

- The signs of relinquishment are the same as those Jesus experienced: new courage, clarity of heart and mind, and peace.

- Relinquishment takes time and the mind needs enough will to persist until the deed is done.

- Suffering is part of the experience of relinquishment, sometimes during and sometimes after.

- The hope of relinquishment is based on God's love and the victory of the cross to overcome all evil in ourselves, in others and in the world.

- Relinquishment prayer is an emotional experience. It does not mean that copious tears are always present. Some people grieve with groans and inner distress. Tears often drive release.

- Relinquishment prayers are for great painful events, but they are also helpful for daily frustrations. It is a lifestyle of bringing to God all one's struggles and doubts.

- The prayer is individual, but it is also communal. Sometimes institutions and communities need to struggle in prayer to let go of dreams, disappointments and injustices.

PRAYER OF RELINQUISHMENT EXPERIENCE

Group Experience

- One experience is for a group to pray collectively a prayer of relinquishment about something that the group discerns is an issue of control or worry. Before the prayer, talk together about a common issue that causes the group concern and usually over which the group has no control.

- If the group is not one that has a collective concern, then do the prayer experience together but have each person identify their own issue. People might pair up and talk with a partner about something that is really bothering them or something they are afraid to relinquish. This could take ten to twenty minutes.

- The leader then begins with two to three minutes of silence in order to prepare for the experience.

- Read the passage in Matthew 26:36-46 while everyone's eyes are closed. If some want they can get down on their knees or on the floor prostrate.

- The group then repeats after the leader with spaces between for reflection,

  - "Abba, Father"

  - "if it is possible, let this cup pass from us" (or "me" if the concerns are individual)

  - "yet not what we (or I) want but what you want."

- If this is a collective concern, have people pray aloud their fears or concerns with the issue. If these are individual concerns, have people pray with their partners, giving them time to verbalize before God their deepest thoughts and feelings.

- When the group prayers or partner prayers are completed, the leader prays, "Stay awake and pray that you may not come into the time of trial; the spirit indeed is willing, but the flesh is weak."

- Have the group repeat after the leader with space for reflection: "Our (My) Father, if this cannot pass unless we (I) drink it, your will be done."

- Then again, "Our (My) Father, if this cannot pass unless we (I) drink it, your will be done." Continue in silence for a couple of minutes.

- Pray together the Lord's Prayer or the leader closes with his or her own prayer for the group.

- At the close of the prayer time, take time to talk together about your experience. How did the prayer impact your feelings or understandings about the concern? How might the group or individuals continue to relinquish to God their concern? Are there any questions or thoughts about this prayer?

Partner Experience

- Talk together about a worry or concern you could relinquish to God.

- Read the passage in Matthew 26:36-46.

- Go back and forth between partners, praying about the issue you want to relinquish. At the end of each vocalized prayer, pray "yet not my will but your will be done."

- Do this three times.

- At the end of the prayer time, pray the Lord's Prayer together.

- Share together and talk about your experience and any questions or thoughts you might have. How might you continue to support each other in your relinquishment prayers?

Individual Experience

- For four days pray the Garden Prayer of Relinquishment for fifteen minutes each day.

- If you can, do this prayer early in the morning or late in the evening when you can be completely alone.

- Think of something that worries you a lot, something for which you are bitter and distracted or something that you have to do but don't want to do.

- As much as possible, imitate Jesus' Garden experience. Get on your knees or prostrate yourself and bring your concern fully to God.

- Follow the pattern of asking for release three times and saying like Jesus, "yet not my will but your will be done." If you need to ask more often, do so.

- Each day you can bring the same thing or different things to God. Journal about your experience or talk with a friend about it. How might you sustain a prayer experience of relinquishing control or fears and worries to God?

PRAYER JOURNEY

Victoria Marty

For most of my life I believed that taking care of my mom was my responsibility and mine alone. She has struggled with mental illness and often wasn't stable or functional. For years she barely got by financially and emotionally. Many times I cried out to the Lord to help her make better decisions and to help her get help, but things only got worse.

A year ago, I took matters into my own hands, believing I was the answer to her problems. After months of talking and planning she moved in with us, hoping she could find a job here and get her own place. It was the worst six months of my life. My mom refused to get a job. She refused to help herself even though we were providing everything she needed to get on her feet. She and my husband fought all the time and finally she and I had the biggest fight ever. A week later her boyfriend from New Mexico came and got her, so she returned with hopes of marriage for the sixth time.

At that moment I realized I had to let her go, completely and totally. I could no longer bear her pain or choices. The only person who could keep her, carry her and complete her is Jesus. I relinquished her to the Lord's keep and I cried out to the Lord to take her, to care for her and to heal her spiritually. And he did! He is so faithful. When I finally came to my wits' end and let her go, he picked her up and has taken care of her ever since. She didn't get married, and she and I are closer than ever. She relies on the Lord for her strength. I could never imagine she would be in such a good place, mentally, spiritually and physically. It took me letting go for God to fulfill his plan.

James Pagels

This week in praying the prayer of relinquishment, I struggled with the location for this prayer. I either pray in my office or while walking. Walking doesn't work for this form of prayer. My office is small, and very cold. I ended up using a hallway. I decided that I would really push myself and lie face-down on the floor while praying—I thought that the position might posture my heart correctly.

The first day I lay there with nothing on my mind but, "I'm cold and uncomfortable—I hope no one comes up here and finds me lying on the floor." Day two I thought, "I'll be persistent in my praying and try again." I still struggled with thoughts of being caught praying like this. I finally said, "God I give in. I'll continue to pray this way until I hear from you." The third day I had a short list of areas where I was holding on to things that caused stress and anxiety in my life. I verbally laid these things before God and left them there.

On the fourth day God began to show me how my greatest desire was to be successful as a church with increased attendance, great worship and plenty of finances. This was no surprise to me, but then he took me back to my interns and my poor loving of them. This was just one way in which holding on to my desire for success caused me to love poorly and damaged my leadership of people toward God. As the weight of this issue began to sink in, I found I didn't want to let it go. I argued with God that things needed to be a certain way, that people wouldn't come to church and then where would we be?

After a while, I realized my fists and jaw were clenched, and I remembered, "I'm here to lay down my anxiety and stress—to let go!" I willed my hands open and said aloud, "Father, not my will but yours be done." Then the floodgates of emotion opened and I cried. I was a mess! Since that day I have daily given this to God and I imagine will have to for some time.

FURTHER READING

Foster, Richard J. *Prayers from the Heart.* New York: HarperSanFrancisco, 1994.

Richards, Fr. Larry. *Surrender: The Life-Changing Power of Doing God's Will.* Huntington, IN: Our Sunday Visitor, 2011.

15

Forgiveness Prayer

Forgiveness lies at the heart of Christian faith.

HER MAJESTY THE QUEEN OF ENGLAND'S CHRISTMAS MESSAGE 2011

His death has accomplished our forgiveness;
very well, we must then pass that on to one another.

N. T. WRIGHT

Resentment is like a glass of poison that a man drinks;
then he sits down and waits for his enemy to die.

NELSON MANDELA, WHEN ASKED WHY HE WAS NOT
RESENTFUL FOR HIS IMPRISONMENT

JESUS AS SAVIOR

We call them heroes—people who risk their lives to save others. We read about them in the papers, see them on TV or in social media feeds. They inspire us. Why would someone risk his or her life to race into a burning building, dive into a fast-moving river or intervene in a street fight to help someone? It makes no sense, but it fascinates us. We marvel that a stranger could love so much. Jesus loves us so much that even though for many he is a stranger, he rushed into our world to rescue us.

Jesus is the Savior of the world: "And we have seen and do testify that the Father has sent his Son as the Savior of the world" (1 Jn 4:14). A Savior is one who can deliver, preserve and protect. Jesus is the one who ultimately delivers us and protects us. After the death of Jesus some disciples walked the Emmaus road and talked with a "stranger." They did not recognize him until they sat around the meal table and broke bread. Their eyes were opened. Then Jesus explained the gospel message, "Thus it is written, that the Messiah is to suffer and to rise from the dead on the third day, and that repentance and forgiveness of sins is to be proclaimed in his name to all nations, beginning from Jerusalem" (Lk 24:45-47).

The Savior delivers us from the suffocation of sin. This darkness is of our own making and is also the result of sin in a broken world. Evil, hatred, violence, destructive thoughts and behaviors, gossip, lying, cheating, stealing, sexual impurities and self-centered decisions are part of our lives. Few people murder and rape, but we all lie, cheat and gossip from seemingly insignificant acts to major immoral decisions. Sinful behavior is rooted in our need to preserve ourselves and enhance our significance with our own power.

Jesus came to deliver us by proclaiming the advent of God's kingdom in a revolutionary new way. He proclaimed the kingdom of God, but not as a place either in Israel or heaven. The term "kingdom of God" meant that *God* ruled, not rulers, governments, politicians, religious leaders, the wealthy or revolutionaries. Jesus called us to become kingdom people, people of the new covenant. As people of the new covenant, we embody love and extend the grace of Christ. We live the hero life of bringing and being the embodied Good News. God's kingdom is relational and based on God's covenant with us. Jesus' death on the cross was God's action to renew the covenant that we had broken. His death and resurrection delivers us from the power of sin and destructive forces in our lives and in our communities.

A covenant is based on an ongoing relationship of commitment and justice. Miroslav Volf, a Croatian theologian, in his book *Exclusion and Embrace* describes the relationship between the cross and covenant:[1]

1. The open arms of Christ represent "*God making space for humanity in God's self.*" God wants to be in relationship with us. "The very *identity* of each is formed through relation to others."[2]

2. Renewing the covenant requires *self-giving*. We broke the covenant with God, yet Jesus with his blood sacrifice made renewal possible.

3. The covenant is *eternal*. God does not give us up, even when we deserve it.

The new covenant of God's kingdom is relational and goes between us and God and toward each other. Volf explains, "Contemporary societies are threatened as much, if not more, by the incapacity of people to keep covenant with one another."[3] Enduring, just and life-giving communities are based on relationships, not rules. Therefore, relational self-giving and sacrifice are key to the kingdom of God. We embrace as God embraces.

Embracing others is rarely easy. To embrace someone who has defrauded, wounded or betrayed us is not simple, clean or easy. It is messy and bloody. It begins with relinquishment in the Garden and clinging to the cross. The prayer of forgiveness is the work of God's kingdom, by renewing covenants with God and with others. The basic act of the Savior was forgiveness. The basic response as Christ followers is to respond in kind to others.

There is a gentleman
with whom I help facilitate a
discipleship program. At one point,
he was mentoring me, yet I felt
abandoned and hurt by how the
mentoring relationship ended.
There were many promises made
that were not kept on his behalf.
This relationship has been rocky
since, and through this time of
intentional pursuit of forgiveness, I
have experienced and felt a change
of heart toward this man. It's not
that I now feel he was justified
in what he did, but I am feeling
the freedom of releasing those
things from myself. I feel a level of
freedom and love toward the man
that I haven't felt in a while.

—Jay Bryner

The ability to forgive is probably one of the greatest powers of all time. It is a journey of understanding and embracing the very nature and mission of our Savior Jesus Christ. Forgiveness is not easy to accept or extend to others, because it is more than a rational act. It is also an emotional act. Reason matters, but the greatest mark of our humanity is our relational lives. Our relational lives are a combination of reason and emotion. Emotions not only matter, they are vehicles for change: "Emotions bring a piece of the world to us and into us, providing unprecedented opportunities for growth."[4] Fosha writes in *The Healing Power of Emotion*, "Emotions are, par excellence, vehicles of change; when regulated and processed to completion, they can bring about healing and lasting transformations."[5]

PRAYER OF FORGIVENESS

When we repent and believe the gospel, we follow Jesus' way. We repent of our compulsion to make it our own way.[6] Sin at its core is choosing our own interpretation of good or choosing our own evil, and not choosing Jesus' way. Jesus' way was a way of peace and forgiveness. During the final meal with his disciples, Jesus spoke of the importance of unity. Christ followers will be known by their love, not by their beliefs and rules. At the center of our sinfulness is the fracturing of relationships. From the first break in the Garden to the betrayal of the cross to the multiple betrayals and breaks in relationships we experience every day, the fracturing of community divides us and evil has its way.

In the Lord's Prayer, asking and giving forgiveness is God's will on earth as well as in the heavens. From Jesus' prayer to forgive others to his own actions on the cross, God's response of a holy God in an unholy world was forgiveness. Jesus' death and resurrection dramatized and made real the radical act of forgiving those who do not deserve it. Forgiveness means to pardon, cancel an obligation and relinquish the judgment of guilt and punishment.

By accepting the good news we are in a constant loop with Christ, accepting his invitation to be Lord in our lives, recognizing sin, seeking forgiveness and forgiving

> **I have always thought** of forgiveness as a discipline, as a requirement, as an act that I do for someone else and for myself. It is entirely different to think of forgiveness as an unmerited gift that God extends to both me and the other, not only at the cross leading to salvation, but in an ongoing relationship with him and with each other. I have often tried to "will" forgiveness. I will have to learn to receive the grace of forgiveness.
>
> **—Jason Sedore**

others. Jesus healed all those whom society had rejected. He healed them by driving out disease and forgiving their sin. We do the same. We seek to keep Christ, our Savior, at the center of our lives, and that is partly done through forgiving.

Forgiveness is a rational and emotional journey. It is easy to know one must forgive, but it is a challenge to feel and experience it. Acts of betrayal or hurt are held hostage in our emotional brains and require an emotional journey to truly arrive at release. Resentment, anger, bitterness and chronic sadness are emotions that wire us toward despair and limited options. Ongoing denial of facing and addressing these issues wires our brains for negativity and fear throughout our lives.[7] Jesus experienced all manner of harm from mocking, lies, betrayal, physical abuse and death on the cross. When we cling to him, we can experience with him a dying to self and rising to new life in Christ Jesus. We then can know possibilities and experience new life, a new covenant. Therefore, forgiveness prayer is fundamental to following Christ. It is a core discipline that delivers us from death and renews covenant. Sincere forgiveness is ultimately liberating.[8]

Because forgiveness is difficult, very similar to the process of mourning, it is helped with sustained prayer, staying attached to Christ. Studies have shown that people who can forgive usually use prayer.[9] Forgiveness prayer allows for a new beginning, like the renewed covenant though the journey is often painful and long. Forgiveness prayer is a journey. It takes time, intentionality, grace, deep self-awareness and a final radical act of love. Forgiveness is closest to the suffering journey of Christ to the cross, his painful death and subsequent resurrection.

> **I was convicted** about all the people I needed to forgive. I questioned whether or not I should call, write to or meet up with them to express my own sorrow for harboring bitterness. Then I realized it's me. I need to forgive me. I'm not mad at them but I'm disappointed in myself. My wound of perfectionism had crept into my relationships with others. I was transferring my own pain into their lives so that I didn't feel the blame. The person that I need to spend an hour forgiving is me.
>
> **—Randall McNeal**

FORGIVENESS PRAYER GUIDELINES

- This prayer is not a naive embrace of evil or a dismissal of the consequences of unjust and immoral behavior of others.

- This prayer does not always mean that a relationship is reestablished. Restoration of relationships is not always possible between people. Sometimes one person will not forgive. Sometimes a person is too dangerous and unhealthy.

- Forgiveness prayer is always possible for an individual or a community whether relationships are reestablished or not. By forgiving, we are able to unhook the emotional power another has over us and to move on with our lives. We have the possibility of a future.

- Forgiveness prayer allows us to let go of the power someone has in our lives to define us and influence us. We exchange our victim identity with our rescued-in-Christ identity.

- We embrace a trust in God's judgment. The goal is not to feel love and warm fuzzies, but to feel release and to relinquish judgment to God.

- Forgiveness prayer requires naming the emotions of anger, rage, confusion or sadness. Sometimes one may feel intense hatred. By bringing the authentic emotions to Christ in prayer, we can release their power to shape us.

> **I can forgive,** but I cannot forget, is only another way of saying, I will not forgive. Forgiveness ought to be like a canceled note—torn in two and burned up so that it never can be shown against one.
>
> —Henry Ward Beecher

- Forgiveness prayer involves four phases: (1) *being with the Savior* throughout the process and, if possible, with trusted others who pray with you, (2) *naming and revealing* the emotional pain,[10] (3) *letting go*, and (4) *waiting and receiving* from the Savior a new picture, vision or words.

- Forgiveness prayer is usually not a one-stop prayer. It is often a multistage process.[11] Most deep wounds take many prayers and sometimes years to completely name the pain and experience the resurrection of new life.

- Forgiveness doesn't happen through effort but through obedience. Jesus forgave us so we forgive others. Forgiveness comes as a grace because of the blood and suffering of Christ. It is a mystery. We are delivered by Christ. We cannot boast except in his glory and grace.

FORGIVENESS PRAYER EXPERIENCE

Group Experience

- Sometimes a group harbors distrust, pain or anger at someone or others because of some event or circumstance. This prayer works well for a group to embrace the hurt, release it to God and experience healing. If there is a common group hurt, first discuss exactly what you want to bring to Christ for forgiveness. Allow fifteen to thirty minutes for a group discussion. Instruct everyone to pay attention to the individual hurt they felt in the collective experience. This is not about counseling, dismissing, denying, perpetuating or redefining someone's experience in the group. The goal is to bring the very real hurt to the cross for healing. If the group is unable to come to consensus on the nature of the hurt, do the prayer as an individual prayer experience.

> **I have an "enemy"** in my life. Throughout the forgiveness prayer experience I felt a numbness and disconnect between my head and heart. I worked through the Scripture, sitting in the dark historic chapel on the college campus. Then I stood in the moonlight coming through the window and wrote on a whiteboard, stating aloud "the hurt." Though I did not feel much emotion, I found some clarity in the hurt. As I moved to step three I felt as though I was pushing against a cold steel wall. I realized that if I want to forgive this "enemy" and grow, this will take prayer and time and submission.
>
> —**Jesse Ellington**

- As an individual experience ask people to reflect quietly and then write down on paper about a hurt done to them and one that they want to bring to Christ. Reflective music in the background is helpful but not necessary. Allow ten to fifteen minutes for individual reflection.

- An assigned guide reads Luke 23:33-35 while everyone has their eyes closed and is listening reflectively.

- *Step One—Connecting with Christ*: Guide, "See yourself as one of the people standing by and watching."

- Guide reads the passage again and allows a couple of minutes for reflection.

- *Step Two—Naming the Hurt*: Guide prays, "Lord, we are at the foot of your cross, and we bring to you the pain of our own betrayal and hurt."

- Guide says, "As you stand at the cross in prayer, write down and name exactly your feelings about the hurt." [If this is a group betrayal or hurt, have people instead say them aloud with their eyes closed in prayer.] Allow several minutes for people to enter into this part of the prayer and name their pain.

- *Step Three—Letting Go*: Guide prays, "Lord Jesus, in your pain you forgave the sin and ignorance of others; help us to let go and trust you."

- Guide says, "Write a prayer releasing the person or event and the pain to Jesus." If this is a common group process, have people reflect individually and then pray aloud a prayer of release. Allow enough time for this step.

- *Step Four—Receiving Jesus' Response*: Guide reads Luke 24:1-6, inviting the group to see themselves going from the cross to the open tomb.

- Guide prays, "Our Messiah, Jesus Christ, we have received your forgiveness for our own sins, and we have asked to forgive others. We listen now for a resurrection perspective on this act of forgiveness." Allow a few minutes for people to listen in prayer and write down anything they might hear or feel from Christ.

- Close the prayer time with the Lord's Prayer.

- If this was a common group experience, have people share about the prayer time and any thoughts they received during step four. If this was an individual group experience, have them pair up or get in small groups of three to four and share their experience. Leave time for group questions or reflections.

Partner Experience

- With a prayer partner, talk together about the experience or person you want to forgive. Most people have several hurts or betrayals in their lives, so talk together about the one that is foremost and is limiting your freedom and growth.

- Take turns serving as the prayer support for each other. One person will go through the process, and the other will be with them and pray with them and help guide from step to step.

- With a partner, the prayer experience can be done aloud.

- *Step One—Connecting with Christ at the Cross*: Read the passage and pray for both to be with Christ throughout the process.

- *Step Two—Naming the Hurt*: One person goes first in prayer to name very specifically the hurt and pain he or she has experienced. A sincere entering into the full extent of the hurt helps bring us into an honest place before Christ. The partner stays in a place of prayer. It might take some time to name all the ways in which the person felt hurt or betrayed.

- *Step Three—Letting Go*: After some silence and when the first person feels that he or she is ready, speak aloud a prayer of forgiveness. This also can take several minutes.

- When the person is finished, the prayer partner can pray for his or her partner.

- *Step Four—Receiving Jesus' Response*: Read the passage at the tomb and sit in reflective silence listening for any perspective from Christ. If any is given, receive it in prayer.

- The support partner closes in prayer. Take some time to discuss the experience and then repeat it the same day or on another day for the other partner.

Individual Experience

- As an individual this prayer can be done multiple times over a week, or a substantial period of time can be set aside to enter into the prayer experience. It usually takes time to uncover all the ramifications of a hurt.

- Each time begin with the Scripture of Jesus on the cross and end with the Scripture of the empty tomb.

- Journal about the feelings as often as you need to. Sometimes it is more effective to speak them aloud to Christ. When you are ready to let go, write a simple prayer such as "Jesus Christ, I forgive so and so," and say it as often as is necessary. Sometimes this can be more a prayer of faith than a conviction of thought.

- Allow time to listen for how Jesus might comfort or guide you. Write any thoughts in your journal. The ones from Christ speak truth to you and change you.

PRAYER JOURNEY

Sue Ramsdale

I prayed for several days over who I needed to forgive, and my mom came to mind each time. I prayed for God to show me what I needed to learn about my mother in order to find true forgiveness. He showed me very vividly a memory of my childhood: me coming home from school early because I had attempted suicide during recess. My dad picked me up from school, and my mom came home from work early. The scene is me waiting in my parents' bedroom and my mom running in and falling on her knees sobbing, alternating between hugging and grabbing me, crying and yelling, "Why would you do that to me? What would I do without you?"

My mother and I have had a rocky relationship, but as the result of counseling we now have a very positive relationship. I thought that God was going to show me a scene from my childhood where I was hurt by my mother, but he showed me a scene where I hurt *her*, and where her love for me is undeniably clear, and that I need to look at her in a way where I can still see that love and welcome it.

Franklin Mains

As I sat with the forgiveness prayer, I had difficulty thinking of someone who caused hurt or betrayal in my life that I've not already forgiven. I kept coming up blank. Even continuing to work through the exercise was unhelpful. As I imagined myself looking up at Jesus, bloodied, battered, disfigured, and heard him whisper, "Father, forgive them," it seemed ludicrous that I would drag someone to the cross because they had hurt my feelings or had been dishonest with me. However, the shocking discovery for me was that while I found it easy to forgive others, I find it very scary to ask for forgiveness from others. In forgiving others, I continue to be in control. To ask forgiveness is humbling because I am at the mercy of another. I open myself to rejection and ridicule. It occurs to me that I do have a problem with forgiveness—not giving it, but receiving it.

Katherine Wilson

For several years I served as the chapel coordinator for the seminary where I teach. For one chapel service I designed a worship service on forgiveness. I was very excited about it. It included music, a short homily on the central role of forgiveness in our Christian faith and then a season of prayer. Students, faculty and staff could come to the altar and have a respected local pastor pray for them. The day of the chapel service arrived and I was relieved at how well it was going. I could sense the presence of Christ as we worshiped.

I was sitting engrossed in prayer for others when the Lord spoke to me and said, "You need to go forward." I was shocked. "Me? Why do I need to go forward?" The Lord replied, "You need to forgive your mother." Internally, I began a wrestling match with God, "Lord, I don't need to forgive her. I've already done that. I've been in counseling for five years to work through the destructive nature of my mother." I sat for some time and then asked, "Lord, what do I need to forgive?" There came into my mind the hurtful memory of my mother trying to choke me as a very small child. The whole scene played out in my mind. "Lord, I don't want to forgive her." But eventually, I went forward. I approached my favorite pastor and mumbled something about, "I need to forgive my mother." Though I said little, Pastor Bob prayed a beautiful prayer of forgiveness and release as if he knew all about the situation. Today I don't remember any of the words, and at the time I didn't really feel anything except relief at having been obedient.

I went back to my seat and returned to prayer. As I sat the Lord unexpectedly drew me back into that room and time when my mother grabbed me and started strangling me on the couch. But this time, instead of watching myself on the couch from the door of the room, as I usually did whenever it came to mind, I was standing at the end of the couch, watching her choke me. I was in the form of me as a little girl. Jesus Christ was standing directly behind me, watching her too. Then I experienced from Jesus through me his love and grace for my mom. I saw her as he saw her. I saw her as she truly was in all her brokenness and frail humanity. I was filled with his grace and felt sad and sorry for her. I forgave her. At that point I experienced a new kind of personal freedom. Something was unlocked in the closet of my soul.

FURTHER READING

Horrobin, Peter. *Forgiveness: Pray the Most Powerful Prayer on Earth!* Lancaster, UK: Sovereign World LTD, 2009.

Wuellner, Flora Slosson. *Forgiveness, the Passionate Journey: Nine Steps of Forgiving Through Jesus' Beatitudes.* Nashville: Upper Room, 2001.

16

Sacrament Prayer

From childhood on I have had the dream of life lived as a sacrament . . .
the dream implied taking life ritually as something holy.

BERNARD BERENSON

The lack of incarnational presence by the church and its leaders
is what causes the world to think that we're trying to sell them something
instead of simply inviting them into the life we live.

HUGH HALTER

JESUS AS HEAD OF THE BODY

We all have physical bodies that have a shelf life and that need to be protected and cared for on a daily basis. We feed our bodies with staples like bread, rice or beans, and we need water to drink. We can't live without these basic physical necessities. When our bodies die, we no longer exist in this physical world. We eat and drink so our bodies will live as long as they can. Our life experience is contained in our bodies, so it is fascinating that Jesus referred to himself as the bread of life and the giver of living water. He is the living Body.

In Matthew 26:26 Jesus took bread, blessed it and gave it to his disciples saying, "Take, eat; this is my body." In John 6:51 Jesus says that anyone who would eat his bread of life would live forever. He also spoke of giving living water to any who would ask. The image of body has significance. Jesus shed his blood and his body was broken as physical reminders of our reconciliation. Through his act we are transferred from being complete aliens and hostile to God to a position of being in the very eye of God's favor as new creations. We die and are buried and raised again with Christ. Jesus' gift of life is very physical, not only spiritual and mystical. Life is for today, not some future time after death.

Jesus and Water

Water is a symbol of new life and freedom. In the Old Testament Moses was rescued from the river as a baby. God separated the waters from the dry land at the Red Sea and provided water in the wilderness. In the New Testament Jesus submitted to water baptism. Jesus turned water into wine at a marriage celebration. He spoke of giving a cup of water to the least of these. Jesus called Peter to walk to him on the water. He poured water into a basin and washed his disciples' feet. On the cross when he was pierced, water and blood poured from his side. Water is necessary for our life journey.

The experience of baptism, coming through the waters, is how the church re-enacted the death and resurrection of Christ. Jesus' death was his final baptism into life. Those baptized today confess their sins (or the parents do if an infant is baptized) and are purified, as N. T. Wright explains, "through the water into God's new covenant."[1] Baptism reminds us of the covenant journey from the world of sin into the world of new life and hope. The baptized are now members of God's family and eager to follow Jesus.

Jesus and Bread

Jesus ate many meals with his followers, with the hungry and curious and with the marginalized. In the Old Testament unleavened bread symbolized preparedness and haste for the faith journey. Jesus used bread as the symbol of our daily necessity and his fellowship with us. He ate bread with sinners. He broke bread and miraculously fed hundreds. He broke bread again after his death and his disciples' eyes were opened. In some cultures it would be rice or beans. In the physical act of eating and drinking we are reminded of Jesus' sacrifice and his kingdom message of good news for all people.

The Eucharist, the Lord's Supper, means thanksgiving. It is the ongoing sacrament reminding us of our new state in Christ and of its cost and its blessing. Jesus' sacrifice was complete. Our redemption lacks nothing. Jesus' final meal with his disciples was celebrated during the Jewish Passover, where Jews

> I experience great joy in the symbolism of art. To me, God comes alive in the expression of his nature and power through his creation. Sipping water as I focused on the Living Water caused me to look forward to the day when thirst will rule my life no more. The bread reminded me of how dependent I am on its sustenance and how God wants to be that for me.
>
> —Morgan MacPherson

> **Sacraments are the hinges**
> between the spiritual and material
> worlds. I experience this when I sit
> through a traditional high church
> service with the candles, the smell
> of the incense, the well-worn
> phrases that remind me of who I
> am, what I believe and what we are
> doing. The procession and chancel
> readings, the images and words
> on the walls, the vestments, the
> sourness of communion wine and the
> reception of the host, the mundane
> announcements, singing together,
> processing together, praying in
> silence—in the midst of all this
> human sensual experience of material
> things, there is a spiritual encounter. I
> need more of these to remind me of
> this wedding between worlds.
>
> —Patrick Miller

remember and retell the story of the exodus. Jesus had come to the end of his physical journey. When we eat bread and drink the wine in the fellowship of our faith family, we remember his liberating love. We experience his grace. Jesus was the body given for us, and now he is the head of the body bringing the people of the new covenant into one unified whole. We are the "living" bread and water in our world.

As one body we are led by Jesus, whose eyes, ears, thoughts and passions we adopt. We are immersed in his life by always looking to Jesus throughout our days. We also experience love and growth as we function together as the church, the living presence of Christ.

Body and Sacraments

The experience of the sacraments of baptism and communion remind us of who God is and how much God loves us. We receive his grace. As Gerald Sittser writes in his book *Water from a Deep Well*, the main point of baptism and communion is to remind us of Jesus' saving act. The sacraments "join material and spiritual together into a seamless whole, just as the incarnation does."[2]

> They [sacraments] are institutions of Christ, the Head of the Church, as well as ecclesial actions manifesting His saving act in the world. Their effectiveness comes from Him. They are used by the Church to convey His healing power to His Body of believers. Through them Christians experience growth that is based on Christ's saving events.[3]

Upon receiving baptism or communion, the Eucharist, we are sent out to be the bread of life and living water to others. We incarnate Christ's love and sacrifice through our own willingness to love and sacrifice.

SACRAMENT PRAYER

As sacraments are usually administered in a church or at least in a gathering of believers, sacrament prayer, practiced outside formal sacramental experiences, encourages a daily reminder of how the will of God is made manifest between the spiritual and the physical. Sacrament prayer is a prayer that uses physical elements such as bread and water. These physical elements remind us in prayer of our calling to be the sacrament of bread and water in our families and communities.

The purpose of the prayer is to remember Christ's role as head of the body providing our spiritual nourishment and also to seek the unity of Christian believers everywhere. In sacrament prayer we are reminded of this call on the community of believers to have a common unified commitment to Christ's person and mission.

The body of Christ is global, diverse, strange and beautiful. Yet we often assume it to be individual, uniform (like "me" theologically), predictable and acceptable. We all need water and bread, and we all travel together on a pilgrimage ever toward God. Therefore, sacrament prayer reminds us who is the head and where we are in the body, as one small part. Sacrament prayer reminds us to seek for love and unity and to pray for others.

> **Sacramental prayer** is one that is often lost in our churches. We spend a lot of time talking about our problems and praying for each other, yet forget to mention that in all things we are being united with Christ. Most recently I've noticed many Christian organizations responding to social justice issues with facts and critical thinking. I've yet to see one suggest we turn to prayer so that in our unity with Christ we may know how to act. What if church became less about us and more about Christ?
>
> —Randall McNeal

SACRAMENT PRAYER GUIDELINES

- Sacrament prayer is concrete and active. As the body of Christ we incarnate Christ's presence in life-giving and nourishing ways.

- Sacrament prayer requires an intentional focus on being in the sacred presence of Christ in a distracted and carnal world.

- Using objects to remind ourselves of the physicality of our faith is a part of sacrament prayer. These objects might be a small cross, a rock, a prayer bracelet, a prayer shawl, a Scripture verse one carries, a picture or icon or the traditional symbols of water and bread.

- It is also possible to create a prayer altar, a sacred space area, where you are reminded of Christ's presence as you go about your day. The altar can be anywhere, at home or work, and can be any size, such as a couple of objects to a designated seating area. The objects are anything that reminds you of Christ and his sacrifice and love.

- Since sacrament prayer reminds us of the grace given and our responsibility to live out grace to others in the daily routines of our lives, it is best practiced daily, or at least as often as possible.

- Sacrament prayer is not about being kind or doing something good for others. It is a prayer that draws us into the sacred and compels us to be like Jesus.

- Because sacraments are linked to the exodus and Jesus' pilgrimage on earth, the prayer involves a sense of journey. The journey is a pilgrimage for seeking more of Christ's presence in our daily lives. Practicing the presence through movement and attention to Christ reminds us of our calling.

- Sacraments remind us of the sacramental lordship of Jesus Christ and our call to be unified in Christ. Sacramental prayer urges us to meditate on and pray for the unity of the church worldwide.

SACRAMENT PRAYER EXPERIENCE

Group Experience

- This experience needs a large enough space to accommodate the group and to create four sites for a prayer journey. These sites can be set up on small tables or on a cloth on the floor. People can either stand or sit on a chair or the floor at each journey site. It can be as simple or as complex as you desire. Though people are on a journey from site to site, they are also in community together.

- The first time this experience is done can take thirty minutes or more depending on the size of the group. It can be repeated often in a few minutes to remind the group that Christ is the head and they are the body together.

- *Opening Instructions*: "Whenever you go on a journey, you need food, drink, companionship and shelter. Our spiritual journeys need the bread and living water of Jesus Christ, the fellowship of believers and the leadership of our Lord. Take this sacrament prayer journey in silence, following the instructions at each site. You can begin at any of the four sites."

- The four prayer sites are:

  - *Site One—Bread of Life*: Have a small loaf of bread or pieces of bread in a basket or on a plate (this is not the consecrated bread used in communion, but representative bread).

    - Print out the following verses or have a Bible open to these verses or have people look them up with their own Bibles when they arrive at the site. The verses are John 6:35 and John 4:47-51.

    - Instructions for site one: "Read the verses and sit in quiet prayer for three to four minutes meditating on the words. Take a piece of bread to eat when ready and pray, 'Jesus, thank you for your sacrifice. I receive your bread of life.'"

- *Site Two—Living Water*: Have a pitcher and small cups for water.
  - Print out the following verses or have a Bible open to them or have people use their own Bibles. The verses are John 4:11, 13-14 and John 7:37-38.
  - Instructions for site two: "Read the verses and sit in quiet prayer for three to four minutes meditating on the words. Take a cup of water and pray, 'Jesus, thank you for your sacrifice. I receive your living water.'"

- *Site Three—Head of the Body*: Place a picture of Jesus at this site. It can be art or pictures on a computer screen, and so on.
  - Have the following verses available: Colossians 1:18-24 and Ephesians 1:22-23.
  - Instructions at this site: "Read the verses and sit in quiet prayer for three to four minutes meditating on the words. Make a list of all the areas of your life that need the lordship of Christ. Pray, 'Lord, I confess I have not given these areas to you. I give them to you now. Be the head of my life.'"

- *Site Four—Unity of the Body*: The first time the group does this sacrament prayer journey, you might have a project that allows each person to create a neck or wrist band or object that identifies the group as a group. It should be something that everyone can wear or carry with them. You can get a few simple beads or a cross for people to string and prepare for themselves, or have a rock on which to write "unity," "one in Christ" or whatever you want. The idea is to create something that will symbolize the group as a group together.

  You can also have people put prayer requests in a basket. When a person comes to the unity site, he or she can write down a prayer concern and then pray for other concerns left in the basket. Prayers for growth in Christ and unity of the body are encouraged.
  - Have the following verses available: 1 Corinthians 12:25-27; Ephesians 2:13-14, 19-22; and Ephesians 4:15-16.
  - Instructions at this site: "Read the verses and sit in quiet prayer meditating on the words. Make the object that represents the group's desire to be one in Christ. Pray for unity and growth for the group."

- *Possible closing prayer for the journey*: "Almighty God, who alone can bring order to the unruly wills and passions of sinful humanity: Give your people grace so to love what you command and to desire what you promise, that among the many changes of this world, our hearts may surely be fixed where true joys can be found through Jesus Christ our Lord. Amen."[4] The group might also develop its own prayer for unity.

• Allow time at the end to process the experience together as a group discussion.

Partner Experience

• With your partner or small group follow the experience above but go in order from site one to four. Have the objects on a table in four areas in front of you. Read the Scripture texts aloud together. Be in silence as you meditate at each site. You can use the prayers above or make your own at each site when you pray about receiving the bread, the living water and the lordship of Christ, and about growing in unity together.

• Before you do the prayer experience, determine together what object you want to make to represent your relationship in Christ. The object will serve to remind you of your spiritual partnership and to pray for one another. The bread, water and picture of Jesus can be gathered from items common to a household.

Individual Experience

• For four days use your prayer time to go through the sacrament prayer journey of bread, water, Jesus as head and believers as the body, doing one section for each day. Read the Scriptures listed above for each section, meditate and pray. After each reading and meditation, journal your thoughts.

• You can also make a personal prayer altar. Items can include the objects for this prayer time each day. Put meaningful art, verses or objects that remind you of Christ's sacramental journey for you and the believer's call to unity and growth.

PRAYER JOURNEY

Michael Mahon

The use of my senses while handling and eating the bread and drinking the water helped my connection to God come alive. Though I prefer to take communion in the company of others, I was immediately transported to a Eucharist-connection with God. I also took time to med- itate on Christ as the head and what that meant in my life. I thought through how I steal control away from Jesus in most areas of my life, including work, family, finances and plans for the future. I prayed for help to see how he is in control and to help me rest in the peace of that truth. I am happy to say that God has helped me find a place of peace and steadfastness in my life that I do not believe I have ever experienced.

I wonder if this is his way of answering my prayer, allowing me the space to freely loosen my grip on items in my life.

Jesse Ellington

What most impacted me in the prayer experience was bringing the tangible into the world of prayer. Bringing water, bread, my junk-store-purchased blue-eyed Jesus from college and my newly created unity rock into my prayer life was good for me. It brought the physicality and focal points of liturgical worship without the authority and ritual closer to me. I was especially struck by the power that drinking water and eating bread in the morning can have on the meaning of the words I

am praying. I don't know that I've ever personally prayed for the unity of the church. I saw how the academic value of division and distinguishment in my work environment bleeds into the classroom and chapel. My image of Christ was the most challenging to find meaning. I went online, looked at a couple of small icons I have and settled on a large picture. I realized that I don't think of Jesus as an actual person often. It was a little off-putting. I'll keep praying about that.

David Stewart

I built a little altar in my office out of two chairs. There I placed a clear pitcher of water, a loaf of French bread, a cross and a little model church I have from our building campaign. These props served as aides to help me receive Christ daily as my source of spiritual nourishment and called me to join in his body and the work he is doing in the local church here in Sunnyside. My prayers were

very focused and passionate for Jesus to bring a greater unity here in Sunnyside among the various churches. I began to visualize our ministerial association doing great outdoor worship services in the local park and feeding all the hungry and homeless with food left over to spare. This was a great opportunity for me to grow in a desire to become more one with the body of Christ.

FURTHER READING

Claiborne, Shane, and Jonathan Wilson-Hartgrove. *Becoming the Answer to Our Prayers: Prayer for Ordinary Radicals.* Downers Grove, IL: InterVarsity Press, 2008.

Clifford, Catherine E., ed. *A Century of Prayer for Christian Unity.* Grand Rapids: Eerdmans, 2009.

DeSilva, David A. *Sacramental Life: Spiritual Formation Through the Book of Common Prayer.* Downers Grove, IL: InterVarsity Press, 2008.

Losso, Christian, and Elizabeth Hinson-Hasty, eds. *Prayers for the New Social Awakening.* Louisville: Westminster John Knox, 2008.

PART THREE

God the Holy Spirit

17

Prayer Language—Tongues

It is right, then, that the doctrine of God should precede that of prayer
and that we should deal with prayer in the context of pneumatology,
for the Spirit alone enables us to pray and gives us strength to do so.

WOLFGANG PANNENBERG

Let us thank God heartily as often as we pray that
we have His Spirit in us to teach us to pray.
Thanksgiving will draw our hearts out to God and keep us engaged with Him;
it will take our attention from ourselves and give the Spirit room in our hearts.

ANDREW MURRAY

THE HOLY SPIRIT AS ABIDING PRESENCE

When two people stand before their faith community and pledge themselves to each other, they promise to stay in union until "death do us part." They vow to hang in there no matter how hard it gets financially, physically or relationally. We thrive when we can trust that the other will be there for us. And when that occurs a couple slowly develops their own language. They understand each other through much more than words. Inside jokes, certain phrases and looks or gestures can speak volumes. When the two break out laughing, usually no one else really gets it. When we know each other so well, there is a deep unspoken bond of oneness and love.

The Father, Son and Holy Spirit are One God, the same being and three persons in a *perichoretic*[1] embrace, a dance of love. From the Trinity we see the profound importance of the mystery of God's love, the sacrificing grace of Jesus' life and the Holy Spirit's abiding presence. Through prayer we connect to the Trinity and acknowledge the particular role the Holy Spirit plays in our daily lives.

The Holy Spirit is found in the Old Testament from creation to the charismatic ministry of the Judges[2] to the prophetic books that introduce the Messiah and his empowerment by the Holy Spirit. In the Old Testament the Holy Spirit is called *ruach*, meaning in Hebrew wind, breath or spirit. The force behind the word is the idea of moving air. In the New Testament the Greek word is *pneuma*, which also means breath, wind or soul. It too carries the idea of movement, of blowing. The Holy Spirit is active.

In the New Testament Jesus spoke of the Spirit of the Lord coming upon him (Lk 4:18-19), anointing him to bring good news and freedom. Jesus was baptized by the Spirit and empowered by the Spirit. Jesus promised his followers that they too would have the baptism and empowering presence of the Holy Spirit. "And I will ask the Father, and he will give you another Advocate, to be with you forever. This is the Spirit of truth, whom the world cannot receive, because it neither sees him nor knows him. You know him, because he abides with you, and will be in you" (Jn 14:16-17).

Jesus spoke those words during their final meal together. He promised his disciples that he would send a comforter, someone to be with them and in them. This *parakletos*[3] would guide them in remembering his teachings and life. This would be the Holy Spirit poured out on Pentecost on believers gathered in the upper room waiting and praying as directed by Jesus and the angels after his resurrection. Jesus told his disciples in Acts 1:4-5, "This is what you have heard from me; for John baptized with water, but you will be baptized with the Holy Spirit not many days from now."

The disciples were questioning Jesus about what would happen next, and Jesus replied that they should wait to receive the power of the Holy Spirit. They wanted to know what to expect and when he would return. Jesus said they did not need to know the "times and periods" (Acts 1:7). When we pray, we often want answers, guidance and assurance that we are right, but Jesus gives us instead a relationship with the Holy Spirit. In the same way that Jesus' followers waited and prayed in the upper room, we wait and pray for the Holy Spirit.

The infilling of the Holy Spirit is described in Acts 2:1-4 where a mighty wind and tongues of fire and ecstatic speech marked the event. The indwelling presence of the Holy Spirit is a mystery. The spiritual fills up the material with an experienced sense of God's presence and power. Something is received that the world does not see or understand. Something happens in which a transforming power is evident in lives and events.

The early church caught on fire after Pentecost. After Peter's sermon three thousand people believed and miraculous signs were normal. The dramatic infilling of the Holy Spirit—the sounds, the fire, the languages coming spontaneously from every mouth—marked the transition from the presence of God as a physical Jesus Christ to the indwelling presence of God as the Holy Spirit. Heaven and earth were joined together through the Holy Spirit.[4] The purpose of the Holy Spirit was to enable believers to follow Jesus into the world and to proclaim the gospel.

For Paul, receiving the Holy Spirit was the sign of baptism into the body of Christ. Without it, a person's faith journey was incomplete. Paul wrote in Romans 8:9, "But you are not in the flesh; you are in the Spirit, since the Spirit of God dwells in you. Anyone who does not have the Spirit of Christ does not belong to him."

TONGUES AND PRAYER

Throughout church history the role and manifestation of the Holy Spirit is often debated. For some the Holy Spirit's role is minimized, while for others the Holy Spirit is highly treasured and they rely on it. Of particular difficulty is the early church's sign of the Holy Spirit as the gift of speaking in tongues, called *glossolalia*. Though churches and believers have various interpretations of the importance and expression of a prayer language, speaking in tongues is found in Scripture and did demonstrate the presence of the Holy Spirit. It is also clearly connected with prayer.

In Romans 8:26-27 we learn that the Holy Spirit prays on our behalf with passionate intent. The Spirit interprets our needs to the Father with sighs and groans that are beyond words. The Holy Spirit comes to our aid and lends a hand, and the Spirit does this for whatever weakness whether physical, emotional or relational or due to inner poverty or incapacity. To intercede means that the Holy Spirit rescues us when we are in trouble. In prayer we have a special relationship with the Holy Spirit, a relationship that sometimes has its own language.

When we embrace the Holy Spirit there is a spiritual submission that is deeper than cognitive expression or controlled emotion. A spiritual language is possible. In the New Testament the root meaning of the word *glossolalia* is "tongue" and refers to language, but in the plural form the word can refer to ecstatic speech. Jesus himself spoke about *glossolalia* in Mark 16:17, "And these signs will accompany those who believe: by using my name they will cast out demons; they will speak in new tongues."

Though tongues as a prayer language is found throughout church history from the first century to today and is often connected to revivals of faith, many are suspect of the experience. Some conclude that tongues were a gift only for

During a personal retreat, I had an intense desire to seek God. I went to a labyrinth where I spent several hours in prayer. As I persisted, my prayer turned into singing Scripture, and then I was praying deeply in a prayer language that I cannot describe the intensity of—I prayed and prayed knowing that God was meeting needs and answering prayer; eventually it subsided and I went back to singing Scripture. It took a while just sitting there to even want to stop and get back to my normal self. I know that God met me there in a special way and I am so grateful.

—Eunice Oyungu

the early church. Some believe it is linked to hysteria and emotionalism, which detracts from a thoughtful faith. However, researchers have discovered interesting things about the nature of tongues and prayer.

Dr. Newberg, who led a team of scientists at the University of Pennsylvania, tracked the blood flow in the brains of people who prayed or sang with words and then when they spoke in tongues.[5] Dr. Newberg's team and other researchers discovered three things. First, the person speaking in tongues is still self-aware, so it is not a blind trance. Studies show that people who pray in unintelligible words are still aware of themselves and their environment whether the experience is ecstatic or quiet and subdued. They also found that most people who regularly practice a prayer language are emotionally healthy.

Second, people do give up some control over motor and emotional areas of the brain. Even though they are self-aware they are relinquishing control of their speech and emotions. Third, the frontal lobe is the active area of the brain when speech is involved. The frontal lobe lights up when a person is in control praying with words or with song. However, when a person is praying in tongues the frontal lobe is quiet. This is the same brain pattern seen when people are experiencing their deepest moments of faith. People studied say they regularly experience peace and a feeling of God's presence. As people report the benefits of speaking in tongues spiritually, science confirms what is happening neurologically.

When we receive Christ, we have the Holy Spirit available to us. The Holy Spirit is our greatest advocate and comforter. We are loved. Prayer is how we are mindful of our love relationship with the Holy Spirit. Augustine, the great early church father, used I John 4:7-16 to conclude that "the primary presence of the Holy Spirit is love, not knowledge."[6] The Holy Spirit helps us with groanings too deep for words.

The Holy Spirit at Pentecost came with physical manifestations of the presence of God. Tongues of fire and a mighty wind filled the space while observers recognized their own languages spoken by foreigners (Acts 2:11). Sometimes the gift of tongues is the gift of a spoken language so that God's grace might be proclaimed. Other times the gift of tongues is unintelligible, though when used publically the Holy Spirit gives understanding to others for interpretation (1 Cor 14:27). When it is unintelligible and personal, it is a prayer language for the believer (Eph 6:18 and Jude 1:20).

Made-up, spontaneous singing can approximate a spiritual language experience for individuals or a group. People start singing their own prayer to God, and others join with their prayers. Though actual words are used, the spontaneity and creativity of it often approximate an actual *glossolalia* experience. We can tell the value of prayer language when it results in spiritual fruit in our daily lives. In 1 Corinthians 14:2-17 the benefits include communing with God concerning the mysteries of faith (v. 2), being built up and strengthened (v. 4), and praying, singing and praising God in union with the Holy Spirit (vv. 14-16).

PRAYER LANGUAGE GUIDELINES

- Prayer language is biblical, though its use can vary from being a part of public worship to being a private part of an individual's prayer life.

- Prayer language is an expression of the indwelling presence of the Holy Spirit. It is not the test of the Spirit's presence in us. It is a gift. It can't be fabricated or forced. Some people do not experience *glossolalia* even though they sincerely try. It is not a requirement to be closer to God. It is a help.

- Our minds desire control and predictability. Prayer language is a means of giving space for the Holy Spirit to be expressed physically in our lives.

- Speaking in tongues is based on a deep trust in the indwelling presence and power of the Spirit.

> **Prayer language** by music is one of my favorite ways to experience the movement of the Spirit. I close my eyes during music and stop singing to hear the people around me. Being attuned with God I can feel the Spirit moving from person to person, connecting people in a way that is sometimes forgotten in daily life. I did prayer language by music with my junior high youth group. Naturally, they felt awkward at first. As more and more joined in, their timidity left. The Spirit moved in them.
>
> —Matt Wimer

- The use of tongues is especially helpful when we don't know how to pray or we are too overcome with distress to pray. We come in humility to a God who loves us and whom we can trust.

- Listening to people pray in other languages is a way to engage spiritually and rest the control part of the mind. Making up songs of praise using simple phrases is another way to pray in the Spirit.

- When we pray in the Spirit we experience God's transforming love in our own lives and we respond in love to others.

- Speaking in tongues in prayer is peculiar to the individual. There is no correct sound.

- Prayer language is a trust relationship, falling into the Spirit's presence and letting go. If you are concerned with outside evil influences, begin your prayer asking for the blood of Christ to cover you and the Spirit of Christ to surround you.

PRAYER LANGUAGE EXPERIENCE

Group Experience

- Since prayer language is often a private experience and since not all faith communities practice prayer language in worship, this experience is a moderated one.

- You can choose one of two avenues and the amount of time you give can vary from setting to setting. However, it would be helpful to have enough solitude and reflection time to allow the prayer experience to work.

  - *Creative Singing*: Creative worship singing is a type of prayer language. Everyone sings their own words at their own pace but aloud in community. Some people close their eyes to focus on prayer. Standing helps orient the body in praise.

  - A leader begins singing words like "Glory to God" or "Spirit fill me" or "Jesus is Lord" or "Hallelujah." Any affirmation or praise statement works. You can also use a simple Scripture phrase of three to four words. Use the one phrase over and over so that you are not thinking about words but allowing the Holy Spirit to fill you with praise. The melody is made up as you listen to and respond to the Spirit.

  - As individuals feel ready, they join in using the leader's words or their own, singing their melody aloud.

  - The singing can last anywhere from five to fifteen minutes or more depending on how the group embraces the experience and how the Holy Spirit guides.

  - The experience affirms the movement of the Holy Spirit in community. It also is one that works better if you try it several times so people are more relaxed and know what to expect.

- *Languages*:[7] Listening to prayer in other languages not your own is another way to experience prayer language in community. If you have a group that speaks different languages, you can have everyone pray aloud in their own language at the same time. If your group only speaks one language bring in a recording of prayers in other languages (Hawaiian prayers sound very beautiful) or use songs of praise in other languages.

  - Before playing the recording, tell the group not to try and understand the words but to listen for the Spirit.

  - Play a few praise songs or prayers for five to ten minutes.

- Upon completion of either the singing or listening to prayers in other languages, have the group process and share their experience. Do they have any questions or thoughts?

Partner Experience

- With your partner or small group you can do either of the group prayer experiences above. Decide together which one. Sit in silence to prepare your hearts and then either sing or listen to praise or prayer in another language. Take time afterward to share about your experience.

- Or you can agree to try to pray in the Spirit privately and then talk about it to-gether when you meet next. Praying in tongues involves three steps:

  - Ask for the infilling of the Holy Spirit. This is a sacred request.

  - Relax the mouth and body. If the mind and body are trying to control this, it likely won't happen. When you relax, you are physically humbling yourself.

  - Open the mouth and begin saying whatever syllables come out. A leap of faith happens when you simply begin to express whatever comes out.

  - If nothing happens, don't worry. Begin singing a simple phrase of praise like "grace and truth" (Jn 1:17) and spend fifteen minutes singing however your body leads you. You might add walking in a small area of your house while you sing.

- When you are together, reflect on your experience. What did you feel? What made it difficult? How did you experience God?

Individual Experience

- For four days allow fifteen minutes a day for prayer language. If you already use prayer language, you might try spiritual singing or listening to prayers and praise of other languages.

- Guidance for spiritual singing is found in the group section above and for praying in tongues in the partner section.

PRAYER JOURNEY

Caleb Jackson

I was betrayed by my business partner of fifteen years. He swindled me and took $500,000 set aside for expansion and left the country with my trusted secretary. I was so bitter, angry, em-barrassed and frustrated that I didn't see this coming. I had to let people go who had worked for us for a decade. I felt like a broken clay pot stomped into the dust. I wanted justice.

Two years after he left, I still couldn't wrap my mind around it nor move forward. I kept busy trying to reestablish my business and assure customers. But at night the torment was real. My small group leader, who stood by me throughout, suggested I go on a retreat and spend some time in prayer to bring this before God. He arranged for a pro-fessional counselor and spiritual guide, Allyn, to go with me.

I flew to southern California where I met up with Allyn, and we drove to Rancho Capistrano, a retreat center. I decided to receive from

Allyn whatever God might have for me and to honestly use this time to get unstuck. On the second morning he asked me to read and meditate on Isaiah 30, especially verses 15 and 18: "For thus said the Lord GOD, the Holy One of Israel: In returning and rest you shall be saved; in quietness and in trust shall be your strength. . . . For the LORD is a God of justice; blessed are all those who wait for him." The words pierced my soul. I read those words over and over as I sat outside under a tree. I was ready to move on. I started walking and praying aloud and asking God to help me trust him for justice and to return to his quietness and strength. I wanted to feel God's mercy and to be a blessing to others. I didn't want to be trapped anymore by my anger. I kept praying out loud for the Lord to fulfill this promise in me and for me to give to the Lord all my pain.

About halfway up a steep hill I started speaking a prayer language. I don't do that much—maybe once or twice before—but it overwhelmed my body and came out in a torrent of prayer to God. I prayed and prayed and trudged up that steep hill. When I got to a little meadow on the way up I stopped. I knew I had to forgive my business partner and secretary. I started bearing witness to God that I

forgave them both. I called out over and over, "Lord God, I forgive them. Jesus Christ, I forgive them. Holy Spirit, I forgive them." Then I began praying a whole litany of prayers, "You birds of the air, bear witness that I forgive them," "Rocks, bear witness that I forgive them," "People in the cars going by below, bear witness that I forgive them." I realized later that I was giving the Holy Spirit permission to cleanse my soul, my mind and emotions, my body of all bitterness.

I walked up even higher and the Holy Spirit led me to begin praying for my partner and secretary. I prayed for them in every way that I could think to do. When that was expended, the Spirit led me back down and led me to pray for myself, my family and especially my business and all the people connected to it. About halfway down the prayer language came back and I allowed the Spirit to take my innermost desires and intercede to the Father for me. It was the strangest but most liberating experience. I did not plan it. The Spirit led it. When I reached the bottom and was back under the tree, I knew that something had shifted deep within me. It was true; in returning and resting I was saved from my bitterness.

Anna Jones

I will openly admit that I never really believed in speaking in tongues. I

had always assumed that the apostles were enabled to speak other people's native languages in order to spread the gospel. I was very suspect of the modern usage and exploitation of it. However, I tried going into this prayer experience with an open mind and spirit. I requested the Holy Spirit to dwell in me and relaxed myself and started to pray. I first started to say regular prayers with a very relaxed mouth, and so they came out a little jumbled. After about five minutes, something changed. I felt warm all over, and a little anxious, and my tongue became like a bird flapping itself out of a locked cage. When I projected sound it was another language, and when I held back sound my tongue continued to move rapidly though silently. I had almost no control over it. I vocalized this for as long as it continued to happen. I did not feel any particular emotion during that time, except for surprise. I'm still bewildered by it, and I don't understand what happened spiritually during that time, but I do understand that it was a gift.

FURTHER READING

Hartley, Fred A. *Prayer on Fire: What Happens When the Holy Spirit Ignites Your Prayers.* Colorado Springs: NavPress, 2006.

Heidler, Robert. *Experiencing the Spirit: Developing a Living Relationship with the Holy Spirit.* Ventura, CA: Renew Books, 1999.

Keefauver, Larry. *Experiencing the Holy Spirit: Transformed by His Presence.* Nashville: Thomas Nelson, 2000.

18

Conversational Prayer

If you then, who are evil, know how to give good gifts to your children,
how much more will the heavenly Father give the Holy Spirit to those who ask him!

LUKE 11:13

It is in fact the most normal thing in the common Christian life to pray together.

DIETRICH BONHEOFFER

THE HOLY SPIRIT AS COMPANION

One of our most fundamental needs is for friendship and companionship. We marry with this hope. We spend time developing friendships with others. We all need people to share life with us, understand us and commit to us. Unfortunately, friendship is becoming harder to come by. Recent studies have found that 20 percent of the population is chronically lonely, and the percentage is increasing.[1] Jesus himself walked his life journey with companions, some very close to him. He loved them and they loved him. They did life together. They were on mission together.

Jesus didn't want to leave his beloved disciples without companionship. During their last meal together Jesus spoke to them about the coming of the Holy Spirit.

> If you love me, keep my commands. And I will ask the Father, and he will give you another advocate to help you and be with you forever—the Spirit of truth. The world cannot accept him, because it neither sees him nor knows him. But you know him, for he lives with you and will be in you. (Jn 14:15-17 NIV)

Jesus is speaking to all of his disciples. The Father gives the faith community then and now the Holy Spirit. This Comforter will be "with you" forever. The "with you" means he will be in your midst. The word for "lives" means to remain. It carries a sense of permanence. The second phrase "with you" is different from the first one. This one means "beside." The Holy Spirit is among you and beside you, and then finally the Holy Spirit is "in you." The "in" means a stable presence, non-movement. The spherical presence of the Holy Spirit emphasizes the completeness of the Spirit's presence among, beside and in us.

After Jesus' resurrection, he met with his disciples around a meal, and "he breathed on them and said to them, 'Receive the Holy Spirit'" (Jn 20:22). Jesus passed the Holy Spirit from himself to his followers to remain with them in the same way that he himself was with them. Both times that Jesus spoke about the Holy Spirit, they were in community around a meal together. Both times the Holy Spirit was promised and given to them all as a companion presence of Christ in their community.

The Holy Spirit is not a presence that comes and goes like magic smoke. The Holy Spirit is always around and is around in a special way in community. In Acts whenever the Holy Spirit fell, it fell on all who were gathered together (Acts 10:44-46). The Holy Spirit is especially sent to the church and is especially potent and present in the community of believers. Paul and Luke emphasize the "communal aspect of the Spirit's ministry."[2] The Spirit abides with them and empowered their signs and miracles. They spoke with authority. They healed. People were transformed. The signs and wonders, the love the Christ followers had for each other and the power of their words were so compelling that the church exploded in growth.

The Spirit of *koinonia* was with them all. *Koinonia* means close association, communion and fellowship. It carries the idea of generosity and sharing. The Holy Spirit binds us together in unity (Eph 4:3) into one body: "For in the one Spirit we were all baptized into one body—Jews or Greeks, slaves or free—and we were all made to drink of one Spirit" (1 Cor 12:13).

CONVERSATIONAL PRAYER

Western cultures believe that identity is primarily individually constructed. People are free to make their own choices about their personal lives, their careers, their spouses, even whether or not they take responsibility for something, such as aging parents. However, in many other cultures and in first-century Palestine, the focus was on identity in community. An individual's role was based on his or her place in the community. If you were a fisherman's son, you would be a fisherman. If you were a woman, you would be a wife, mother and home businessperson. If

Once I overcame my initial hesitation I found conversational prayer to be wonderfully insightful and engaging. A natural undulation of the Spirit flowed between my three friends and me and a subtle intimacy connected us. The statements and requests and responses were uncontrived. One topic naturally ebbed into another. I have never experienced such dynamic group prayer.

—Shaun Short

you were the firstborn son of a scribe, you would become a scribe as an adult. These were not debated, except by Jesus. Jesus reframed Peter's responsibility as a fisherman to his earthly father to be instead toward his heavenly father.

> The community-forming activity of the Holy Spirit challenges us to move beyond the contemporary assumption that the Spirit's actions center exclusively, or even primarily, on the individual soul. Not only does the Creator Spirit renew particular lives, but the Spirit is the source of all life in creation.[3]

Because of the individual orientation to identity, Westerners are often more task-oriented than people-oriented. We often see prayer and prayer requests as tasks rather than as community opportunities to be oriented toward each other and the Holy Spirit. Instead of seeing prayer needs as goals to be accomplished through asking, prayer needs are opportunities to come together around what hurts or matters to us. There is trust that the Father and the Holy Spirit that watches over us will handle these things well on our behalf. For that reason there is special power in group prayer.

An orientation toward individualism and tasks puts the responsibility for outcomes on an individual's shoulders. Jesus clearly put responsibility on the group. The Holy Spirit was poured out on everyone gathered, male and female, old and young, slaves and free. Therefore, the group bears the responsibility for bringing requests to God in partnership together and with the Holy Spirit, who takes the requests to God knowing God's will. There are thirty-eight references to prayer in Acts and 60 percent of them occur in community. The pervasiveness of prayer in the early church clearly marked it as a praying church (Acts 1:14; 2:42).

> To come into the presence of the Holy Spirit with a community of people was a new concept for me. I was part of a whole without losing my identity. It was a very healing experience and a gift that I will always treasure. I felt truly connected to the body of Christ.
>
> —Sandy Bass

Praying in community does not mean the pastor or leader prays for the group. Praying in community is a conversation shared together about the community's needs and conducted in sync with the Holy Spirit. We often relegate prayer to the professionals or to private times alone. The Holy Spirit was sent to be with us, among us and in us. At all times and in all places we can connect to the Holy Spirit.

One of the primary roles of the Holy Spirit is to intercede on our behalf. The Holy Spirit is directly related to our prayer lives. We are called to always pray, but it is the Holy Spirit that packages the prayer according to the will of God. The obedience in prayer is to pray, not to pray a certain way or to get a certain outcome. We often assume that prayer isn't worth it when we pray and nothing seems to happen.

However, through the Holy Spirit we know that it is not our business to make anything happen. That is the business of the Holy Spirit through God. Our business is to pray, especially together.

CONVERSATION PRAYER GUIDELINES

- Essential elements in conversation prayer are an embrace of the Holy Spirit's presence and a dependence on the Holy Spirit to guide the prayers.

- Conversation prayer is praying with a group using a direct, simple and brief conversational style.[4] Conversation prayer is natural and scriptural.

- The prayer is based on the premise that God is concerned about everything in our lives.

- Conversation prayer is a combination of listening and asking.

- The prayer begins without the usual sharing of prayer requests. Often we gather for prayer and spend fifty out of sixty minutes sharing. Then a few people pray in the last ten minutes. Instead, requests are shared within the actual prayer time.

- The prayer is not a monologue of one person speaking for several minutes and then another person speaking, but a one- to two-sentence named request, such as "Lord, help me with my finances," followed by reflective responses. The second person prays a response such as, "God, help X with her finances," and the third might pray after listening to the Spirit, "Lord, help X trust you with her everyday needs."

- Short one- to two-sentence prayers reflect conversation. The conversation is between the group and the Holy Spirit. We sometimes use prayer time to teach others or share our wisdom or life experience. Conversation prayer is not about us, but about a complete dependence on listening to and responding to the Holy Spirit. If you are emotionally eager to pray next or you pray too long, you probably are listening to yourself more than to the Holy Spirit.

> **My first experience** with conversation prayer was with four strangers, so I constructed a solid barrier around my heart. I did not want to expose the pain and worry that clouded my mind. I didn't know if I could trust them, and I was deeply afraid of letting them see my vulnerability.
>
> As we began to speak short prayers of praise and adoration, my heftily constructed walls began to give way. As each person humbly and transparently shared their brokenness, I had no recourse but to do the same. Five people sat around a table as strangers and forty-five minutes later we were deeply bonded to each other and to God.
>
> —Lori Allen

- The prayer responses come from listening. You don't need to go around the circle, nor does everyone need to respond to every request. Listen to the Spirit.

- There are small spaces of silence to listen to the Holy Spirit for guidance between requests and responses. The silence also helps us to focus on the person's words rather than trying to get ready for our own contributions.

- This type of prayer works best in a group of three to five people. Comfort matters. Conversation prayer takes thirty to sixty minutes depending on the group's experience. Don't sit on the floor or hold hands. If you become uncomfortable, it will be difficult to listen to the Holy Spirit.

- The value of conversation prayer is that it is a natural and easy way for people to pray together. There are no experts or "saint." We all talk and we can all talk to God together.

- Another value is the recognition of the movement of the Holy Spirit among us. It is not about our success but the Holy Spirit's presence with us.

CONVERSATION PRAYER EXPERIENCE

Group Experience*

- A leader takes time to clearly explain the prayer experience and to model it before the group. It is biblical but not natural for us to pray in this manner, so care is needed to describe and demonstrate how the prayer time happens. Having a handout can help each person follow along and then the sheet serves as a guide when groups pray.

- After the explanation, break the group into smaller groups of three to five. Tell them that the leader will watch the time, so people can completely enter into the experience. Make sure that all cell phones are off and watches are put away. The steps are as follows:

  - *Step One*
    - Say together Romans 8:26-27.
    - Then pray Ephesians 6:18: "Lord, we 'pray in the Spirit at all times in every prayer and supplication. To that end keep alert and always persevere in supplication for all the saints.' Guide us as we pray."

  - *Step Two: Thank you, God, for . . .*
    - *Silence*: Begin in silence for one to two minutes, reflecting on the Spirit's presence.
    - *Give thanks for God*: As you are led, thank God for whatever is brought to

---

*Many people have the personality type that enjoys clarity and structure. Some people prefer more spontaneity. Feel free to tailor the conversation prayer experience toward the preferences of your group. The guidelines above provide clear structure. However, conversation prayer can also be highly effective with a more organic approach.

your mind and heart. Examples: "Thank you Jesus for saving me." "Thank you Lord, for creating this beautiful world." Each person will most likely have several or even many short prayers of gratitude toward God.

- *Give thanks for others*: As led, thank God for others in your life. Examples: "Father God, thank you for my friend who stood by me." "Thank you Jesus, for my mom." "Thank you for the life and inspiration of Nelson Mandela." Again, there will be several responses from each with silence in between.

- *Step Three: Help, God . . .*

  - Throughout this time there are spaces to listen to the Spirit for guidance. Listen and then pray for whatever request comes up. After someone introduces a request, the rest listen for how to add their prayers to it. Sometimes you might even pray a couple of times for a request. Sometimes you don't have any clarity. Then just hold the request before the Holy Spirit.

  - *God, help me*: As you feel led, share the personal requests in your own life. Examples: "Lord, help me to stop obsessing about success." "Jesus, help me forgive the coworker who yelled at me." "Spirit, help me sense your presence in my life." Give space between requests to listen for how the Holy Spirit leads you to respond. It is like a threaded discussion.

  - *God, help others*: When there are no more personal requests, move to praying for others' needs. Examples: "Lord, I am worried about my brother who's been drinking again." "Jesus, help my dad find work." "God, my friend at school is very depressed." Listen for responses to each request.

  - *God, help the world*: When the needs of others are finished, move to praying for broader concerns in the world. These are global concerns for which you probably don't have a direct connection. As priests to the world, we pray for the needs of the world. Examples: "Jesus, watch over the innocent children in Asia." "Spirit, help us to find a spirit of unity with people different from ourselves."

- *Step Four: Thank you, God . . .*

  - The leader will say when five minutes remain. At that time transition from the request prayers to again thanking God.

  - When the time is over, the leader prays something like, "Holy Spirit, thank you for hearing our prayers and interceding on our behalf."

  - Close with a blessing such as, "The grace of the Lord Jesus Christ, the love of God, and the communion of the Holy Spirit be with all of you" (2 Cor 13:13).

- Take time to have the group share about their experience. Are there any questions?

Partner Experience

- A smaller group can pray this way even if there are only two of you. Begin by going through the guidelines and making sure you understand how it works. When you decide to experience a conversation prayer, be sure to avoid taking time at the beginning to check in and share updates. You can do that after your prayer time.

- If there are only two of you, it might take less time, such as fifteen to twenty minutes, but not necessarily. Agree together on how much time you want to take and set a timer so you can relax and be present to the prayer experience.

- When completed, talk about your prayer time. What was the experience like for you? Was the silence and flow of the experience comfortable? Where you able to listen for the Holy Spirit?

Individual Experience

- Since this is a community prayer experience, it isn't possible to experience it without others. If you can, find a friend or small group to teach them and then pray in this manner. It is also possible to find prayer places online that practice community prayer. It might not be this model, but it would be an opportunity for you to listen to the Holy Spirit and experience praying with others.

- Journal on the impact of the experience for you.

PRAYER JOURNEY

Katherine Woodston

I talked Melanie into going with me to a gathering of Christian women. She didn't really believe in Jesus as the Son of God, but she was my friend and was curious about us. There was a guest speaker talking about the theology of formation, and she was really interested in hearing someone with a PhD talk about the rational aspects of faith. I remember that it was a great talk, and Melanie was engaged the entire time. Unfortunately, at the end of the talk the speaker wanted to give the women a formational experience, and she chose conversation prayer as that experience. Melanie was in a panic as the speaker began to share how we would be praying together. She whispered to me, "I believe there is probably a God out there, but I've never prayed or tried to address God. What am I going to do?"

I wasn't sure myself, but I assured her that it would be okay. She didn't have to participate. We were divided into groups of six and Melanie panicked again. She leaned in and said, "I can't not pray! They'll think it's weird that I'm not participating, and then they'll think something is wrong with me. Give me some words! Tell me something to say." I said, "Melanie, just use your own words. It's simple speech. Nothing fancy. Just say something that is on your heart and mind."

I thought I had blown it with my friend, and she would never come again to one of my Christian events. However, it was not like that at all. We had fifteen minutes to pray. We settled and then the simple thank yous and requests came naturally.

After about five minutes Melanie actually prayed, "God, help me discover who you are." Then later she asked God to help bring peace to the Middle East. She thanked God for creating this wonderful world. She really entered into it!

At the end, we talked about it. She said, "It was so refreshing. It's not what I expected prayer to be. I thought someone would drone on and on with lots of words trying to guilt me to Jesus." She added, "I actually felt close to God, and that has never happened to me before. I would do this again." I learned that prayer is a door for everyone and I can trust the Holy Spirit with my friend.

Josh McMann

I really disliked group prayer. People get all serious, scrunch over in their chairs, and begin a long, elaborate beseeching for God's cure for someone or God's favor on someone else for a job or whatever. People go on and on. They quote Scripture and usually end with "in Jesus' name" or "not my will but yours," so if the prayer doesn't work, "No problem. It's God's fault, not my prayer." What is supposed to be prayers on behalf of others becomes grandstanding. And if you're praying and someone says, "yes, Lord," the prayer goes on even longer. Then there are the mumblers who pray and you can't hear a lick of anything they say. I understand that some of this is really sincere, but

there is so much that is not. I didn't want any part of group prayer.

Then one weekend on a retreat, the retreat pastor had us get into small groups of men to pray conversationally. My stomach knotted up and I was looking for a way to escape to the beach. I wanted no part of this. But some men from my church were eager to give this a try, so I decided I would just get through it.

Ben, the retreat pastor, took some time to explain conversation prayer. I wondered if maybe this could work, but I knew the temptation to strut your spiritual stuff was powerful. The other three men in my group all agreed to follow the guidelines and keep our prayers short and listen for the Holy Spirit. I had never thought about the role of the Holy Spirit in group prayer and especially never had heard that we should listen for guidance. Seemed pretty fantastical to me. Ben said he would give us thirty minutes, to which I thought, *thirty minutes?*

It was one of the most holy community experiences I have ever had. A quiet spirit bound us together as we began to praise and thank God. The silences were like time-outs with a coach. Intense listening and trust in the Spirit to lead us. When it came time for personal prayers, I shocked myself by praying, "God, help me see my wife as you see her. Help me to love her when she is depressed and not push her away." I was immediately embarrassed, but the other guys started praying for me. One asked for Jesus to be my eyes. Another saw the Spirit resting on our home. I felt a peace and a hope that I could be a better husband as she struggled with her abusive past. These guys and I agreed to meet once a month to pray for our families and our community after we got back. We've been meeting now for three years. It's still a great experience. Every now and then one of us starts waxing eloquent and we just tap his shoe with our feet. He gets it.

FURTHER READING

Rinker, Rosalind. *Learning Conversational Prayer.* Collegeville, MN: Liturgical, 1992.

Jackson, Neta. *The Yada Yada Prayer Group.* Nashville: Thomas Nelson, 2003. (This is a fiction series about the transforming power of a prayer group. Though it is not directly about the style of prayer explained in this chapter, it does exemplify the power of community prayer.)

19

Breath Prayer

Sin is a disorder in our relationship with God.
Error is a disorder in our relationship with truth.
Sickness is a disorder within ourselves.

HAMISH MCMINN

Those in whom the Spirit comes to dwell are to be people
who live at the intersection between heaven and earth.

N. T. WRIGHT

THE HOLY SPIRIT AS INNER HEALER

My husband likes to say that "normal" is only a setting on the dryer. None of us are "normal." We are all messed up internally by any combination of individual, family, relational, work, church or general life dysfunctions. Our inner selves eventually get complicated and slopped up with all sorts of brokenness. In Psalm 51:7 and 10, the psalmist prays our common yearning for a clean inner self, "Purge me with hyssop, and I shall be clean; wash me, and I shall be whiter than snow. Create in me a clean heart, O God, and put a new and right spirit within me." We want to be normal—clean and uncluttered.

The use of hyssop for cleansing is documented throughout the Old and New Testament. Hyssop is a small climbing bush used in purification rites. It has a wonderful smell. The branches were gathered into a bunch and used for sprinkling rituals. Hyssop is first mentioned in Exodus 12:22, when Moses commanded the Israelites enslaved in Egypt to use hyssop branches for sprinkling the blood of a slain lamb on the lintel and the two doorposts. The blood protected the household from the loss of their firstborns. In the New Testament hyssop branches dipped in sour wine were offered to Jesus when he cried out with thirst (Jn 19:29).

The psalmist desires a clean heart and a new and right spirit. The "heart" refers to one's entire inner life, both the emotions and the will. It is the center of one's inner being. The cry is for a pure and morally sound center. The "spirit" is also the center of one's inner life. The word for "put" means to dedicate or inaugurate a fresh beginning and alludes to the blood sacrifices in the temple for purification. Jesus came as our final blood sacrifice.

Though Jesus is no longer physically present, the Holy Spirit was given to precisely remind us of our status as a new creation. The Holy Spirit not only reminds us, but helps us with our every weakness and infirmity. The Holy Spirit intercedes on our behalf. We are forgiven and are new creations continually being renewed by the Spirit of life residing in us. Before Christ, the Jewish people would go to the temple for sanctification, a ceremony for purification from sin. Now the Holy Spirit is the one who renews us (Heb 10:15-18).

Renewal, the sanctifying presence of the Holy Spirit, is in the inner person, not just outward behaviors. The Holy Spirit lives in us and leads us into righteousness and peace. We know internally how we ought to be. The law is written on our hearts and minds, where decisions and desires dwell in perfect harmony with a perfect God (Tit 3:1-7).

Because of this renewal, some believe there is nothing else to do. The heart and mind and body are purified by the Spirit once and for all. We are no longer the sinners we once were. Therefore, sin is not possible, and if sin happens it is because the "devil made me do it." Others say that sin is not a concern because we can ask for forgiveness. Another group says, "I can't help my anger or my drinking or my depression or my gossiping," though they are Christian. Throughout Paul's letters, he still admonishes and teaches new believers to be a holy people. There is a standard of behavior, not based solely on outward right actions but inner purity and dependence on the Holy Spirit (Eph 4:29-31).

In Ephesians 4:30 Paul writes, "And do not grieve the Holy Spirit of God, with which you were marked with a seal for the day of redemption." We grieve the Holy Spirit or quench the Holy Spirit when we live as unbelievers, as though we were still solely in the flesh without the indwelling presence of the Spirit. The word *grieve* suggests real emotion and sadness. The Holy Spirit is wounded by our neglect and transgressions. Ephesians 4:17 through 5:5 lists sinful behaviors and thoughts. In Galatians 5:16 Paul encourages believers, "Live by the Spirit, I say, and do not gratify the desires of the flesh."

The struggle is that we often try to manage our outward behaviors, and are sometimes fairly successful, but managing our inward attitudes and thoughts is much more difficult. We experience this when, in the heat of an emotion, we act out in sin by insulting or gossiping to others. To deal with the inner person, we learn to walk in the Spirit and live by the Spirit (Gal 5:25). As the Holy Spirit is with us 24/7, we can lean on the Spirit for help. Prayer reminds us to live by the Spirit.

BREATH PRAYER

Breath prayers help us to depend on the Spirit for help with our weaknesses. They are short prayers that we repeat over and over when we need them. Usually when we stumble it is not during our set-aside prayer times, but during our busy working times. Therefore, breath prayers are a meaningful way to live by the Spirit. The phrase "breath prayer" comes from the biblical word for Spirit meaning breath. Breath prayer is based on the underlying premise that the Spirit is active in our lives. Breath can't be seen but is necessary for life. The Spirit goes where it will and is necessary for our life in Christ. Each physical breath is a short simple inhale and exhale, reminding us of the breathing in of the Spirit and the exhaling of the sinful self and all its traps.

> "Holy Spirit, come focus me." As I pray this, there is a sense of peace that comes over me. I don't know why I am surprised. Yesterday I was substitute teaching in a fourth grade classroom, and before the kids got there I began to pray this prayer. When class started I was focused and ready to teach. I was in great spirits and led with joy. I found myself praying this prayer throughout my day, and it keeps me focused.
>
> —Joel To

Short prayers are found in Scripture. The psalmist used short prayers such as, "Lord, have mercy." Jesus' repeated prayer in the Garden, "Your will be done," is another example of a breath prayer. The early desert fathers and mothers practiced short prayers that would carry them through the day and night. One of the most famous breath prayers is the Jesus Prayer: "Lord Jesus Christ, have mercy on me a sinner." It is often shortened to "Lord Jesus, have mercy." The story of the healing work of the Jesus Prayer is told in the famous little book *The Way of the Pilgrim*. Throughout the Bible and church history, breath prayers would fill minds and invite the Holy Spirit to transform the inner selves.

The attention to our inner emotional and spiritual world is an important aspect of keeping pure and growing in Christlikeness. Neuroscientists who study the brain have demonstrated that emotions, particularly those of fear and anger, often triggered by stress, can override the more thoughtful brain processes.[1] Laurence Gonzales, who studied people who survived danger, wrote, "Rational (or conscious) thought always lags behind the emotional reaction."[2] Elite athletes, performers and military personnel know they need to condition their bodies. They condition themselves to respond instinctively when challenges come rather than trust their rational mind to respond appropriately. To do this elite per-

My breath prayer came to me clearly: "Holy Father, I need your peace." I have prayed this many times and have felt my body relax. Truly, the Holy Spirit knows what my body needs. I have struggled a long time to make sense of the command to pray continuously. Breath prayer makes this task less daunting. The more I make breath prayer a part of my life, the more it becomes part of my unconscious prayer life. The prayer is so simple, yet so transformational.

—Brian Youd

formers take explicit learnings and practice them over and over until they become implicit learnings.

Explicit learning happens in the reasoning part of the brain. When we study our Bible, listen to a sermon or read devotional books *information is stored in the reasoning part of our brain* about how our faith works. However, when we are threatened and stress factors are triggered our thinking becomes fuzzy. Plus all of us have unresolved issues from childhood, hurtful relationships or tragic events. Because these are difficult emotionally, we tuck them away and avoid thinking about them. Whenever we are stressed, the tucked away emotions are triggered and we are less able to manage our behaviors. Implicit learning—learning that results in instinctive behavior—is *information stored in the body* because the action is done over and over. The body remembers and if stress occurs, the body is able to function as the mind wants it to function.

Therefore, breath prayer is a way to be continually aware of the presence of the Holy Spirit and our desire to be Christ's lights on a hill. By repeating a prayer that speaks to our deepest desire in Christ, we imprint the message on our heart and mind and body. The Holy Spirit has access to all of us—not just the part we bring to the Spirit when we're rational and in a good space. Breath prayer can help purify us as the Old Testament use of hyssop did: "Or do you not know that your body is a temple of the Holy Spirit within you, which you have from God, and that you are not your own?" (1 Cor 6:19).

The Holy Spirit's role in our lives is to intercede on our behalf for every weakness. The weaknesses are physical, mental, emotional and spiritual. Breath prayer has great healing potential allowing the Holy Spirit to dwell in our innermost beings. We give the Holy Spirit permission to open closed closets of the heart and to bring deep healing. The deepest miracle of prayer happens when the Holy Spirit dwells in our inner being. The signs and wonders our churches need today are not only physical miracles, but miracles of the heart. The Holy Spirit guides us in our deepest desire and we can construct a prayer that we carry throughout the day to pray for ourselves and others.

BREATH PRAYER GUIDELINES

- Breath prayers are a way to pray in the Spirit. They are like spiritual breaths, and they keep us focused on God.

- Breath prayer is a prayer of intimacy and reminds us of God's presence: "And remember, I am with you always, to the end of the age" (Mt 28:20).

- With breath prayers we pray without ceasing: "Rejoice in hope, be patient in suffering, persevere in prayer" (Rom 12:12).

- Though breath prayers are to be used throughout one's day, they are discovered through a period of reflection and quietness.

- Breath prayers are formed by listening to the Holy Spirit for our deepest desire and then allowing the Holy Spirit to respond.

- Breath prayers work particularly well for people who are in distress. We often use too many words when praying for people and assume we know what they need. A breath prayer allows the person to name his or her own need and then allows friends to pray that need over and over. We pray with someone rather than pray for someone.

- Breath prayers bring comfort and order out of chaos.

- The breath prayer is a prayer that is soaked into the body by remembering and saying the words again and again.

- Breath prayer is not a magic formula. It is a way to live in the Spirit.

- The value of the prayer is its brevity. It's easy to remember. The prayer is a simple request of one's deepest desire to be formed and whole in Christ.

> I felt stagnant and stuck with God. One day I sat by a stream and prayed "God, help me to see." I needed God to grant me inner healing and help me to see where my stagnation began. God showed me that moment and lifted the burden of judgment that I felt off of my shoulders. For ten years I equated the bad experiences, harmful relationships, stress and personal struggle with God's judgment for a mistake I made. My pain, I thought, was necessary for me to earn back God's favor. Sitting on that bank by the stream I didn't hear or see, I felt God's voice and presence tell me, "This is not my judgment."
>
> —Jim McLaughlin

BREATH PRAYER EXPERIENCE

Group Experience

- *Discovering your breath prayer*: The leader guides the group through the following steps. Begin by explaining the prayer process if this is the first time. After explaining the process, go through the steps as a prayer. The prayer time usually takes ten minutes. Allow space for reflection and stillness.

- In a seated position, get comfortable so you are less aware of your body.

- Close your eyes and be still. Focus on your breathing and the verse, "For the kingdom of God is not food and drink but righteousness and peace and joy in the Holy Spirit" (Rom 14:17). Say the verse together as a group several times.

- After a short period of silence, imagine God is calling you by name. Perhaps Jesus is standing before you and calling your name. He then asks, "What do you want?"

- Answer Jesus directly with what honestly comes from your heart—a single word or simple phrase.

- Choose then a name for God that is meaningful to you at this time (Jesus Christ, Holy Spirit, Lamb of God, Shepherd, Father God, Creator and so on).

- Combine your name for God with your answer to Jesus' question and create a simple prayer of five to seven syllables. Examples:

  - I need peace. Name is "God." Prayer is "God, I need your peace."

  - I need rest. Name is "Shepherd." Prayer is "Shepherd, I rest in you."

  - I need healing. Name is "Holy Spirit." Prayer is "Holy Spirit, heal me."

  - I need cleansing. Name is "Savior." Prayer is "Savior, cleanse me."

- After the prayer experience, have people get into groups of three to four and share their prayers. They might need help with getting the prayer into a short format. You can also have people pair up, share their prayers with each other and then commit to pray each other's prayers. For instance, if Jeff's prayer is "Spirit, guide my path," his partner Luke would pray regularly Jeff's prayer, "Spirit, guide Jeff's path."

- Talk together as a group. Have one or two share their experience with the larger group. Give time for questions. This prayer experience needs a follow-up time when the group can meet again and share experiences of praying their prayer and praying the prayer for their partner.

- Breath prayers can also be created for a group. A group can decide on a desire together, construct a short prayer and agree to pray it regularly as a group.

- Give time at the end for questions and conversation about the group's experience.

Partner Experience

- Partners or a small group would follow the same pattern as described in the group experience above.

- This is a way for prayer partners to pray for each other throughout a long period of time. Often breath prayers matter to the individual for several months.

- Sometimes the initial breath prayer is not the deeper desire. Therefore, check in with each other to make sure that the prayer is the one for the individual.

- Talk together about how the prayer helps you be more like Christ.

Individual Experience

- Follow the guidelines in the group section.

- Journal about your experience. How has it helped you be more Christlike? What does the prayer tell you about your inner world? How might you use the prayer to manage emotions, memories or behaviors that interfere with your desire for righteousness, joy and peace?

PRAYER JOURNEY

William Gaultiere[3]

Some years ago Kristi and I were on a retreat with a group of Christian leaders and I found myself feeling jealous of three people. They each had wonderful opportunities to serve God in powerful ways that I'd like to do.

I was disappointed in myself—I didn't want to be that way. I thought that I had worked through that issue in my prayers already. Besides, these people were my friends and they were serving the Lord. I felt discouraged and guilty.

Later when talking with another friend, he brought up Paul's words in Philippians 2:3 about Christ's *kenosis* or self-emptying love: "Do nothing out of selfish ambition or vain conceit, but in humility consider others better than yourselves."

That could have heaped more guilt and pressure onto me, but actually it focused me on Jesus and how in his incarnation and life of service he humbly ministered to me. Jesus, the Lord Almighty and King of kings, picked up a towel, got on his knees and washed my dirty feet (Jn 13:1-17). I wanted to serve others as he served me.

As I meditated and prayed on this the Lord led me to form a breath prayer: "In Christ's humility, consider others better than yourselves."

I kneeled before the Lord in quiet prayer, waiting to breathe, hands raised high in worship before the Lord who humbly served me. I prayed, "In Christ's humility," breathing in deeply and pulling my hands toward my chest, receiving the Lord's generous, gracious love. Then I prayed, "Consider others better than yourself," exhaling and extending my hands outward, overflowing with Christ's consideration and esteem for those I had been jealous of.

I prayed this breath prayer for each person I had been jealous of, asking God to bless each one in his or her life and ministry. And my soul smiled with delight. I was happy for these people to be in the spotlight. I realized I was blessed to be in the background and to affirm and intercede for them.

Carol Vanderford

I've been practicing breath prayer under another name for a long time. I've called this kind of praying my Beetle Bailey prayer. Years ago a popular comic strip featured a scrappy Army private named Beetle Bailey, who was trying to survive the rigors of boot camp by staying one step ahead of the lovable but thunderously tough "Sarge." At least once a week, Beetle would get pummeled by Sarge and the comic would show a squashed pile of limp uniform, topped by a tottering helmet, with a wimpy, white "I surrender" flag flapping out of the human debris pile of Beetle Bailey. I found that picture so humorous because I could relate to that debris pile. It triggered a reminder of myself when I go through a really tough time. So that picture of Beetle, surrendering, waving his little flag, became to me a word picture of prayer. When I would feel pummeled, as if I were nothing more than a heap of human debris, when I'd have no energy to think, much less pray, when my pain, confusion and desperation would overwhelm me, I'd whisper, "Beetle Bailey here, Lord."

It was an immeasurable relief to recognize that God knew my situation, my heart and my need. I did not have to explain. All I had to do was call out to him, acknowledge my desperation, and this word picture became our special form of communication. God would meet me. I would sense his peace, his assurance that he was in the center of my concerns and in control and loved me. "Beetle Bailey here, Lord." Just a breath away.

FURTHER READING

DelBene, Ron, with Herb and Mary Montgomery. *The Breath of Life: A Simple Way to Pray.* Eugene, OR: Wipf & Stock, 2005.

Jordan, Edna G. *Breath Prayers for African Americans.* Colorado Springs: David C. Cook, 2004.

Mathewes-Green, Frederica. *The Jesus Prayer: The Ancient Desert Prayer That Tunes the Heart to God.* Brewster, MA: Paraclete, 2009.

20

Healing Prayer

For I am the LORD who heals you.

EXODUS 15:26

A person who wholly follows the Lord is one who believes
that the promises of God are trustworthy, that He is with
His people, and that they are well able to overcome.

WATCHMAN NEE

THE HOLY SPIRIT AS INTERCESSOR

When circumstances beyond our control overtake us, we are desperate for help. Most of us have at one time or another cried out to God to save us or save someone we love. Cancer, accidents, home or job losses, and natural disasters overwhelm our sensibilities. When we can do nothing else, when we've done everything we can possibly do, we need divine intercession. We need God's power, and we pray and ask others to pray for God's help.

We know God does help. Throughout Scripture signs and wonders are indicators of God's activity. In the Old Testament a sign is a distinguishing mark that demonstrates God's power, reminds people of God's covenant and announces things to come. When Moses talked with God in the burning bush, God had Moses use his staff to create signs for Pharaoh (Ex 4:17). The signs and wonders were testimonies to the Israelites that God was leading them and loved them (Deut 26:8; Ps 65:8; Jer 32:20; Dan 4:3).

Jesus used signs to demonstrate his love and capacity to rescue (Jn 2:23). Jesus not only did many miraculous healings, he told his followers that they would do more than he: "the one who believes in me will also do the works that I do and, in fact, will do greater works than these" (Jn 14:12). Jesus declared that signs will demonstrate

My mom for years had a torn rotator cuff in her right shoulder. She had no insurance and no money for surgery. It was horrible to see her in pain and not be able to do something about it. During that fall our church had a Tuesday night prayer ministry. Sometimes they would pray aloud and sometimes they would lay hands on people. One Tuesday she decided to go to the prayer meeting and ask for prayer. While she was there, they all laid hands on her, anointed her with oil and asked the Lord to heal her shoulder. Though we had prayed individually, this was the first time people laid hands on her and prayed together. She was completely healed. Over five years later, she is still healed.

—Victoria Marty

their faith (Mk 16:17-18). During Jesus' teaching at the final Passover meal with his disciples, he spoke several times of their doing wonders in his name. Jesus said, "I will do whatever you ask in my name, so that the Father may be glorified in the Son" (Jn 14:13).[1] These verses are particularly difficult for some to grasp especially as they relate to healing ministry and signs today. However, it is clear that God and Jesus performed signs.

The Holy Spirit came with signs, fire and the sound of a mighty wind, and the early church performed signs and miracles (Acts 2:43; 5:12; 8:13; 14:3). Healings continued to occur centuries after the early church. Augustine (354–430 C.E.) in his book *City of God* writes detailed reports on healings. Scholars have found that healing was a normal part of the ministry of the church.[2] Healings also occur today.

"UNANSWERED" PRAYER

With the intercessory purpose of the Holy Spirit and Jesus' admonition to heal, prayer for healing and intercession is part of the ministry of believers. However, the biggest roadblock to intercessory prayer is the problem with unanswered prayer. When prayers go unanswered, people may believe that prayer wasn't worth the effort or they don't have the faith to do it or God doesn't care about them.

There are two challenges to this problem: what does it mean to pray "in Jesus' name for whatever you ask" and why are some prayers answered and others not? These are serious and complex questions. They aren't easily answered with statements such as, "There is a lack of faith," or "God is punishing people for sin." To suggest that God allows disasters such as 9/11 or the tsunami in Japan to happen in order to bring people to faith is to trivialize both God's power and love.

Karlene Clark, a pastor and church planter, expresses her frustrations with healing prayer, which, if we're honest, match many of our own frustrations:

Intercessory prayer is something I struggle with though I pray this way every day. I pray for family and friends, for specific needs and general ones, for people suffering tragedy in the world, for a housemate facing a specific need. I sincerely care about people and the pain that life brings them. I pray because it is the only thing that I can do much of the time.

But I have to make this confession—I'm not sure how much confidence I have in intercessory prayer. I wish I had more. If Christ loves these people more than I do and earnestly cares about their pain more than I am capable of feeling, why do these intercessions seem to go unanswered more often than not? Some counsel that prayers are unanswered because of the need for God to cooperate patiently with humans exercising their free will. But if me and 500 other people are praying every day that God will relieve the pain and suffering of my friend—who was paralyzed in a car accident last July and is now in constant, excruciating pain so that she is disconnecting from reality—then what good is intercessory prayer? This situation is certainly out of the realm of human will or decision. Prayer is the only option left for her pain, and yet her pain continues. I want to know why the intercession of Christ at the right hand of God is not effective in this situation.

It may sound like I'm having a faith crisis, and I really am not. What I'm questioning is whether intercessory prayer really has much value. I cannot help but ask this question. When a godly woman is crying out day after day, "Oh Jesus, please help me!" in excruciating pain, why is Jesus silent?

"Why is Jesus silent?" First, none of us has the wisdom and sovereign oversight to answer this question. We cannot trivialize the sincerity of this lament with simple answers, though people do. We sometimes feel compelled to fix the problem. Some use biblical passages as the answer, such as the ones that say, "If you haven't asked properly in Jesus' name, then the prayer isn't answered. There is a lack of faith."

Praying in Jesus' name is not a magic phrase but a theological one. In John 14, 15 and 16 Jesus says six times, "ask in my name." These passages are often taken out of context and applied to healing prayer requests. Jesus says if you believe in him, you will do the same works as him. The works will be cumulatively greater as they impact people throughout time and place. This means that signs and wonders will happen. Therefore, ask. In John 14 the purpose of asking in Jesus' name is to glorify the Father. In John 15 Jesus says asking in his name results in the bearing of much fruit. In John 16 the result is complete joy. Asking in Jesus' name assumes an intimate love relationship with the Trinity and a desire to glorify God and do the work of God. The outcome is fruit and joy. Asking in Jesus' name is directly correlated to accomplishing the mission of God as partners.

To pray in someone's name in first-century Palestine meant to have that person's authority and power. It also meant that a person belonged to the one named and that person's whole purpose was identical with the one named. In this context Jesus is preparing the disciples for the continuation of his kingdom mission. The "praying in Jesus' name" is not an objective exercise to get something, but rather a subject-centered experience where we connect with someone, the Trinity, and become one in passion and purpose.

Another passage that creates confusion is found in Matthew 21:20-25, the story of Jesus and the withered fig tree. The disciples were stunned that a perfectly healthy tree would wither in a day from the roots up because of Jesus' words. His response, "Whatever you ask for in prayer with faith, you will receive" (Mt 21:22). This passage is sometimes used to support a radical view of healing prayer that says, "Anything will happen if you have faith. So if it doesn't happen, it is because you don't have enough faith." During these times faith refers "to the social glue that binds one person to another, that is, the social, externally manifested, emotional behavior of loyalty, commitment, and solidarity."[3] Jesus is asking them to stay loyal to him and thus to God. It is not about mental willpower.

The withering of the fig tree was a sign in Jesus' journey motif between Bethany and the temple. Jesus raises Lazarus and then enters Jerusalem triumphantly. He goes back to Bethany and on the return to Jerusalem he curses the fig tree before entering the temple and cleansing it. The fruitless tree symbolized the fruitless temple. The lack of fruit is alien to God's character and mission.[4] Jesus is not talking about getting things or healing, but about the astonishing capacity of faith, a faith characterized by trusting that God is God, to break in God's kingdom. There is fruit. Right after these words, Jesus speaks about the necessity to forgive. The lack of forgiveness breaks relationship with others and with the Father.

> Previously, intercession has been more like a grocery list of things to check off for me. However, now I am more invested in the suffering in our world. In the last ten days, our church lost two beautiful kids due to long, courageous battles with cancer. I was inspired to fight for these families in prayer, like a relentless widow persistent in her requests. I found strength in prayer and felt a sense of urgency in praying for healing and wholeness in our broken world. If God is acquainted with suffering and grief, intercessory prayer draws me into this.
>
> —Dave Sugawa

Jesus did heal and Jesus told his followers to heal in his name. Though 87 percent of people believe that God answers prayers at least some of the time, 13 percent lost faith because of unanswered prayers.[5] That makes the problem of unanswered prayer a serious concern. A response is theological: What is the nature of God? What is the nature of the world God created? What is our role in the world? Do we have free will? We know from Scripture that God is good and loving. God created a world that is highly complex and interdependent with good and evil dwelling together. God gave us the freedom to make choices. We are invited to be part of God's kingdom purposes.

Our penchant for individualism and need for simple cause-effect answers often overlooks or underestimates the interrelatedness of life. Science has taught us otherwise. An illustration is from chaos theory and is called the *butterfly effect*,[6] the term coined by Edward Lorenz, a meteorologist at MIT. The butterfly effect means that myriad small events can have large consequences, and we cannot predict how one tiny thing might impact another. Newtonian science was based on the idea that things happen by cause and effect. Nature can be figured out and managed. People can be understood and managed. If we figure out how things work, then we can accurately predict, repair and have power over natural processes. This affects how we see prayer. If we pray right, we get the right answer.

However, with the development of chaos theory, scientists saw the universe as much more complex, interrelated and less predictable than thought. Scientists can measure probabilities, but we can't always be sure of the specific causes for every effect. For instance, global warming might contribute to increased tornadoes in the Midwest, but we can't be sure that it caused a specific tornado that destroyed a specific town.[7] This has important consequences for how we understand the world God made and when and why some prayers are answered and others seem not to be. Dr. Wink explains it this way:

> In this [integral] worldview, the whole universe is a spirit-matter event, and the self is coextensive with the universe. We are not like solitary billiard balls, as materialism sees us; from the very beginning we are related to everything. . . . We are related to every other self in the universe. In such a world, we no longer know the limits of the possible. Therefore we pray for whatever we feel is right and leave the outcome to God. We live in expectation of miracles in a world re-enchanted with wonder. Intercessory prayer is a perfectly rational response to such a universe.[8]

HEALING PRAYER

Prayer is one of the means that God uses to accomplish his will. In his eternal purpose God has given his children the privilege of participation in his mission for establishing his kingdom on earth.[9] Since the center of all things is God the Father, Jesus Christ the Son and the Holy Spirit our Intercessor, and God

In Japan, there is a word *te-ate*. *Te* means hand and *ate* means put. I do not know when and why the word was made but many Japanese people know that putting a hand on a person works for healing. When I was little and had a stomachache, my mother would put her hand on my stomach and the ache went away. When I bumped my head, my teacher put her hand on it and I felt better. When my grandmother had an ache on her leg, she asked me, "Could you put your hand on it?" and she felt better. None of us knew about Jesus or healing prayer. Now I feel so thankful because I think this is evidence that we were made by God and he loves us and works in us even when we don't know him!

—Hatsue Aizawa

calls us his children, we are under the care of the Almighty. As we are connected with people everywhere, good that happens to us can result in disaster for another. If you receive a heart transplant, someone else had to die and others were not chosen. If your student receives a scholarship, another one did not. Think of it as a baseball hit into the stands filled with forty thousand people. Only one person catches the ball. We do not see the scope of the universe or the outcome of time. Only God is sovereign and watches over all throughout time, and only God is trustworthy for eternity. Therefore, we pray in faith that God will be God.

Take into consideration these ideas:

- If the world operates with probable patterns, then we can accept those patterns as natural (the sun comes up; clouds cause rain; germs cause illness; storms happen). God sometimes overrides them, so we pray.

- Since we have free will, then we bear the consequences of free will when in sin or ignorance; we do things that bring harm to ourselves or others. God sometimes intervenes on our behalf, so we pray.

- Since sin and evil are let loose for a time and the end times have not arrived, then evil and sinful people will hurt and destroy the innocent. We still pray.

- Though Jesus Christ overcame evil on the cross, suffering is still the fabric of everyone's life. God is uniquely manifested in suffering. We pray for the suffering.

- Since God created us and a good world, sometimes the evil prosper and the good suffer (the rain falls on the just and unjust). God has promised a day when there will be no more tears.

When we allow the Holy Spirit to take our prayers to the Father for the Father's will, in faith we trust:

- God's timing as inscrutable and loving for eternity

- God's righteousness and justice

- God's mystery and universal sovereignty as preeminent

- God's worthiness of our praise and trust

On *60 Minutes* a thirty-eight-year-old man who had a recurrence of a brain tumor after an eleven-year remission was asked, "Do you ever ask, 'Why me?'" He answered, "I have good things in my life— friends, a job, skills, and I have never asked God 'Why me?' Why should I ask now when things go wrong?"

The Scriptures tell us to pray for others. So we pray. We pray in faith. We are called to pray, not to take responsibility for answers. So pray fervently, with hope, with specific desires and with confidence in a God who loves us and died for us and a Holy Spirit who intercedes for us. As priests for a world desperately needing intercessors, it is the role of the individual and church to pray. We are not asked to take responsibility for the outcome of prayer. We pray urgently and freely for the needs of our friends, family and this world. Intercessory prayer is a prayer of participation in God's will.

HEALING PRAYER GUIDELINES

- Intercessory prayer for healing of body, land, nation or family is a biblical responsibility.

- Intercessory prayer demonstrates the power and presence of God, but it is not just an object lesson. Jesus has compassion on us. The Holy Spirit intercedes with sighs and groans too deep for words. It is a response of love.

- Intercessory prayer transcends the boundaries of the natural world. Intercessory prayer links heaven and earth in a dance of love.

- Everyone can pray intercessory prayers. We are all to pray for others. We stand before God in a priestly ministry of intercession relying on the Holy Spirit for guidance. Some people are given the gift of healing.

- Intercessory prayer compels us to face evil and not avoid pain, which only God can overcome. We have nothing to fear.

- Intercession is first listening and then praying and then listening some more. Intercession isn't a torrent of words and fervent emotions. It is standing quietly before a sovereign God and asking through the Spirit for God's intervention.

- A New Testament call to intercessory prayer is found in James 5:13-14.

  - Begin with identifying the need. Many start praying without asking the person what is their need.

  - When we gather around someone in need, we become family to them and validate and identify with their struggle.

  - Oil is often used in healing prayer. In the Bible oil symbolized God's approval. So anointing with oil was a gesture of fellowship with God's power to heal supernaturally. A finger is dipped in oil and then the sign of the cross can be applied on the forehead or hand.

  - Praying in the name of Jesus means to pray in faith and love.

- Intercessory prayer joins us with God's mission to bring his kingdom to earth through signs of God's activity.

- Intercession is often not a one-time experience. Prayers of intercession are characterized by a persistence to seek God's will. Continue with prayer as often as is practical or as the person desires or the need continues.

- Intercession is an act of faith approaching the throne of grace through the interceding power of the Holy Spirit. Therefore, the prayers are left at the altar. We do not take emotional or mental responsibility for the outcome.

HEALING PRAYER EXPERIENCE

Group Experience

- This experience can take place in a nursing home, hospital, home of a sick person, the church or really any location. Healing prayer in the context of worship prepares everyone for the sacredness of intercession.

- Any type of healing service can be created. Following is an example of one.

  - *Music*—Choose two to three songs of praise and invitation.

  - *Scripture*—Psalm 103 is a thanksgiving song for God's goodness. It can be read with a leader and group response beginning with the leader and then the group reading every other verse.

  - *Homily* (very, very short)—such as Matthew 8:1-3 where Jesus cleanses a leper. The passage is about (1) coming to Jesus, (2) humbling yourself before Jesus and (3) trusting Jesus' compassion.

  - *Healing prayer*—There can be music in the background. Any people who desire healing can come forward (unless you are in a setting with a specific person).

    - Ask the person, "How would you like us to pray?"

    - Gather around and lay on hands (be sure and not crowd the person).

    - Be in silence to listen to the Holy Spirit for a few minutes.

    - Have two to three pray aloud as they are led. Pray for God to heal in the name of Jesus and ask the Holy Spirit to come on the person.

    - One person anoints with oil. The person can say, "I anoint you with oil in the name of the Father, and of the Son, and of the Holy Spirit."

    - This can be repeated for as many people as need prayer.

    - If a group does this for themselves, each one should bring a specific request for healing or a request for some other need.

  - *Music*—Close with a praise song.

  - *Prayer*—A leader can close in prayer.

- After you have prayed for someone, check in with them in the next day or two. The purpose is not to ask "Did it work?" but rather to assure them of your continued care and to ask how they are doing, and to pray again if asked.

- Talk together as a group. How did you experience the prayer time? When did you feel most clear and close to God? Did you ever feel confused or do you have questions? Whenever a prayer is answered, it is celebrated. It is a sign of God's grace and love. Tell the story of it. The stories are for the encouragement of the community.

Partner Experience

- You may pray for each other and/or you may go together to pray for someone who needs prayer.

- The process is to (1) Identify the person's need (ask them specifically); (2) sit in silence to center on the Holy Spirit and listen; (3) place hands on the person and pray for him or her as you feel led; and (4) anoint with oil. More details are in the section above.

- Talk together about your experience. How did you experience the Holy Spirit's presence? Did you feel anxious or afraid? Share about it.

Individual Experience

- You may choose to go and pray for someone that needs prayer as detailed above.

- Or you may set up a small altar to remind you that you are coming before the throne of God, and then pray intercessory prayers for people and needs. Listen first to the Holy Spirit for whom or for what he wants you to pray. When you are clear—it is usually one or two things—pray. Continue to pray until your heart feels clear or an answer is given.

- Write in your journal about your experience. How does it shape your understanding of your mission in the world? How does praying for others shape you and your faith?

PRAYER JOURNEY

Victoria Marty

In 1999 my husband was diagnosed with multiple sclerosis and we fell into financial disaster. By 2001 his MS had gotten so bad he had to stop working. We thought we would lose everything. To make matters worse Social Security denied his disability claim seven times, and we were forced to get an attorney. He could not work, and I could not financially support us. But with lots of help from God, our church and family, we were able to get by. Every day I would pray to the Lord that "whatever the outcome is, that it would be a fair and just ruling." I trusted God and had faith he would see us through.

It took us two and a half years before Social Security would hear our case. As the years wore on it was harder to have faith, but I would just keep praying the same thing every time I would get scared or hopeless: "Whatever the outcome is, Lord, I pray that it would be a fair and just ruling." I never told anyone this prayer, not Tony nor our lawyer. On the day before our court hearing our lawyer called. He was surprised and joyful. He said the judge reviewed Tony's case and that we did not need to go to court the next day. The only thing he said was Tony has been awarded full disability, and then he said, "I believe this is a fair and just ruling." I nearly fell over. The Lord is faithful.

Elaine Proff

One morning I got up as usual, made my coffee, and went down to the mailbox to pick up my paper. I took it back to the kitchen and spread it out on the breakfast bar. As soon as I did, I saw the story on the front page of a young girl, about ten years old, who had been abducted the afternoon before by a stranger. She was walking home from school. He opened his pickup door and grabbed her. Some witnessed the event but no one got a license number. I've read lots of front-page stories but this one was different. God said clearly and forcefully, "Pray for this child." I laid my hands on the paper and I started praying. I prayed and prayed. I prayed for the protection of the child. I prayed that the Holy Spirit would compel the man to let her go and would soften his heart. I don't know how long I stood there and prayed, but afterward I went throughout the day praying. The next morning I opened the paper and on the front page was another story about the same little girl. After many hours of driving around, the man finally drove into a gas station, let the girl out unharmed and turned himself in. I felt as if I were part of God's miracle in that little girl's life and in that man.

Janee Walker

I felt stymied with intercessory prayer. It just felt very overwhelming to be praying for problems that, when I am honest about my feelings, I really doubt will be healed. No person is beyond God's power, but healing a person with illnesses like alcoholism or Alzheimer's through me? That is where my faith is shaky on healing prayer.

Then my teenage daughter accidentally cut her foot on a frame that had been sitting on the floor. I looked at it and put a Band-Aid on it for her. The cut was between her toes and hard to reach. Two days later she complained that it still hurt. She looked at it and announced to me, "It's not healing." God immediately nudged me. "Pray for her foot." I'm thinking, "God, her foot? You've got to be kidding." I looked at her foot. It did look much the same as on day one. I didn't pray. He continued to nudge, pointing out to me that this would indeed be starting out small. Later in the day I prayed for her foot while I put on another Band-Aid. I asked him to heal the cut, relieve her pain and her worry over the lack of healing, and released this injury to him. The next morning she announced to me that it was significantly better, but the words she used? "Mom, my foot is healing." I felt like God was saying, "Trust me."

My daughter, Emily, and I are very close. Her faith is strong, so much so that as an eight-year-old, when she had a tonsillectomy and was unable to take the pain medication, it was her first thought to ask me to pray for pain relief. She couldn't talk, but she would tap my arm and fold her hands. Over the initial three days post-surgery she required repeated doses of "pain relief prayer." I would pray and ask God to take her pain while laying my hands on her. I could feel her little body all tense with the pain, and as I prayed she would slowly drift off to sleep. Her trust in him and in me was complete. Pain relief came to her over and over. I had forgotten all about this until the foot incident.

I need to trust more, open myself more, listen more and trust God's path more. I am praying less for diseases to be gone and more for the person. I am holding them before God, releasing them to his will and praying for my will to align to his.

FURTHER READING

Atkinson, David. *The Church's Healing Ministry: Practical and Pastoral Reflections.* London: Canterbury Press Norwich, 2011.

Campolo, Tony, and Mary Albert Darling. *The God of Intimacy and Action: Reconnecting Ancient Spiritual Practices, Evangelism, and Justice.* San Francisco: Jossey-Bass, 2008.

Manning, Brennan. *Ruthless Trust: The Ragamuffin's Path to God.* New York: HarperSan-Francisco, 2002.

21

Meditative Prayer

To pray is to descend with the mind into the heart,
and there to stand before the face of the Lord,
ever-present, all seeing, within you.

THEOPHAN THE RECLUSE

And the Spirit is the one
that testifies, for the Spirit is the truth.

1 JOHN 5:6

THE HOLY SPIRIT AS TRUTH WHISPERER

Often churches and faith communities are rocked with controversies about what is true and what is not or if there are multiple paths to truth. There was a time when tattoos, purple hair and women wearing pants were highly controversial. Now these are ridiculous issues. More serious ones do occur. We've had culture wars over worship styles and heated debates over Bible translations. Churches split over differing biblical interpretation of controversial passages. The essentials remain: God created us and loves us; Christ is our center and saved us; and the Holy Spirit guides us to be part of God's mission in the world today. Yet controversy over less essential beliefs sometimes overwhelm the essentials. Each generation discerns afresh what is true in regard to the less essential testimonies of their faith. Though controversy and confusion are normative, gracefully seeking the Spirit of Truth and finding a way forward together is rare.

Before the disciples' world was rocked and all sorts of assumptions were shattered, Jesus took them with him to the Garden of Gethsemane where he customarily went to pray. He spoke his last direct words to them before he was betrayed and arrested. In all three Synoptic Gospels, Matthew, Mark and Luke, Jesus warns his disciples to continually pray in order to avoid temptation. He said to them, "Stay awake and pray that you may not come into the time of trial; the spirit indeed is willing, but the flesh is weak" (Mt 26:41).

Some translations use "watch and pray." The word for watch means to be alert, to stay awake. The "time of trial" was coming for the disciples when their Master would be crucified. Everything they had hoped for would seem to be lost. We know the end story of Jesus' triumphant resurrection, but they were in a fog.

Their time of trial was the loss of their Master; ours is different. The time of trial for us is any temptation that entices us to take control of God's truth and battle for its rights without seeking truth in prayer. Only the Spirit can lead us into truth. And we can only hear the Spirit if we "watch and pray." Jesus promised the Holy Spirit so we would not be left as orphans, without guidance and parental safety. Jesus said, "But the Advocate, the Holy Spirit, whom the Father will send in my name, will teach you everything, and remind you of all that I have said to you" (Jn 14:26).

The Holy Spirit is a very special Advocate for us. Not only does the Holy Spirit intercede on our behalf, but the Holy Spirit is also the Spirit of Truth who dwells in us and reminds us of Jesus Christ's words. We are fortunate to have the Bible, which is God's written Word. We can read and study this Word and internalize the teachings. However, sometimes we focus on the thought processes of truth and forget that truth without integrity, lived out in behaviors, is not truth.

The problem with the weakness of our humanity is that we take ownership for the truth. This can lead to the temptation of self-sufficiency and pride. We take control of our lives. We decide what is righteous and what is not righteous. A slow rift begins between our talk and our walk. Because of this, we sometimes have spiritual leaders who are stellar in public and sinners in private. The Holy Spirit whispers to us living truth. The Holy Spirit reminds us of the person of Christ and the words of Christ. The Holy Spirit keeps us humbly attached to a holy God.

When we are tempted, the Spirit of Truth reminds us of our holiness in Jesus and helps us to "see" more clearly. Darkness or blindness is often a result of the desire to rely on the flesh and not the Holy Spirit. We think we know what is best for us, *or* we know it's not best, but we want the comfort that comes from yielding to the temptation. This is especially true when we feel threatened or insecure, and we succumb to an addiction. An addiction is any activity or substance that we turn to for comfort or control and which has these characteristics: (1) difficulty controlling the use of the activity or substance, (2) preoccupation with using the substance or doing the activity, (3) continual use despite damaging consequences and (4) denial that it is a problem. The consequences are usually a short-term gratification with a long-term adverse result.

In our fast-paced, high-stress culture, addictions are rampant from small problems such as compulsive use of social media, compulsive shopping, over-exercising or over-eating to larger even more destructive habits such as drug, alcohol and sexual addictions including the use of pornography. All these addictions are prevalent among

Christians. Addictions of any kind are very serious, not only because they are personally and relationally destructive, but because the object of our desire consumes us and we are unable to freely love God and clearly see God's truth. Addictions are a complex issue not easily routed out with a simple desire to stop. It does take desire, but it also takes a community, a plan and the help of the Holy Spirit.[1]

Whether our temptation is an ongoing addiction or any sin, such as anger, gossip, bitterness, hatred or immorality of any kind, the temptation indicates that the weakness of our flesh has overcome our desire to live according to the Spirit. Jesus says to be alert and pray. The Holy Spirit is the Spirit of Truth that helps us with our weaknesses (1 Thess 5:19-23).

MEDITATIVE PRAYER

The Spirit of Truth does not yell or force us to be like Christ. The Spirit of Truth whispers, reminding us of our true spiritual desires and warning us of danger. Therefore, the Spirit is best heard when we listen, and we listen best when we pray. Meditative prayer is a perfect medium for listening to the Spirit using Scripture. Meditative prayer creates "the emotional and spiritual space which allows Christ to construct an inner sanctuary of the heart."[2] In our interior spirit, we allow the Holy Spirit to speak truth into our lives. Meditative prayer allows the Holy Spirit to transform our inner lives. From that place we have a more grounded perspective on the everyday. Desperation, striving, untamed desires and insecurities are submitted to the soothing living waters of the Holy Spirit's presence. An ungrounded, chaotic life leads to imbalance. An ungrounded, chaotic community leads to conflicts. Meditative prayer invites us to a centered place with a desire rooted in Christ's love (2 Tim 1:14).

Months ago someone gave me Psalm 15 as a prophetic message from God. I was called to be a man who can "dwell in [the Lord's] sanctuary" (Ps 15:1). I allowed this passage to soak into my soul. I sensed the Lord challenging me in how I think about others. Psalm 15:3 says a man who dwells in the Lord's sanctuary "casts no slur on his neighbors." I don't think I verbally put down people, but I often do in my thoughts. I'm trying to take captive those thoughts and think instead on whatever is true, noble, right, pure, lovely and admirable (Phil 4:8).

—Brad Rohr

The Holy Spirit provides a living presence of the Word. The living Word was Christ in the flesh. The written Word is the authoritative Word of God we can use in prayer. The Holy Spirit guides us as we read Scripture and reflect on its meaning in our lives. Reading, studying and reflecting on Scripture is another avenue for discerning God's voice, for receiving guidance and for experiencing God's healing.

We hear truth from God's perspective.

The use of Scripture for prayer has an active and a passive element. We engage the text in study and reflection and then in prayer we listen for the Spirit's guidance. By listening, we develop the ability to perceive God in the everyday. We slow down and are less distracted. To perceive God we commit to the discipline of nonattainment. We pray to be with God, Christ and the Holy Spirit, and the Scriptures give us a foundation.

The purpose of meditative prayer is less about solving a problem and more about relinquishing control to Christ and listening to the Holy Spirit. We are a people who often seek a quick fix or a definitive answer. The Holy Spirit is timeless and truth is difficult to separate from our own needs for safety and significance. In meditative prayer we commit to listening for as long as it takes. We wait to make sure that we are not coming into the temptation to judge rather than love, to control rather than serve, to be right rather than to be connected to Christ and others.

Meditative prayer is a prayer of the imagination rooted in the Word of God or at times the writings of other saints. We need focused time to meditate on God's Word. Jesus said in John 6:58, referring to himself: "This is the bread that came down from heaven, not like that which your ancestors ate, and they died. But the one who eats this bread will live forever." Our bread is remembered at the Lord's Supper and the bread is digested when we meditate on Scripture. The second word translated "eats" means to munch on. This cannot be rushed or forced. Meditating on Scripture is not a mental study, but a Holy Spirit–led reflection. It gives space for the Spirit of Truth to keep us grounded in Christ and to seek God's truth and not our own.

We can meditate on small passages for understanding. We can visualize stories of Jesus' teaching. We can bring a disputed text to the Holy Spirit in prayer. This does not replace very careful Bible study, but we are limited and need the mind of Christ to truly understand his Word to us. We can pray this way as individuals or as a community.

My mother died while I was on a flight between Anchorage and Seattle. When I arrived, they had already taken her body to be cremated. I had to fly back to my home in Alaska before her remains were ready to be buried, so I have not seen her grave.

Since then, I have harbored judgment against my sister for keeping my mother's medical condition from me. This morning I was doing a meditative prayer using John 11. As I asked, "Where have you laid him?" all of that came back to me. I saw my sin in judging my sister, putting me behind the rock in a tomb and sealing me off from her.

Lord, I am so sorry for barricading myself in, please forgive me. Thank you for rolling the stone away. Thank you that I will see my mother again.

—Sue Honan

MEDITATIVE PRAYER GUIDELINES

- Meditative prayer is a prayer of listening similar to contemplative prayer (chapter 4) and Scripture prayer/*lectio divina* (chapter 13). Our minds are not trying to produce, ask, seek, inquire or intercede, but rather rest and listen in the Spirit for the Spirit's truth.

- In order to focus the mind on the Holy Spirit, meditative prayer uses Scripture or other sacred readings to open the mind to God. The mind attends to a simple passage, phrase or story until the heart is listening.

- Meditative prayer is particularly helpful in allowing the Holy Spirit to purify our hearts and minds, to help us anchor on the living truth.

- Sacred space and time is important. This is not a "quick, get to the answer" prayer. Like a watchman watches through the night, we watch and pray.

- Begin a meditative prayer time by praying, "Holy Spirit, guide me/us into God's truth and transform me/us into Christlikeness."

- Take any biblical story or a few verses, such as Jesus in the Garden praying, the parable of the prodigal son, the woman touching the hem of Jesus' garment, Peter's vision on the roof, small sections from the Sermon on the Mount or Romans, Colossians, and so on, and read the verses several times.

> I was particularly skeptical of imaginative visualization. For me the Bible has proper uses and abuses. Prior to this week I could not have conceived of any legitimate use of the Bible that did not take into account the historical context and was not an attempt to better understand Scripture. I now see that the Bible can be used in other ways besides just determining what it meant. In meditative prayer I did not gain any exegetical insight, but I did gain insight into myself. The visualization was a profound experience that I am honestly not ready to discuss just yet.
>
> —Jason Goble

- Close your eyes and imagine the story happening before you. Imagine the scene with the sounds, smells, visuals.

- See yourself first as an *observer*, then as a *participant* and finally see it from *Jesus' perspective*.

- Refrain from analyzing it or thinking too much about what it means. See it as a story from God, as bread without needing to know the recipe.

- Give time for the story or the passage to move from a "thought" experience to a "felt" experience.

- Wait for the Holy Spirit to breathe insight, teaching, protection, courage, Christlike desires or whatever it is the Holy Spirit has for you. Meditative prayer goes to the inner rooms of your character.

- Keep the story or the event as small as possible in order to focus better. For instance, the Sermon on the Mount is very extensive in content. Choose a section, perhaps the section on salt and light, to meditate on. When the section is a teaching passage imagine the setting. See Jesus speaking to the crowds. Be an observer and then participant. See Jesus or Paul speaking directly to you.

- If meditative prayer is done with a group it is often called "guided meditative prayer." A person directs the prayer experience. When a prayer like this is guided, any questions the leader would ask are open questions inviting the person to go deeper into the passage. They are not direct questions. See the examples in the group experience.

- In a group you can also bring passages representing theological or social confusion in order to listen for the Holy Spirit's perspective or guidance.

- After a meditative prayer time, write down any thoughts or insights or talk with a friend or spiritual guide. Sometimes there is no special experience or insight, but usually meditative prayer leaves people with an experience of restfulness. If not, it could be there is some unfinished business in the person's life that is interfering with their ability to be at rest with the Holy Spirit. Again if this is so, seek support from a trusted spiritual elder or guide.

- The "truths" are corroborated by experience, the faith community, the whole of Scripture and reason.

MEDITATIVE PRAYER EXPERIENCE

Group Experience

- A designated leader prepares the environment so there is no distraction and the setting is comfortable for people. Make sure people turn off their electronic devices. You will need fifteen to thirty minutes or more for this experience.

- A guided meditation prayer experience works for a wide variety of group sizes.

- Have a chosen passage of Scripture. To demonstrate I will use a passage from the Sermon on the Mount—Matthew 5:43-48, a section about loving our enemies.

- Have everyone get seated comfortably. The meditative prayer guide reads slowly and leaves time between the readings for people to sit in silence and listen.

- Begin with the suggested prayer: "Holy Spirit, guide us into God's truth and transform us into Christlikeness."

- The leader can help people focus by sitting in silence for a few minutes, having everyone relax their bodies and focus on breathing. You might say, "Take slow deep breathes. Inhale the presence of the Holy Spirit. . . . Slowly exhale any thoughts, worries, fears and insecurities. . . . Rest in Christ's love. . . . The Holy Spirit is with you."

- Tell the group, "Jesus is speaking to his disciples and the crowds. He went up on the mountain and sat down and began to teach them. See this happening in your mind. You are watching this take place."

- *Listening as an observer*: Read Matthew 5:43-48. The guide says, "As I read the passage slowly, imagine you are there. See the place in your mind and see Jesus speaking."

- *Listening as a participant*: Read the passage a second time. The guide says, "As I read the passage again, see yourself as a person to whom Jesus is speaking. You are there."

- *Listening from Jesus' perspective*: Read the passage a third time. The guide says, "As I read the passage for a third time, see the experience from Jesus' perspective. Ask for the eyes of Christ to see his point of view."

- Close the meditative prayer time with a prayer like, "Holy Spirit, thank you for the living Word and for your truth to us."

- Divide the group into pairs or small groups of two to three. As much as possible, make sure the groups are safe for the individuals in them. Have them share about their experience.

- After sharing, ask if there are any questions about meditative prayer or if anyone wants to share their experience with the entire group. Encourage them to write their experience down and to remember any truth or insight that came for them.

Partner Experience

- Partners or a small group can do a similar experience as the one above. You can take turns reading the passage. Read it once as an observer, once as a participant and once (as much as possible) from the perspective of Jesus.

- The benefit of meditative prayer with a partner is that you usually know each other well and are secure with each other. This allows you to go deeper into the prayer time and also invites you to be more open about the prayer experience.

- At the close of the experience, talk about it together. Do you have any insights or questions? How might the Spirit of Truth help you live a more Christlike life on a daily basis? How might you carry the passage or story with you throughout the day?

- Sometimes you can use a passage several times in order to allow any resistance or reluctance to entering into the experience to lessen.

Individual Experience

- Meditative prayer is particularly helpful if you are struggling with an addiction, sin or relationship, or simply feel stuck spiritually. Find a story or verses that might help you. Ask the Holy Spirit to guide you to a passage.

- Give yourself thirty to sixty minutes for meditative prayer. It doesn't always take that much time, but you don't want to feel rushed.

- Over a period of several days, even weeks, if necessary (some struggles are particularly resistant to resolution), use the same passage. Ask the Holy Spirit to help you as you begin. Imagine yourself in the passage as an observer until there is some movement. Then see yourself as a participant, again leaning into any movement of the Spirit, and then lastly see it from God's (or Jesus' or the Holy Spirit's) perspective.

- After each experience, journal thoughts, insights and openings.

PRAYER JOURNEY

John Irving

I was attending a conference for denominational leaders that had its combination of plenary speakers and workshops. I decided to attend a workshop on spiritual formation in the church. The information was good and helpful, but at the end, the presenter wanted to demonstrate how spiritual formation might work in a church by leading us in a guided meditation. I was very resistant. Such things seemed to me soft spiritually and could open possibility for the misuse of Scripture. I also don't like to entrust myself to someone I don't know, but this person seemed competent. I told the Lord I would try it, but he would have to protect me.

The presenter used the parable about the farmer throwing mustard seed in his garden. She shared that mustard seed was an unclean plant that wouldn't be put in a garden but would be planted in a designated space. She also said a mustard plant is like a weed, crowding out other plants, and you certainly don't want birds coming to your garden. She then began the meditative prayer experience.

She asked us to imagine a garden that we would really enjoy. She had us walking around in it and I made this great flower and vegetable garden that I had always dreamed of creating. Then she asked us to see Jesus in the garden. Where Jesus is the kingdom of God is active. I was proud to have Jesus in my garden and I was talking to him and showing him around.

Then she said, "Look around. Something is in your garden that you don't expect or want. What is it?" I looked up and my estranged son walked into my garden. I choked. She said let Jesus talk to you about whatever has come into your garden. I turned to Jesus and Jesus simply said, "You need to forgive your son." I started quietly weeping. I did not expect this. We've been estranged for ten years after a bitter argument over his choices. I told the Lord, "Yes, I forgive my son and I will call him."

When the experience was over, I shared with the group. I felt a new clarity and cleanness in my spirit.

Richard Peters

As a New Testament scholar in my denomination, I'm often asked to come to a church and help them sort out a theological or social problem disturbing the congregation. I really enjoy doing this because we often make assumptions about what Scripture means without really studying the passages in the broader biblical context and in the immediate textual context. A well-known church in our area invited me to present on the issue of women in church leadership. I don't support it from a biblical perspective, so they asked me to bring a biblical view on the issue.

I spent quite a bit of time reviewing the pertinent texts and arranging a presentation.

The day after I concluded my work on the presentation, I was in my normal prayer time when I distinctly heard the Holy Spirit say to me, "Richard, are you going to ask me?" I was floored. I thought, *I guess I should.* I sat in quiet and held these passages before the Lord to listen. I can't explain what happened but after a while the whole issue restructured in my mind and I saw the passages in a different light. I saw that the Lord intended for men and women to pray and prophesy and have equal leadership roles. I felt very unnerved by this because now I had a problem. This flipped my theological world and what would I tell the church? I called the pastor to let him know and he asked me to come anyway.

FURTHER READING

Foster, Richard J. *Meditative Prayer*. Downers Grove, IL: InterVarsity Press, 1999.

———. *Sanctuary of the Soul: Journey into Meditative Prayer*. Downers Grove, IL: InterVarsity Press, 2011.

Reinhold, Amy, and Judge Reinhold, compilers. *Be Still and Know That I Am God: 31 Days to a Deeper Meditative Prayer Life*. New York: Howard Press, 2007.

22

Discernment Prayer

God does not exist to answer our prayers,
but by our prayers we come to discern the mind of God.

OSWALD CHAMBERS

I pray that the God of our Lord Jesus Christ, the Father of glory,
may give you a spirit of wisdom and revelation as you come to know him,
so that, with the eyes of your heart enlightened,
you may know what is the hope to which he has called you,
what are the riches of his glorious inheritance among the saints.

EPHESIANS 1:17-18

THE HOLY SPIRIT AS GUIDE

Throughout the stages of our lives we have big decisions to make. As a child it might be which sports to play, which friends to choose and which interests to take up. As we get older the decisions have more important and long-term consequences: Will I marry and to whom? What profession should I choose? Which faith community do I become a part of? Then it becomes where and when do we retire. Since we can't see into the future, it's very difficult to discern which choice is the best. The Holy Spirit was also given to help us discern and to guide us.

The Holy Spirit as the Spirit of Truth guides us, directs our path and enables us to know what is good, acceptable and perfect. Acceptable means what is pleasing to God, like a fragrant offering. The "perfect" means maturing toward the end goal of being conformed to the likeness of Christ. In Romans 12:2 Paul urges Christ followers not to be conformed but to be transformed: "Do not be conformed to this world, but be transformed by the renewing of your minds, so that you may discern what is the will of God—what is good and acceptable and perfect." The result is the ability to discern the will of God. The word for "discern" means to put to the test, examine, discover, approve. The nature of the words suggests a process, a journey to discover. Discernment is a fine-tuning process in order to hear the Father clearly. We want to know the mind of God. To do this we need the Holy Spirit. Paul prayed:

> And this is my prayer, that your love may overflow more and more with knowledge and full insight to help you to determine what is best, so that in the day of Christ you may be pure and blameless, having produced the harvest of righteousness that comes through Jesus Christ for the glory and praise of God. (Phil 1:9-11)

Knowledge is not simply things we know. The word translated "knowledge" refers to insights. The second word, which is translated "insight," means discernment and experience, especially experience that comes from sensory perceptions and intellectual understanding. In this context in Philippians it means that we will have moral discrimination. In other words, the way is not always clear and we need to use our senses and our intellect and the Holy Spirit to help us discern the way.

In Acts we see many stories of discernment and decision making among the early leaders. Discernment was not only moral. The Holy Spirit directed people to next steps, to understand God's will and to prophesy. These more often than not happened through discernment in prayer as guided by the Holy Spirit:

- *Prophecies*: Acts 2:17-18 (fulfillment of Joel 2:28-32)—The Holy Spirit is poured out with new prophecies, visions and dreams. These resulted in a fresh awakening and understanding of God's will and mission.

- *Moral clarity*: Acts 5:1-11—Ananias and Sapphira lied to Peter about the amount of money they received for selling some property. Peter discerned the lie and said, "How is it that you have contrived this deed in your heart? You did not lie to us but to God!" (Acts 5:4).

- *Specific leadings*:
  - Acts 8:25-40—The Holy Spirit directed Philip to the Ethiopian official on the desert road between Gaza and Jerusalem and the official was converted and baptized.
  - Acts 9:10-19—The Lord directed Ananias to find Saul, who was persecuting believers, and heal him of his blindness.
  - Acts 16:1-10—Paul and Timothy were forbidden to speak in Asia and Bithynia, but received a vision to go into Macedonia.

- *New kingdom vision*:
  - Acts 10:1-48—While Peter was praying on the roof of Simon the Tanner's house, he received a vision and direction to visit the Gentile Cornelius.

- Acts 11:1-18—Peter testified to the leaders in Jerusalem concerning the baptism of the Holy Spirit on Gentiles.

- *Calling and direction*: Acts 13:1-4—Leaders in the Antioch church laid hands on and then sent Barnabas and Saul on their first missionary journey.

- *Doctrinal discernment and innovation*: Acts 15:1-31—At the Council of Jerusalem the apostles and elders debated whether Gentile believers should observe the Law of Moses or not. Peter spoke and then James made a judgment not to burden the Gentiles except on a few points.

- *Preparation for suffering*: Acts 20:17-36—Paul said farewell to the Ephesian elders as he headed toward Jerusalem. He told them he was "bound by the Spirit," using words that suggest being held captive by the Holy Spirit's leading. The Holy Spirit has alerted him to upcoming trials and persecutions.

The guidance of the Holy Spirit is individual, communal and global. Philip was directed to engage one specific man in one specific place. The Jerusalem elders as a community discerned the role of the Law in the Gentile believers' lives. Paul, Barnabas, James and others began to grasp and witness the liberating impact of the gospel to Gentiles everywhere. Therefore, we too turn to the Holy Spirit for guidance in everyday matters, life decisions and community direction.

DISCERNMENT PRAYER

Discernment happens in community and is experienced in prayer. Whether the community is one person with the Holy Spirit or several people with the Holy Spirit, it requires openness to receive input from other sources of wisdom and insight (1 Cor 2:10-12; 2 Pet 1:19-21).

Parker Palmer wrote about the importance of community discernment in his book *Reflections on a Hidden Wholeness*. He calls these discernment communities "circles of trust."[1] These trust circles were safe spaces in community for the inner self to emerge and be known. Since we are all masters at self-protection and denial, it is difficult for us to see clearly when we need to make a decision about a course of action that matters to the kingdom.

God is continuing to challenge me to trust. At one point this week I found myself resisting the prayer, "Holy Spirit, how might I live more fully by your Spirit?" because it just felt like it would be so much work. And yet I know that when I do trust and pray like this, the burden of life is lighter. When I trust I find tangible examples of the fruits of the Spirit in the dysfunction and brokenness of my work relationships. This week ended in a nearly miraculous meeting with my boss that I can only make sense of through God's response to this prayer.

—Patrick Miller

This is especially true when we are invested in a particular outcome or if there is a lot of fear. Palmer names three reasons why we desperately need to discern in community:[2]

1. The faith journey is too taxing to do alone. God created us in community and designed us to be interdependent.

2. The path is too hidden. With others in prayer and conversation, we discover subtle clues and imagine new possibilities.

3. The destination is daunting. Together we encourage each other. We experience courage together.

Because of the challenges of our age, the prayer of discernment is more critical than ever. Today everyone is right and has rights, and the "one" is more important than the whole. Understanding is sometimes difficult and complicated and hard to arrive at together. Jesus yearned for a church known for its love and united around his name. Today the church is often known for its division and strife. This is partly true because we don't know how to pray and discern together. We decide we are right and like the religious leaders of Jesus' time, we fight for that perspective no matter what it might cost. If we pray and seek direction together, it is less possible to dislike the other and more possible to find agreement. Discernment prayer matters.

Discernment does not mean to abdicate responsibility for making a decision, but to listen for the Holy Spirit's perspective on the decision. Group discernment requires a dependence on God and others for making major decisions. What might have happened if the Council of Jerusalem had dissolved into a hopeless argument with two sides accusing the other of heresy? What might have happened if courageous individuals hadn't discerned a moral injustice and risked everything for the rights of others: slaves, the poor, the uneducated, the victims of hate crimes, the mentally ill or the physically disabled? The church is

I was engaged to a wonderful man. However, I felt unclear about whether I truly wanted to marry him or whether we were mainly good friends. He wanted to get married. I was confused. We decided to seek help from our church and a clearness committee was set up. The evening we gathered we took two hours for silence, talking and listening, and prayer and sharing. Though anxious I felt the calming presence of the Holy Spirit and the care of the people with us. In the end, it was clear. I knew and they confirmed that I was not called into this relationship. It hurt my friend, but I knew I was not the one for him and he was not the one for me. Two years later we both had met and married people right for us.

—Emily West

to be the pioneer in correcting social injustice in the same way that Jesus came to preach the gospel and release the captive (Lk 5:18-19). Through prayer and discernment the church can take the lead in making a difference.

One of the church's best traditions for exploring new opportunities is discernment. Discernment prayer creates the possibility for the Holy Spirit to break through our limitations and see new possibilities. When we look back at our history we see men, women and sometimes children led by the Holy Spirit to dream dreams, risk possibilities, endure persecutions and see the dawning of a new day.

Innovation occurs when changes to established things are imagined. The

> Today is a time for redefinition for the church; it is a time for the church to listen to its stories, talk about its direction and identity, and patiently discern the shape of its future life and ministry. Yet people are weary from church business as usual, from church gatherings that do not connect with deeper meanings of their life and faith. The church must draw on its best traditions of faith and practice in order to find new ways of interacting and deciding.[3]

Holy Spirit helps us discern how the gospel might be more fully expressed in our time. Innovation happens in environments that are willing to stretch and willing to fail. When the disciples followed Jesus, they left everything and heard and saw things that took them a while to understand. When Peter went to the house of Cornelius, he took a huge risk. Entering the house of a Gentile was breaking the Law as he understood it. He went because God prepared him to see things differently with the vision of the clean and unclean food. God spoke, so Peter went. We often get stuck in our personal lives or in our communities because our possibilities become more and more narrow, and we limit what God might do. Discernment is a process that allows an innovative approach to a problem to emerge as the Holy Spirit directs the process. We are able to visualize new possibilities.

DISCERNMENT PRAYER GUIDELINES

- Discernment means to distinguish between things. Discernment prayer seeks to answer the question, "God, what is your will?" for individuals and groups.

- Discernment is based on trusting God and believing that the Holy Spirit will lead us.

- Discernment is a communal experience involving the individual, the Holy Spirit, others and Scriptures.

- Discernment prayer is not possible if one or more people are already convinced they know the answer. It is based on a relinquishment of will to the will of God. It requires humility of spirit.

- Discernment prayer requires silence and listening to the Holy Spirit and to each other.

- If the discernment prayer is for an individual who is seeking direction for his or her life, a discernment community focuses on the person and the Holy Spirit. The purpose of the prayer time is not to share personal experiences and insights, but to listen to the individual and the Holy Spirit.

- If discernment prayer is for a group in a decision-making process, the focus is on the decision and the Holy Spirit, not any individual's perceived outcomes.

- Enough time is needed for listening, silence and prayer to discern something. Sometimes discernment happens after weeks or months of prayer.

- Discernment prayer is helped best with a format to create a safe, listening and sacred environment. One form of discernment prayer is a clearness committee.[4]

  - Before the discernment experience, someone is chosen to guide the process. The guide is someone who is spiritually mature and comfortable with this process.

  - Decisions made before the gathering include:

    - What exactly is the discernment question? For instance, an individual might be deciding between several possible directions on his or her life. A larger group such as a denomination might be trying to discern a change in direction. The question should be short, clear and easily understood by all. A question such as "What shall I do with my life?" is too broad.

    - When, where and for how long will the group meet? The place should be without distractions and comfortable. The time should be adequate for the question. Usually two hours are needed.

    - Who should attend? If an individual is discerning a question, he or she should select four to five people who are spiritually mature and who know how to pray and listen to the Holy Spirit. They should not be invested in a particular outcome. If it is a group process, everyone invested in the outcome or the primary leaders should be present.

    - When those decisions are made, the leader notifies everyone of the details for the discernment prayer experience. Everyone prepares by praying for their time together.

  - The discernment prayer gathering process includes these steps:

    - *Introductions and opening prayer*: Introductions are made if necessary. Then a simple restatement of the purpose of the gathering occurs, followed by prayer.

    - *Explanation of the process*: Explaining the process assures that everyone understands what will occur and understands their role.

- *Introduction of the question.*
  - The person shares his or her question and takes ten to fifteen minutes to explain the situation.
  - If it is a group question, then the leader reviews the history leading up to the question.
- *Clarifying questions.*
  - If this is an individual discernment process, then people can ask the individual clarifying questions. Wise, open questions help someone understand the situation better or know the person and context better.
  - If this is a group experience, clarifying questions help make sure everyone understands the issue or concern in the same way.
  - It is the guide's responsibility to intervene if the questions asked are leading or betray an agenda. The guide also intervenes if someone is talking too much.
- *Prayer of listening:* After the question is shared and other questions asked, participants sit in prayer of silence, listening for the Holy Spirit and holding the person or question before God. Silence is maintained for ten minutes or more.
- *Sharing:* After the silence, each person in the group shares what came to their awareness while in prayer. Sharing may be thoughts, impressions, Scripture or word pictures. Have someone take notes to give to the person or group at the end of the gathering.
- *Summary:* The leader summarizes the discernment of the group. The larger the group, the more time is needed to discern the primary themes.
- *Clarification:* The group clarifies the discernment. If there are still questions, concerns or ambiguity, the discernment prayer is repeated at another time. There is no rush or timetable. Sometimes there is a lot of emotional investment so it takes more time to let go and listen.
- *Closing prayer:* A closing prayer is offered especially thanking the Holy Spirit for the experience and for the words shared and heard.

- Sometimes unhealthy or unwell individuals interrupt a discernment prayer process with a repetition of fears or views that they refuse to submit to a discernment process. Or sometimes people are unable to listen in prayer and bring again and again their perspective. Discernment prayer needs to be led well, and sometimes that means managing in love a disruptive voice.

- Discernment prayer is helpful not only for discerning direction but also for discerning the nature of one's personal spiritual walk and life. Questions might be, "God, what do you desire of me?" or "Holy Spirit, how might I become more like

Christ?" or "Jesus, guide me to see what you see." Groups may also seek discernment on these types of spiritual questions.

DISCERNMENT PRAYER EXPERIENCE

Group Experience

- Before the prayer experience, the group (or group leader) decides whether there is a specific issue they need to discern together or if they wish to discern in prayer, "Holy Spirit, how can we become more like Christ?"

- Once the question for the discernment prayer is clear, set a time and place that allows for adequate time with minimum disruptions.

- Follow the process explained above in the discernment prayer guidelines section. If the group is larger than ten to twelve people, the *Sharing* step can be done differently. After the listening prayer time when people are invited to share, have everyone write their thoughts, insights, Scripture verse or word picture on a Post-It note or on paper provided. Post their notes on an open wall space or tape their papers on the space. Then for the *Summary* step, have a few people organize the thoughts into thematic groups. During the *Clarification* step, talk together and discuss which thing/s are the priority concerns from the Holy Spirit for the group. This involves another type of discernment through conversation and listening together for when the group "quickens," when the group knows together this is what we should be about, pay attention to, change or try.

- Close in prayer. This prayer can be an individual or several people who want to thank God for the discernment prayer experience.

- Have time for people to ask questions or share perspectives on their experience of discernment prayer. Discuss questions such as: "How do you distinguish between the voice of the Holy Spirit and your own self-talk?" "How do you distinguish between the Holy Spirit's guidance and the guidance of others that might come from bias or brokenness?" "What if you hear from the Holy Spirit, but you don't want to do it?"

- Follow-up on this prayer experience is important. If the group discerned a direction, made a decision or came to understand God's will in a fresh way, then the community will want specific steps toward fulfilling the insights. These too can be discussed together.

Partner Experience

- If each one of you has an individual discernment question, take turns and follow the process as described in the guidelines section. If you want to enhance the experience, consider inviting two to three other people to meet with you. These people should be people of integrity, prayer and faith. Explain the process to them and invite them to listen with you. For whoever brings the discernment question, the other partner or another person in the group guides the process.

- If no one has a discernment question, follow the process using the question, "What is God's will for me at this place in my life?" or "Holy Spirit, how might I become more like Christ?"

- After prayer, talk together about your experience.

Individual Experience

- If you have an individual discernment question, ask someone to help lead a discernment prayer experience for you. Find someone who has experience with the process or who wants to learn with you but is mature enough to lead the process.

- Otherwise, for several days, use Galatians 5:16, 22-23, 25 in this manner:

  - *Opening prayer*: Ephesians 1:17-18

  - *Question*: "Holy Spirit, how might I live more fully by your Spirit?"

  - *Prayer of listening*: Reflect on Galatians and listen to the Holy Spirit for the insight regarding the fruit of the Spirit in your life. Take at least ten minutes to listen. At the end of the prayer of listening, pray, "Holy Spirit, thank you for the gift of your guidance."

  - *Sharing*: Journal on your experience. If you have a spiritual friend or guide, you might share any insights you receive from the Holy Spirit.

  - *Summary*: Repeat the same prayer experience over several days, preferably a week. Then summarize what you discovered about living more fully by the Spirit.

PRAYER JOURNEY

Eric Muhr

One summer, during a trip to my grandparents' home, I felt God challenging me to reconsider my path: would I continue to seek a future in the public eye (politics) or would I be willing to set aside what I wanted (wealth and influence) in order to serve others? It felt like a calling. I struggled in prayer over what kind of a life I should lead and what kind of a person God was creating me to be.

During that process, many others joined me in discernment praying for clarity and for strength to choose well. Today, nearly two decades later,

I have trouble remembering why it was such a hard choice and why it felt like I had so much to lose. In the process of prayer—a daily practice of moving closer and closer to the center—I've found both clarity and community. I can't even begin to imagine going back.

Eunice Oyungu

This week has been a difficult one— traveling to visit my grandchildren in addition to being sick. I did not have the quiet, predictable environment I am used to. However, it was amazing that in the midst of all this God gave me moments of focused silence to listen.

In the course of planning my travels, I realized that my small group leader had some DVDs we had used in our class that I always wished my son and his wife could listen to. Earlier I tried to get them both to a conference, which did not work out. I borrowed the DVDs and took them with me for the visit. I had mentioned to my daughter-in-law that I would bring them along, if she had the time to watch them alone since my son is deployed. My prayer for discernment concerned these DVDs. I wondered if I should have her listen to them or if I was putting too much pressure on her about this issue. When I got to their house, I knew that I was not to mention the subject. It was so clear; it was amazing.

May Wallace

I learned about the importance of discernment prayer through the loss of my closest friends. I spent most of my life in a ministry relationship with Dorothy and Jean. Dorothy was the Christian education coordinator and writer for our denomination. Jean was my ministry partner when I was pastoring. She played the piano, taught Sunday school and helped out with everything from roofing to praying in my church. Over the years we three became even closer friends and depended on each other. When Jean was called to work as a teacher for several missionary families in Peru, I supported her 100 percent. It was tough to be alone, but she blossomed in faith. She always felt called to serve God crossculturally. Dorothy also moved away to do her work. I really missed them. I didn't know what to do except I knew I had to get closer to God. I had to spend more time in prayer, reading the Bible and listening to the Holy Spirit for direction. At first, I didn't notice much of a difference, but then after some years, I would wake up and know what I was supposed to do that day. I felt called to the day and I didn't feel alone. God was with me.

FURTHER READING

Barry, William A. *Discernment in Prayer: Paying Attention to God.* Notre Dame, IN: Ave Maria, 1990.

Gallagher, Timothy M., OMV. *Discerning the Will of God: An Ignatian Guide to Christian Decision Making.* New York: Crossroad, 2009.

Smith, Gordon T. *The Voice of Jesus: Discernment, Prayer and the Witness of the Spirit.* Downers Grove, IL: InterVarsity Press, 2003.

23

Watch Prayer

So the first requirement in God's work is a pure, not a powerful spirit.
Those who neglect this, though their work may be done in power,
will find it destroyed due to the lack of purity.

WATCHMAN NEE

Discipline yourselves, keep alert [watch].
Like a roaring lion your adversary the devil prowls around,
looking for someone to devour.

1 PETER 5:8

THE HOLY SPIRIT AS POWER

No one likes the feeling of powerlessness. No one chooses slavery as a way of life. God designed us to be creative and free as individuals in community. We all like to have some control over our destiny and our well-being. In free countries this is an inalienable right. However, sometimes circumstances and evil are more powerful than we are. Sometimes we are not enough, and we need the strength, will and protection of the Holy Spirit against evil.

The Holy Spirit is the power of God in us. Jesus was filled with the power of the Spirit (Lk 4:14), and he gave his disciples the same power over evil: "Then Jesus called the twelve together and gave them power and authority over all demons and to cure diseases, and he sent them out to proclaim the kingdom of God and to heal" (Lk 9:1-2). In Luke and Acts the bestowing of the Holy Spirit is associated with power (Lk 24:49; Acts 1:8).

Through the power of the Holy Spirit, Christ's message and witness were proclaimed. People came to faith. The Holy Spirit's power also had authority over evil.

Demons were driven out. Sin was renounced. Righteous power from the Holy Spirit is dependent on maintaining, as much as finite humans can, a clean inner house. We are expected to stand firm in faith and holiness (Acts 10:38; 1 Thess 1:5).

For many educated people in industrialized countries, the idea of evil as a real spiritual force is often dismissed as a product of myth and ignorance. Evil beings are good for stories but not real in everyday life. Though they recognize that evil exists in the world, it is the result of mental illness, personal brokenness or social evil from unjust behaviors. However, throughout the Bible evil is a force in the world. Jesus said to Simon, "Simon, Simon, listen! Satan has demanded to sift all of you like wheat, but I have prayed for you that your own faith may not fail; and you, when once you have turned back, strengthen your brothers" (Lk 22:31-32). Paul and Peter also spoke of evil as the power of the air, the devil and the god of this world (2 Cor 4:4; Eph 2:1-2; 4:27; 1 Pet 5:8).

There are many passages in Scripture that speak of powers and principalities and rulers. Walter Wink in his three-volume work, *Engaging the Powers*, did a study of powers and principalities in the New Testament. He came to the conclusion that "powers are both heavenly and earthly, divine and human, spiritual and political, invisible and structural," and that "these powers are both good and evil."[1] The whole of the universe is entirely spiritual and natural. Evil is something people choose and evil is constituted in corrupt governments, families, even religious institutions. There is an unseen power that tempts people and groups to choose the darkness and abhor the light (Eph 6:10-12).

The Old and New Testament do not tell us *why* there is evil or *why* God has allowed evil and injustice to exist in our world. The Testaments do tell us that evil does exist, and we have a responsibility to combat it. We combat evil with love and justice; we choose the light and not the dark. Therefore, we need the power of the Holy Spirit to stand firm.

Jesus overcame evil by healing, eating with sinners and prophesying a new vision of God's kingdom. Jesus cast out demons as a sign of the coming of God's kingdom (Mt 12:28). He demonstrated his complete authority over all things dark. He died precisely to overcome evil at every level. Human or spiritual evil, individual or institutional evil had no power to defeat Christ. Christ rose from the grave so that one day there will be a new heaven and a new earth, integrated and whole without the presence of evil.

Therefore, since we have been buried and raised with Christ, we have the same responsibility to take evil seriously and to engage it. This is evil in our own lives, in our communities and in our nations. Jesus promised and sent the Holy Spirit so that we would have a Helper in this cosmic struggle. The gift of eternal life is not about safety but power to fearlessly follow in Jesus' footsteps. N. T. Wright spoke of it this way: "What was accomplished in Jesus' death and resurrection is the foundation, the model and the guarantee for God's ultimate purpose, which is to rid the world of evil altogether and to establish his creation of justice, beauty and peace."[2]

WATCH PRAYER

A powerful force against any type of evil is praying in the Spirit. God intended for us to be partners in the battle against any power that inflicts hate, cruelty and destruction on individuals and communities. Without Christ and the indwelling presence of the Holy Spirit, our tendency as people is to bend toward the dark. Jesus called us into the light. The Holy Spirit's power enables us to stand firm.

A category of prayer against evil is a specialized type of prayer called "spiritual warfare" prayer. Spiritual warfare prayers are deliverance prayers used to cast out demons from people and places. Spiritual warfare prayer is a prepared, lengthy prayer battle with unseen forces. Though there is historical and present value for this type of prayer, it is also often misused. It can lead to creating environments of fear and hysteria rather than power, love and rational confidence (2 Tim 1:7). Some people become overzealous, "demonizing" every type of behavior and sin. Another criticism is the dualism it creates between body and spirit when every sin and ill is labeled as demons in residence. People then don't take responsibility. They spend a lot of time fighting demons and not addressing the sin in their own lives or injustice in their communities.

Spiritual warfare prayer is a dangerous prayer. In Acts Jewish exorcists were using Jesus' name to cast out demons, but they were not Jesus' followers, and the demons attacked the exorcists (Acts 19:13-17). Engaging the spirits with a lack of wisdom, self-awareness and spiritual maturity is a recipe for the loss of one's own spiritual wholeness. Evil is often disguised as light and is embedded in the world at all types of levels and degrees. Discernment, unwavering centeredness in Christ and humility are necessary qualities for engaging in spiritual warfare prayer. Some people are called and particularly gifted and suited for it (1 Cor 12:4-11).

This chapter is about the role of the Holy Spirit and prayer as a way to watch and stand firm against evil and injustice in the everyday. Jesus gave us the Holy Spirit as Protector and prayer as a weapon to combat evil in our lives and in our world. In the Bible and in church history there are several stories of people who used prayer to combat evil. Daniel prayed in the lion's den. Jesus prayed on the cross. Paul prayed in prison. During the reign of Caesar, Christians would not bow down to him and so were thrown into Coliseum. There they bowed down in prayer, not praying for their own safety, but for Caesar, and eventually Caesar fell: "It was a contest of all the brute force of Rome against a small sect that merely prayed. Who could have predicted that the tiny sect would win?"[3] Believers wrestle against the powers and principalities in two arenas, the personal and the social. Prayer is the means by which we beseech God through the power of the Holy Spirit to overcome evil in whatever form.

This type of prayer is called "Watch" prayer to distinguish it from spiritual warfare prayer. Jesus said in the Garden, "Stay awake [or watch] and pray that you may not come into the time of trial; the spirit indeed is willing, but the flesh is weak" (Mt 26:41). "Stand firm" is taken from passages such as:

Therefore take up the whole armor of God, so that you may be able to withstand on that evil day, and having done everything, to stand firm. (Eph 6:13)

Keep alert, stand firm in your faith, be courageous, be strong. Let all that you do be done in love. (1 Cor 16:13-14)

Stay awake and keep alert means to pay attention and watch like a watchman in the night. Stand firm means to literally stand and figuratively to be steadfast, unwavering. It carries a military sense to hold a watch post or to protect a critical position on a battlefield. Being watchful and standing firm requires courage and faith. It protects us from submitting again to the slavery of sin: "For freedom Christ has set us free. Stand firm, therefore, and do not submit again to a yoke of slavery" (Gal 5:1).

There are two types of watch prayers. One is social, linked to evangelism and justice, and the other is personal, linked to righteousness and engagement. Prayer is needed to combat evil's intent to prevent people from becoming believers and to address injustice in the world (2 Cor 4:4). Chuck Lawless wrote, "Evangelism is more than just a strategy, technique, or program; rather it is taking the gospel into the kingdom of darkness. To evangelize is to march into a spiritual battle."[4]

Evil works with many types of deceptions and confusions. C. S. Lewis's famous *The Screwtape Letters* allegorizes this struggle with the story of two demons trying different tricks to keep people from trusting God. Jesus told his followers, "But you will receive power when the Holy Spirit has come upon you; and you will be my witnesses in Jerusalem, in all Judea and Samaria, and to the ends of the earth" (Acts 1:8). The power of the Holy Spirit helped Jesus' followers to be his witnesses so that the entire world might know God's love and justice. When people were filled with the Holy Spirit, they spoke God's word boldly (Acts 4:31). The great evangelist Paul saw evil as the force interfering with hearing and receiving the gospel message of hope and love. Therefore, evangelism and justice need women and men praying for people to stand firm against the forces of evil.

The second type of watch prayer is linked to protecting our own lives and social circles from evil. It is a form of discipleship and spiritual formation. Watch prayer

> There are several justice issues I brought to my watch prayer. I spent time overseas working against the sex-slave trade, particularly in Asia, so I prayed against that darkness. What also came to my heart was praying for God's protection on the lives of those who are mentally challenged, along with their families. My family was a foster family who took in special needs children, and I know the temptation and depression that sets in those families by the enemy, so I prayed for protection of their households.
>
> —David Huffman

> **As a young Christian** I was very cocky and self-assured. I was called and I knew it, but somehow I turned the call on my life into God needing me. Then I turned God needing me into God will not let me do anything that would endanger the ministry he called me to do. Then I fell hard. I sinned and everyone knew it. People stopped talking to me, and I realized that I used authority to alienate and abuse others. It was not from God. I didn't want that kind of authority again. Praying in the authority of Jesus must be prayed with the utmost caution and respect. The one praying must remember that authority does not belong or rest with them but in the One whom they call upon.
>
> —Jim McLauglin

provides support and understanding to walk daily with Christ in the power of the Holy Spirit. People who do not stand firm can develop a shallow understanding of righteousness and the sacrificial life in Christ. Watch prayer is the place where people are in communion with a Father who loves us, a Savior who receives us with grace and a Holy Spirit who empowers us to live as people of light in a dark world. We are to watch and pray in the Spirit and to stand firm with Christ (Jas 4:6-8).

Watch prayer requires a humble spirit. Often the root of evil is not particular bad behaviors but pride. Pride is essentially self-righteousness, which takes satisfaction from one's particular views, choices and piety. A person sets himself or herself apart as being particularly special or worthy. They come to rely more on themselves and less and less on God.

Because of evil in the world, the Holy Spirit gives us power to stand against the forces of darkness. Whether these forces are seen or unseen, Christians are called to be strong in the Lord and ready to stand against evil. The act of standing against evil's effort to destroy the innocent and the good is an ongoing battle in the world. The watch prayer prepares us for standing firm in the Lord and praying at all times and in all places for all people (1 Jn 4:2-6).

WATCH PRAYER GUIDELINES

- Watch prayer depends on the power of God's Word and the Holy Spirit.
- In watch prayer we stand firm in the light and stand against the dark. The dark may be spiritual or natural, social or individual, minor or macro.
- Watch prayer especially combats forces that lie about the character and calling of Christ.
- The purpose of watch prayer is to persevere in Christ's character and purpose despite suffering and the onslaught of evil.

- Watch prayer is active rather than passive. The pray-er is alert and rests on the power of God to overcome evil of any form. It is an intercessory prayer.

- Watch prayers might be prayed for people, towns, countries, governments or even places.

- Watch prayer requires humility and confession. We confess our need for God and for God's protection and righteousness.

- Like a guard who watches in the night, watch prayer is vigilant, paying attention to the movement of God.

- The pray-er stands on the foundation of Christ's grace and truth, and puts on the new creation of having been raised to new life in Christ.

- Praying aloud and movement helps the praying person externalize the power of the Holy Spirit.

- Watch prayer leads to action. When Jesus cast out demons, people recognized God and many came to faith. People choose light rather than the dark.

- Watch prayers are bold prayers based on an unwavering trust in God's love and sovereignty over evil.

- These prayers are often most useful when prayed over a season of time. They are not formula prayers, but prayers where we partner with God against evil in our time. God desires our prayers with him.

WATCH PRAYER EXPERIENCE

Group Experience

- The group experience can take several forms and usually takes about thirty minutes. Decide whether you want to focus on evangelism and justice or to focus on protection and purity. If you focus on evangelism and justice, pick a particular country or issue before the prayer experience and make sure everyone has some knowledge about the situation. Take five to ten minutes to present information on the focus of the prayer experience. For instance, you can focus on the problem of slave trafficking, racial divisions or drugs, or on a country where people are starving or dying because of an unjust government. You can also choose to pray for a country or people to experience Christ's message of grace. Take a few minutes to bring information on the country or people group. If you focus on protection and purity, share why this is important for the group.

- *Optional opening experience:* Read out loud together Ephesians 6:10-13.

- *Watch prayer*

  - Standing together and praying aloud, each person is invited to pray for the Holy Spirit's power to overcome whatever evil for which you are interceding.

You can pray using Scripture verses or your own words. The prayers are short sentence prayers such as described in the chapter on conversational prayer.

- After each individual prayer, everyone prays aloud, "Lord, we watch and stand firm in the power of the Holy Spirit."

- The prayer continues until there is a feeling of release.

- If it is feasible, you can also go as a group to an area where a darkness persists and silently walk and pray: "Lord, we watch and stand firm in the power of the Holy Spirit to bring the word and life of Christ into this place."

- If the watch prayer is for protection and purity, stand together and pray aloud, each person for the Holy Spirit's purifying power in your own personal lives and in the community. Again after each prayer, pray, "Lord, we watch and stand firm in the power of the Holy Spirit."

- *Close with a blessing:* Evangelism and justice—Jude 1:20-25; Purity—Ephesians 3:14-19.

- After the prayer experience, give time for the group to debrief. What was the experience like for them? Are there any questions or insights? What does it mean for you to pray in the Spirit against evil?

Partner Experience

- As partners or as a small group decide whether you want to pray a watch prayer for purity or one for justice and evangelism. Whichever one, follow the guide above in the group section. Try praying for the same concern over a period of time. You might also walk and pray a watch prayer in your neighborhood.

- Another possibility is to pray for protection over your house. If you do this type of watch prayer, light a candle to remind yourselves that Christ is the light. Go from room to room together and pray for light and protection in each place. As you pray, think about what happens in the room and how would the light of Christ fill the room and influence all the people and experiences that might take place in the room. Stand quietly in the center of the room and take turns praying three to five minutes in each room.

- When you have completed your watch experience, talk together about its impact on you. How did it help you experience God? How might the Holy Spirit's power be unleashed? Did you have any concerns with this type of prayer, and why?

Individual Experience

- For four days in one week, pray a watch prayer for fifteen minutes a day. The watch prayer is described in the guidelines section and in the group section. Tailor the experience to your situation.

- *Day One:* Pray a watch prayer for protection over your house as described in the partner section above.

- *Day Two:* Pray a watch prayer for purity in your personal life. Use Ephesians 6:10-18 to visualize in prayer the Holy Spirit placing on you all the gear needed to combat evil and protect yourself. After each piece, see the Holy Spirit helping you put it on and ask the Holy Spirit to help you to watch and stand firm. If needed, confess when you need to confess.

- *Day Three:* Choose a group or country to pray for the light of Christ to bring hope and peace. Pray in quiet confidence for the people and the possibilities for bringing light to that group. Pray for their protection from the deceptions of evil.

- *Day Four:* Choose a justice issue close to your heart and pray for the power of God to intercede on behalf of the concern. Pray against the dark forces, whether spiritual or institutional, that perpetuate the injustice. Pray for the ones caught in the evil, the victims and the perpetrators. Pray for Christ's will to be done on earth as in heaven.

- Journal each day about your experience. How has praying in power with the Holy Spirit impacted your personal life? What insights have you gained? How are you being led?

PRAYER JOURNEY

Dorothy Lou French

We bought a charming though old house in a working-class neighborhood for our first home years ago. That house was so full of good things. Our three children grew up in grade school and went off to college in that home. All the meals, celebrations, tears, dustings, accomplishments, laundry loads and prayers in that house are hard to enumerate. Particularly special were the times we sat around the breakfast table each morning and read the Bible together and prayed for everything from a test in school to a war in a far-off country. Then every evening we would kneel with each child by his or her bed, review the day and pray. Our children and Christ were the fabric of that home.

But then, we needed to sell the house and move. Work was across town now and the driving was taking too much time and money. The kids were adults and out on their own. Selling the house was easy and hard. It was easy because it went on the market one day and we had a buyer by the end of the week. It was hard because the buyer was a difficult, rough man. He was rude and complained about everything. He didn't seem to really care about the house, and for some reason, he didn't really like us. He tried to cheat us on several occasions, but our realtor was wise and experienced and caught each one. It was a difficult transaction. We felt anxious and sad. I really didn't want my house to go to this man.

I carried the concern in my heart until the Spirit told me to pray a watch prayer throughout the house. When we were all moved out and the house was empty and clean, I took a candle and went from room to room to pray. I thanked God for all the good things that happened in that room, and I prayed that it would be filled with light and love. I went from the kitchen to the bedrooms to the living room, and in each room I asked the Lord to bless the family moving in and to protect them from evil. I prayed for the new owner that he would experience peace. I don't know what happened to the new buyer and his family. However, I felt a release and was able to leave the house in peace.

Alec Sandu

This past November in Ethiopia, we had a crusade. I am so thankful for many sincere prayers on our behalf. We were expecting much spiritual resistance and without prayers and strong words of encouragement I don't believe that the revival would be successful. Many people came from different tribes. God gave our speakers boldness to preach the Word and to cast out demons. Many people rededicated themselves or re-turned to the Lord.

Others who were sick were healed through God's grace. A day before the crusade, I met a nonbeliever whose wife was a Christian. He told me that his wife had painful legs and had difficulty walking. He had taken her to the doctors for treatments but she could not be healed. He promised to bring her to the revival in an ox cart to be prayed for. After being prayed for, she was able to freely walk and dance for the Lord. We all praised the Lord of miracles.

There was also a demon-possessed woman who had terrible headaches. She came forward for assistance. When hands were laid upon her, she fell to the ground screaming and tossing. When the demon was asked who it was, it said it was Joseph and had come to inflict pain on the woman. The demon was violent but could not withstand God's power. After about ten minutes praying, the Lord freed the woman from the bondage of the evil spirit. She became one of the happiest people at the revival. On the last day, the pastor and others commented that the crusade was the best so far. There is a lot to be done. When we join our hands together nothing will be impossible in the Lord.

David Manfred

Not all pastors do this, but I like to research and write articles to help my fellow pastors, so I keep files of my research, some of which result in publications. There was one large area for which I had never written any articles. Though I had traveled across states and taken pages of notes and had bins full of recordings, I never felt released by God to publish any results of the study. I was captivated by the possibilities of the church to be a place of healing, so I had visited a particular church that had an amazing healing ministry. The church welcomed me and allowed me to attend meetings and interview members. I had saved everything believing that the time would come when it would be clear to move ahead and write.

However, while I was going through these materials, God told me to throw all of it away. I proceeded to do so. His voice was unmistakable. I hauled several boxes of material out to the recycling bin, and I tossed the recordings in the trash. From this simplifying act, something happened in me and in my office. I felt a darkness leave. It was clear to me the next day that I needed to pray a cleansing prayer over the entire space. I lit candles and prayed that the light of Christ would fill every corner and space in my office space and claim it for God's redemptive purposes. I never imagined that sorting stuff in prayer would be a journey toward freedom. I am more at peace in my space.

FURTHER READING

Otis, Don S., ed. *Watch and Pray: Standing in the Gap for Your Nation and Community.* Grand Rapids: Chosen Books, 2002.

Spurgeon, Charles. *Spurgeon on Prayer and Spiritual Warfare.* Kensington, PA: Whitaker House, 1998.

Wagner, C. Peter. *Warfare Prayer: What the Bible Says about Spiritual Warfare.* Shippensburg, PA: Destiny Images, 2009.

24

Rejoice Prayer

Joy is a net of love by which you can catch souls.

<small>Mother Teresa</small>

And the disciples were filled with joy and with the Holy Spirit.

<small>Acts 13:52</small>

THE HOLY SPIRIT AS JOY

Joy is a very physical feeling that fills up in us when all is well in our world. Two potent places of joy are at the altar when a couple pledges themselves to each other and in the birth room when a father or mother holds their newborn child for the first time. Sometimes we feel joy on Christmas morning, sometimes when a child kicks that goal on the soccer field and sometimes when we finally complete that marathon or lose the weight we wanted to lose. Joy is a universal human emotion of well-being and contentment. The Holy Spirit is associated with this feeling.

The Holy Spirit as joy calls us to a place of gratitude for all God has done on our behalf both for ourselves and our world. Prayer does not stop at the tomb. It begins with joy before a stone rolled away. Jesus' last prayer for his disciples was for them to know his joy (Jn 16:20-22). The Holy Spirit's indwelling presence reminds us of our great joy in Christ and calls us to a unity of peace. The fruit of the Spirit, the sign of the Spirit's work and presence in us, is "love, joy, peace, patience, kindness, generosity, faithfulness" (Gal 5:22).

The primary occasion for joy in the Old Testament was God's saving acts and covenantal love. Joy was a sensation in the soul expressed during feast and worship celebrations that focused on one's devotion to God. Joy was a mark too of the eschatological expectation of God's final triumph and future glory. Joy in the New

Testament occurred when God's kingdom flourished despite suffering and difficult times. Jesus linked joy with suffering and the coming of God's kingdom. Paul, on the other hand, linked joy to faith. The Greek word for joy is part of the family of words meaning "grace," "bless," "gift" and "thanksgiving."

In the New Testament:

- Joy is finding God's kingdom (Mt 13:44)

- Joy is witnessing the power of God's kingdom (Lk 10:17; 19:37)

- Joy is a sign of the kingdom of God (Rom 14:17)

- Joy occurs when people become believers (Lk 15:7; Acts 15:3)

- God's hope fills us with joy (Rom 15:13)

- Worshiping Christ gives us joy (Lk 24:52; Jn 3:29)

- Joy leads to generosity despite affliction (2 Cor 8:1-2)

- Joy is the result of love among believers (Phil 2:1-2)

- Joy occurs when we imitate Christ despite persecution (1 Thess 1:6)

- Joy comes when difficulties lead to spiritual maturity, a sign of the redemptive nature of our God (Jas 1:2-4)

- Joy is the happiness we experience when we walk in truth (1 Thess 3:9; 3 Jn 1:4)

According to the Bible joy is a feeling linked to our relationship with God. Joy is the peace and hope we experience receiving Christ's grace, the Father's love and the Holy Spirit's presence. Joy is not abstract but a real visceral sense of wonder and goodness.

Joy is a rare experience for people today. The obsession with consumerism disrupts the joy found in simple pleasures, because consumerism depends on dissatisfaction. With dissatisfaction we will keep buying. Gratitude helps us to embrace a simpler life. We begin to experience the joy of our salvation, and the joy of a new car, dress, phone or TV is no longer compelling. We embrace the value of the far more important elements of life—a love relationship with God, others and our beautiful world.

A branch in the field of psychology, called positive psychology, researched why some people thrived and were happy while others did not.[1] Why did

Singing has long been how I adore God. Like Eric Liddell, "I feel the pleasure of God." I decided to spend four days just picking up my guitar and singing whatever was in my heart. It was wonderful to return to this old habit that my new life as a senior pastor has lead me away from. I fell into the presence and pleasure of God immediately and found that one of my grateful places is no place at all but in an action— singing and playing the guitar.

—James Pagels

some individuals live satisfying and fulfilling lives despite their circumstances and others did not? The researchers found that wealth, education, beauty or fame did not equal happiness. One researcher, George Vaillant, completed a longitudinal study of Harvard graduates to discover which aspects contributed to successful living. The research results pointed to three things: physical health, close relationships and handling well difficult circumstances.[2]

Of particular interest are the latter two. Health is not guaranteed in this life, but relationships and how one handles troubles are personal choices. When Christ invites us into a personal relationship with him, we are filled with the Holy Spirit and we have the Holy Spirit's help. Jesus expected that believers would be in a rich community of love. These close relationships are a source of joy. Managing difficulties well is something Jesus modeled and Paul spoke about on several occasions.

> I reflected on Galatians 5:22 in prayer and the word *joy* kept popping up in my mind. My life has been so busy, crazy and stressful lately, and people are noticing my discouragement and depression. I cannot force joy in my life, so I spent a great deal of time reflecting on all the things I should be joyful for, and things naturally came to mind. In the end I felt a desire to be more joyful in my life. I want people to see an outward expression of what is going on in my heart. I want people to see Christ in me as I go about my everyday ordinary tasks.
>
> —David Huffman

REJOICE PRAYER

Joy is a positive emotion that comes from a place of strength and virtue. It is possible to be happy as a swindler, liar or gossip, but it is not possible to experience joy. Joy is a sacred emotion when the inner self is at peace with our Creator and at peace with our circumstances. Joy leads to optimism based on a relationship of trust in God's goodness. Joy may be expressed outwardly or carried within as a silent hope. What the secular world has discovered is that one of the ingredients for lasting change is joy; "joy is a more powerful motivator than fear."[3]

Fear, especially anxiety, is the most common emotion people experience when they are distressed. If there is a threat of any sort to one's value or safety, including the safety of belonging, the body reacts with anxiety. The anxiety urges the person to either run or hide or find some sort of comfort. It's interesting that joy is associated with our relationship with Christ and not fear. Fear stifles hope. Worry keeps us up at night and makes us reactive during the day. Joy says my hope is not in my own strength, but in God's love and the Holy Spirit's power (Phil 1:18-19).

Rejoice prayer is a prayer of thanksgiving and gratitude. It lifts our eyes to the hills from where our strength comes. It reconnects us with God who delights in our praise. By praying with gratitude we are lifted in spirit and we are given a broader perspective. The Holy Spirit comforts us and reminds us of Jesus' love. The Holy Spirit gives us wisdom to see beyond trials to the power of the cross to turn on the light in every place of darkness.

Even in the secular world people have found that thankfulness completely changes your perspective on your life. Those who are grateful are joyful. John Kralik's life was in shambles. His law firm was failing as well as his second marriage. He felt distant from his children. On a hike he felt inspired to write a simple thank you note, and then he decided to write one every day for 365 days. It unexpectedly and dramatically changed his life.[4] As believers we have so many more reasons to be thankful.

The most basic response to God for all that God has done for us is gratitude. Paul writes, "Devote yourselves to prayer, keeping alert in it with thanksgiving," (Col 4:2). Devote means to persist and hold fast. We watch and pray in an attitude of thanksgiving. There is nothing else we can offer back. God made us and loves us. Jesus saved us. The Holy Spirit partners with us. Gratitude as a response reminds us of the many gifts and graces

> **All week I have been** struggling with an interpersonal conflict that has been heating up between friends in our small group. I have felt like anything but rejoicing. This morning I put on my headphones and headed out to the local greenbelt. I feebly sang, but I couldn't muster much. At times I could feel my spirit lifting and a bit of joy coming in, but then the weight would return. The praise was a conscious effort and when I was not engaged in it, my mind soon returned to the darkness of the issue. Even so, after the time of rejoicing, I came away feeling strengthened and hungering for more.
>
> —John Ray

we have received. It generates a thankful heart and openness to the Holy Spirit's movements in our lives and our days. The most basic response to life is an appreciation for its goodness. The most basic response to others is thankfulness for their place in our lives. The most basic response to God is gratefulness.

REJOICE PRAYER GUIDELINES

- Rejoice prayer is an affirmation of God's goodness and a response of gratitude for Christ's love and sacrifice (1 Thess 5:16-19).

- Rejoice prayer is not a naive dismissal of evil and injustice. It is a declaration of confidence in God.

- Rejoice prayer is not meant to cover up difficulties. All difficulties need prayer and reflection with the Holy Spirit. Talking with others and, when necessary, getting help allow you to grow in faith and self-understanding. Rejoice prayer is an affirmation of faith not a bandage for denial.

- Rejoice prayer is an ongoing mindset rather than an occasional prayer.

- The psalms are examples of rejoicing while praying. The psalmist cries out his troubles, concerns or expectations and always concludes with gratitude to God.

- Rejoice prayer can be spontaneous such as when one holds a new baby, but it also is a conscious decision to be grateful.

- With practice we can become people of grace and gratitude. Rejoice prayer creates in us a more generous and loving nature.

- It invites us into the mystery and goodness of the present, to relinquish the past to God and to trust God for the future.

- Being ungrateful is a form of quenching the Spirit. The Holy Spirit is ever interceding on our behalf, and our joy and gratitude unleash power. Rejoice prayer replaces fear with hope.

- In whatever circumstance prayer of gratitude helps refocus us and strengthen us.

> **We bought a** second car for $1,650. Lily picked it out. After two weeks she pulled into our driveway and all the radiator fluid poured out onto the ground. We towed it to a nearby garage. I prayed that it would not be serious, and I was surprised that I did not say one word about the car being her choice. As it turned out, it cost $814 to replace a motor mount, get a new battery and a new radiator. I know what my usual reaction would be. I was shocked when I found myself thanking God that we had the money, that she broke down in front of our house instead of on the highway and that this happened now instead of in November when we'd drive to California. The Holy Spirit is working in me.
>
> —Rick Adams

REJOICE PRAYER EXPERIENCE

Group Experience

- The experience will take ten to twenty minutes or more depending on how long you take for each section. If possible, begin with worship songs that focus on thanksgiving, gratitude and praise. If you don't have worship leaders, bring in some music to listen to that reminds you of God's goodness. You can sing or listen.

- A leader prepares the group by saying: "Rejoice prayers are short prayers of thanksgiving. Paul called us to rejoice always and to pray without ceasing. Jesus wanted his followers to have in them the same joy he has." Read 1 Thessalonians 5:16-19.

- If you want, put a potted tree or branches in a pot and place it in the center of the group. You can also clear a wall to use. Pass out small pieces of paper or Post-It notes. Have everyone write down thanksgiving prayers and then place them on the tree or post them on a wall. (If writing and posting the prayers won't work, pray the thanksgiving prayers aloud.) While they are writing, you can have worship music in the background. Do the rejoice prayers in this suggested order:
  - *Prayers for God and the saints*: "Write down rejoice prayers for God and for people who have influenced your faith. Write as many as you want. Place them on the wall (or tree)."
    - Leader says: "Let's pray simple thanksgiving prayers for each thing you wrote down." "Lord, I rejoice in X. Thank you."
    - Allow enough time for everyone to pray several times.
  - *Prayers for difficult circumstances and trials*: "Write down difficult circumstances or trials in your personal life. Place them on the wall (or tree)."
    - Leader says: "We will pray prayers of rejoicing despite these circumstances. We trust the Spirit for deliverance." "Lord, I rejoice in you and trust you for X. Thank you."
    - If people are uncomfortable naming difficult circumstances in front of the group, have them write their prayers in silence.
  - *Prayers for family and friends*: "Write down the names of family and friends for whom you are grateful. Be specific as to why you are thanking God for them, such as "I thank Jesus for my friend who believes in me."
    - Leader says: "Let's pray simple thanksgiving prayers for each person you named." "Lord, thank you for X."
    - At the conclusion of the prayers, give people an opportunity to write a note of thanks to one of the people named.
- If desired, conclude with worship songs and a blessing.
- Debrief with the group. What was your experience like praying rejoice prayers? How did you experience God? What was hard about this type of praying? How can we maintain a spirit of gratitude?

Partner Experience

- With your partner, spend time giving specific thanks in each area: (1) God and the saints; (2) difficulties and trials; (3) family and friends; and (4) community, nation and world. The prayers are short prayers of gratitude. Allow enough time for reflection and verbal prayers in each area. This is not to pray for answers or guidance or intercession. The time is dedicated to solely giving thanks.

- Have a conversation with your partner about how the call to "rejoice always" might become a part of your daily life. Is there anyone for whom the Spirit is leading you to write a note of thanks or to call and thank?

Individual Experience

- For four days focus on different areas for rejoice prayer. Spend at least ten minutes actually giving thanks. Before you pray, make a list for each day below. Then name them aloud to God and give thanks as specifically as possible for each item on the list. If more come up while you're praying, give thanks for those too. If you want, sing songs of praise before and after the rejoice prayer time.

  - *Day One*: Give thanks for God and for people who have influenced you in your faith over the years.

  - *Day Two*: Give thanks for difficult circumstances. This will not be easy. Make a list of the primary circumstances, and then reflect on how you were shaped and how you grew in faith because of the situation. Then rejoice as authentically as you can. Ask the Holy Spirit to guide you in giving thanks.

  - *Day Three*: Give thanks for friends and family. Think about how these relationships have influenced you, how they have loved and cared for you.

  - *Day Four*: Give thanks for your neighborhood, community and government. Bless them. This is not the time to pray about all the things that are not going right, but for rejoicing always as God calls us to do.

- Journal about your experience. At the end of the rejoice prayer time, write a short email or letter or use social media to express thanks to someone from that time of thanksgiving.

- At the end of the week, reflect on how rejoice prayer is linked to praying without ceasing. How might you incorporate rejoicing into your daily life?

PRAYER JOURNEY

David Beck

I have served as the vice president for marketing at our company for fifteen years. It's a great company to work for. I believe in our products. I like the people I've been working with. They aren't all Christians, but they respect my faith and are good, hard-working people. A year ago I had to take a leave of absence for six months because I had cancer. I needed surgery and follow-up chemotherapy. I wanted to work as much as possible, but my boss said they needed me to focus on my health. He said I would have a job with the company when I'm better.

When it was clear at four months

that six months wouldn't be enough, the company president called me and said they didn't want to lose marketing momentum. They gave my job to a peer. I understood, but I was angry. It seemed like I was being pushed aside. I had worked hard to create a marketing campaign that would run through the next several months. I even said I was willing to work part time to create the next phase. The president said no.

Not only did I lose my position, I learned from a colleague who came to visit that the new VP had completely changed my marketing strategy. I felt like I was being kicked while I was on the ground. I know that it wasn't about me, but I couldn't get over how I felt. I was worried about my attitude as the time for returning to work loomed closer.

I made an appointment to meet my pastor for coffee and told him I needed help. This was keeping me awake at night and I was having trouble liking these people. My pastor said, "David, go home and read Philippians 1:12-19. While Paul was in prison in Rome, he learned that in Philippi some were preaching Christ from goodwill and some for personal ambition. Now Philippi was Paul's baby. However, he came to the conclusion that he would rejoice and continue to rejoice. He

would trust the Spirit for his deliverance. Go home and spend some time rejoicing and thanking God for what happened."

Giving thanks for losing my position seemed like crazy talk, but I decided to give it a try. The next morning after my wife left for work, I opened my Bible and read the passage several times. Then I said, "Well, Lord, here goes." I started rejoicing in the Lord. It was easy to be grateful to God. I was getting healthy and I experienced God's love and strength during my entire illness. Then I just started thanking God for the company, everyone in the company and finally I thanked God for the man who was in my position. I asked the Lord to bless all of them.

I didn't realize that I had been praying for over thirty minutes when my cell phone rang. Later in the day I noticed that something had changed in me. I felt more lighthearted and content. I felt love for the people at the company. I knew I could go back and be okay. It seemed like the Holy Spirit had lifted my eyes to the hills. In fact, I wondered what new thing the Lord was going to do in my life. I realized I was ready for a new challenge. Thank you, Lord, and thanks, pastor, for the help.

Leighton Ford

"In everything give thanks" reminds me of my longtime friend, John Wesley White. He was an evangelist with Billy Graham. I knew him first as a classmate and fellow Canadian at Wheaton College. We prayed together almost daily, played hockey against local schools (he much better than me) and dreamed about our future in ministry. Most importantly, John introduced me (at a hockey game!) to a lovely farm girl from North Carolina who became my wife. For many years John itinerated on his own, preaching across North American and the United Kingdom in large and out of the way places, often with very little income. He led many to Christ, and earned two PhDs. Then about sixteen years ago on the very eve of a campaign, he had a major stroke and, as he says, was "suddenly silenced."

Although his mind was alert, his writing skillful, his attitude positive, speech was limited. When I occasionally called he would laugh, say "Yes, yes." That was all, except he would end every talk with four words as clear as a bell: "Jesus Christ is Lord!" This summer Jeanie and I went to visit him and his wife in Toronto. She was recovering from an illness and they were in two small rooms in a nursing facility. Several family members were present. As we got ready to leave I said, "John, I have always been moved that somehow, in spite of that stroke, you can always say, 'Jesus Christ is Lord.'"

At that he sat up straight and in staccato phrases—almost robotically —said, "In-ev-ry-thing-give-thanks-for-this-is-the-will-of-God-in-Christ-con-cerning-you." Then his eyes moving across the circle, he said, "Betty—Linda—Kathleen—Jeanie—Leighton—and me." How he had to discipline himself to be able to say those words of Paul! What practice over and over it must have taken!

Since our visit his lovely Irish lass, Kathleen, has gone to heaven. I am sure, for all the loss, John Wesley White is still saying those words to himself and others. I remember him as an eloquent and unusual preacher, one suddenly silenced. But no sermon he preached could have been better than those words he spoke to us that hot summer day in that tiny room in Toronto. John, I am seeking to remember in everything give thanks, and I give thanks for you!

Your friend of the years,

Leighton

FURTHER READING

Page, Josephine. *Thank You Prayer.* New York: Scholastic, 2005. (This is a wonderful children's prayer book.)

Stoddard, Sandol. *Prayers, Praises, and Thanksgivings.* New York: Dial, 1992. (This is a prayer book for older children.)

Whyte, Daniella. *365 Days of Thanking God: Cultivating a Heart of Everyday Thanks.* Dallas: Torch Legacy, 2010.

Closing

Simply Pray on the Road of Life

When we pray, we are not sending a letter to a celestial White House,
where it is sorted among piles of others. We are engaged, rather,
in a co-creation, in which one little sector of the universe rises up
and becomes translucent, incandescent, a vibratory center of power
that radiates the power of the universe.

WALTER WINK

There is something you should know about me—I hate prayer.
But there is something else you should know—I now love praying.

JASON GOBLE

God created us to be in relationship with him, so we pray. Jesus names us his brothers
and sisters and made possible our inclusion in a great eternal family, so we pray. The
Holy Spirit is around and in us and intercedes for us, so we pray. As Christ loved us
so we love, and prayer teaches, shapes and encourages us to be world lovers.

In the Bible little is said about how to pray, but the call to prayer is clear. Colossians
4:2 is a simple verse full of insight about prayer: "Devote yourselves to prayer, keeping
alert in it with thanksgiving." The word for "prayer" means customary prayer. It is a
combination of two words; one means "to, toward" and suggests intimacy, and the
other means "vow and prayer." Together the words suggest that prayer is an intimate
and regular face-to-face sacred relationship. The word translated to "devote" also has
two parts—the same part as found in the word "prayer," meaning again intimacy, and

another part meaning "to be strong, to endure steadfastly." The word is sometimes used with martyrdom. We are to endure in prayer. Be strong in it. "Keeping alert" is to be vigilant, awake and is connected with resurrection. When we keep alert in prayer we are brought into life with the Trinity. All of prayer is based on a profound sense of gratitude and thanksgiving for our lives in God.

So what happens if there is a dry well when you pray? Emilie Griffin describes it this way:

> What if nothing happens when I pray? And what if nothing that happens is not the very special sort of nothing, one that I could dramatize as a dark night, but instead the completely vacuous and even boring nothing in which I cannot make any headway at all, in which it seems I have taken a wrong turn, or lost the map entirely?[1]

When we are lost and find ourselves empty and dry, how do we pray? We often cannot. We often then do not. An occasional response to this problem is to label prayerlessness—not praying—a sin problem. The rationale is that Jesus told us to pray, so we should pray. If we are not praying, the solution is to confess and repent and then start praying. "Start praying" usually means attending prayer groups, keeping prayer notebooks and interceding on behalf of others during one's daily quiet time. However, in all my years of teaching prayer in the seminary and in churches, I have found that prayerlessness truly grieves people, and it is not easily resolved with a sin label. When we can't pray, we usually feel shame that we are not as devoted as we believe we should be. We feel that something must be wrong with us.

I don't know that I've ever read or heard someone say it's okay to struggle with prayer. I grew up with guilt from being unable to perform well in prayer and eventually I quit trying. The memories of watching my parents pray are beautiful, yet my inability to follow them in this has been frustrating. Yes, this makes my heart hurt as I want to be as close to God as I possibly can and yet for so long I have been hindered by what I thought I couldn't do.

—Donna Van Horn

The spiritual life is both a hardy and a fragile thing. It is hardy because the God of the universe put inside of us a God-shaped hole that yearns for fellowship with our Maker. It is fragile because the God-shaped hole is in a dust-to-dust body. For that reason, prayerlessness is more often than not the result of a perception that one's spiritual life isn't going anywhere, that it is stagnant or meaningless. When people say they are too busy to pray, distractions are often a cover-up for this hidden fact: When they do pray, there is no sense of God's presence or of any response to their prayer. When that happens, people often get anxious and stop praying. Emotionally, prayerlessness leads to anxiety or cynicism. It happens when we are thinking: What if God isn't really there? What if God isn't really there for me? What if instead of living water I only find a dry well? What then?

PRAYERLESSNESS AND THE DRY WELL

Most of us try to have a meaningful connection with God through prayer. But something happens along the way, and the life of prayer drifts into a dead zone of prayerlessness. I want to suggest that prayerlessness doesn't need to mean that we are stuck or that our spiritual lives are empty. Instead, prayerlessness can be a signal that it is time to begin an authentic adventure. And the journey begins with first naming one's reality: Prayer is dry and empty for me. Metaphorically, this is called the dry well experience. The well is there. The bucket. But when you come thirsty, the bucket comes up empty.

Naming the reality can be difficult because people believe they will be judged or lose status in their faith community or look stupid. Prayerlessness is often perpetuated in churches because we create a culture of shame rather than spiritual adventure. Instead of seeing it as an opportunity for growth and being open about it, we treat it like a disease. As long as the problem is hidden, it cannot be resolved. The only way to move from prayerlessness to prayerfulness is to start where we know we are. When you are lost, the first thing survival experts tell you to do is to stop where you are. If you keep thrashing around, it is more likely you won't be found. Once we have been honest with ourselves, the next step is to understand why we might be in a prayerless state. The following are some possible reasons.

Exhaustion

Exhaustion can be physical, mental or emotional. Exhaustion brought on by stress caused by unending deadlines and life upheavals is a common problem. After finishing a marathon, many runners cross the finish line and collapse to the ground heaving for air. They stretch out their arms and revel in nonmovement. When the body has given its full capacity to some event, it is difficult to be in a prayerful frame. When my stepmother died, who had been the first real mother I ever knew, I was exhausted. The months of care because of her debilitating cancer, the emotional drain of serving her complex needs, standing by her deathbed for hours, put me in an empty space for months. I was emotionally and physically exhausted. Elijah in 1 Kings 18 is an example of how even after spiritual and physical success, he felt depressed and empty. Exhaustion is the most common reason as to why people feel dry in their prayer life. They are dry in their life. The response is to rest, embrace the sabbath and ask the Holy Spirit to discern how your life might have more spaces in it.

Narrow View of Prayer

Prayer practices and types are as varied as an artist's color palette, but most people

are only exposed to one or two ways. In 1 Samuel 3, young Samuel did not recognize the voice of God and three times he ran to Eli thinking Eli had called him.
Whenever I teach prayer, I find that someone is profoundly impacted by a type of
prayer they hadn't experienced before. This is why teaching prayer is so important.
This is why a book such as this prayer guidebook can be so helpful. We need to be
exposed not to just one or two types of prayer, but all types. God is so multifaceted
that God expresses himself in the Trinity. How much more do we need different
ways to engage with God. Temperaments and personalities lead us toward certain
forms of prayer that are more meaningful than others. Liturgical prayers are living
water to some and muddy waters to others. Silence is profound for some and music
feeds the souls of others. In all of Scripture and the history of the church there is not
one "sacred" way to pray. The church carries the honor of teaching people how to
pray. The response is to explore other prayer ways to know God.

Desert Experience/Dark Night

In Luke 4 Jesus was led by the Holy Spirit into the desert for forty days of prayer and
fasting. In the desert Satan sifted the underlying motivations for his upcoming sacrificial life. Desert experiences are traditionally those periods of time when God
feels absent from our lives. Among the saints, the experience of God's absence is
referred to as the dark night. If you experienced God for years in ecstatic worship,
for instance, and then for week after week you feel or experience nothing, it might
be the dark night. The dark night comes when God is giving us an opportunity to
stand in faith no matter what life brings.[2] The prayer response is to enter into the
shaping forces of the dark night. This is helped by getting support from a spiritual
director, sometimes a counselor and close spiritual friends.

Natural Rhythm of the Spiritual Life

The whole of creation tells the story of birth, growth, decline and death. Our
seasons, our need for sleep, the way all of nature has an "on" time and a "down"
time is God's design. The music of life has pauses in it. These are the negative spaces
where we are still and nothing is gained, known or felt. God commanded a period
of rest in Genesis 2:2. That life of rest is both physical and spiritual. This is different
from the dark night, which is often a unique experience of deep shaping. The
natural rhythm of rest is simply downtime. Sometimes a dry well is our fallow time.
The response is perseverance in the routine of daily prayer. This is helped by maintaining the rhythms of prayer through the use of a prayer book.

Sin or Disorder in Your Life

In a few instances the dry well is the result of sin in our life. John wrote in 1 John 1:6,
"If we say that we have fellowship with him while we are walking in darkness, we lie
and do not do what is true." It is not possible to relate to a God of love if in the heart

there is gossip, bitterness or self-indulgence. Despising others in our heart is walking in darkness. Believing that the self-indulgence of pornography or excessive shopping is due to us because of how hard we work for God is the ultimate of deceptions. If these behaviors, thoughts and feelings are not kept in the light of Christ for his healing will on them, a dry well is the first outcome. Sincerity before God is the beginning of relationship with God. A prayer response is confession and accountability.

Lack of Attention/Distractions

In Jesus' last conversation with his disciples, he said in John 15:5, "I am the vine, you are the branches. Those who abide in me and I in them bear much fruit, because apart from me you can do nothing." Abiding in Christ carries the core notion of connection and nonactivity. A branch does no work except to receive from the vine the nutrients and pass them along. For many one of our greatest failures as Christ followers is a lack of attentiveness to the vine. Our busy lives consume our energies, creativity and time so there is little space to be with God. We make the mistake of equating God's will with kingdom accomplishments rather than quiet attentiveness. Finding ways to be still allows for the Spirit to work naturally in our souls without expectation of gain. Sometimes a dry well is an invitation to simply sit quietly with God. A prayer response is meditation and contemplative prayer.

FROM DRYNESS TO LIVING WATER

Prayerlessness is a normal experience. We are used to being entertained, getting instant feedback and having our needs immediately met, so we forget how ordinary a dry well is in our faith journey. If we believe it is not ordinary, the dry well can be a confusing time. If we are not feeling, doing or accomplishing something, we can begin to fear that God is absent from us. And when we begin to fear God's absence, we become ashamed of the dry place. We think it is caused by our failure or spiritual weakness rather than an ordinary part of the journey. The temptation is to drop one's practice of prayer when the experience becomes dry.

A way to avoid this temptation is to disciple followers so that when we find ourselves in a dry place we recognize it, consider the causes for it and take steps to stay connected to the vine rather than drift into continual prayerlessness. Following are some suggestions for moving through the dryness:

1. Healthy Lifestyle—Examine your lifestyle and reorder it so that you can experience rest again. Restore a sabbath experience. Let the natural nourishments our bodies need be the beginning platform for new waters.

2. Ritual of Space for God—Find a time and place that allows you simply to be present with God. This might mean observing the daily offices, painting or sculpting, walking in the woods or down a busy street. The goal is to be with God with no expectation of gain or the accomplishment of spiritual work.

3. Simple Prayer—Create a short prayer or use a Scripture verse as a companion during the dry well. Say the prayer frequently. Carry it with you wherever you go.

4. God in the Everyday—Accept the presence of God in the everyday, especially in nature, music or art. Sitting in a park or at the beach or listening to a great piece of music can speak of God's grace. God in the everyday is a descent into the ordinary wonder of creation that can keep you during dryness.

5. God in Others—Allow God to come to you through others. I have spiritually directed people who have said, "God has never shown up in my life." And then they tell an extraordinary story of someone who sacrificially served them in a dark time. Spiritual friends or a spiritual director are often the face of God during dry times.

A dry well is a place where water was once drawn regularly. Prayerlessness, drifting away from attachment to God, does not need to be the final response. Instead, the dry well can be the desert before the Promised Land, the cross before the open cave, the crossroads to a new well.

> May the God of peace himself sanctify you entirely;
> and may your spirit and soul and body be kept sound and blameless
> at the coming of our Lord Jesus Christ.
> The one who calls you is faithful, and he will do this.
> Beloved, pray for us.
> (1 Thess 5:23-25)

Notes

Introduction

[1]NationMaster.com, "Media Statistics: Television Viewing (most recent) by Country," www.nationmaster.com/graph/med_tel_vie-media-television-viewing.

[2]Pew Internet & American Life Project, "65% of Online Adults Use Social Media," http://pewinternet.org/Reports/2011/Social-Networking-Sites.aspx.

[3]George Barna, "What Effective Churches Have Discovered" (leadership seminar, Portland, OR, February 11, 1997).

[4]Malcolm Gladwell, *The Tipping Point: How Little Things Can Make a Big Difference* (New York: Little, Brown, 2002), p. 9.

[5]Margaret M. Poloma and George H. Gallup Jr., *Varieties of Prayer: A Survey Report* (Philadelphia: Trinity Press International, 1991), p. 47.

[6]Ibid., p. 64.

[7]Richard J. Foster, *Prayer: Finding the Heart's True Home* (New York: HarperSanFrancisco, 1992), p. 13.

[8]Ched Myers, *Binding the Strong Man: A Political Reading of Mark's Story of Jesus* (Maryknoll, NY: Orbis, 2008), p. 255.

[9]Kerry Patterson et al. *The Influencer: The Power to Change Anything* (New York: McGraw-Hill, 2008).

[10]Barna Group, "Top Trends for 2011: Maximizing Spiritual Change," www.barna.org/barna-update/faith-spirituality/547-top-trends-of-2011-maximizing-spiritual-change. The Maximum Faith Project found four barriers to spiritual growth: "lack of commitment, unwillingness to fully repent, confusing activity for growth, and failure to engage in genuine, accountable community."

Chapter 1: Community Prayer

[1]C. Baxter Kruger, *The Great Dance: The Christian Vision Revisited* (Vancouver: Regent College Publishing, 2000), p. 22.

[2]An excellent resource on Jewish prayer: Rabbi Hayim Halevy Donin, *To Pray as a Jew: A Guide to the Prayer Book and the Synagogue Service* (New York: BasicBooks, 1980).

Chapter 2: Creative Prayer

[1]Peter Steinke, *Healthy Congregations* (Herndon, VA: The Alban Institute, 1996), p. 108.

[2]Mihály Csíkszentmihályi has written several books on the concept of "flow," including *Creativity: Flow and the Psychology of Discovery and Invention* (New York: HarperPerennial, 1996) and *Finding Flow: The Psychology of Engagement with Everyday Life* (New York: Basic Books, 1997).

[3]Ronald Rolheiser, "The Grace in Creativity," *Ron Rolheiser, OMI* (blog), May 13, 2001, www.ronrolheiser.com/columnarchive/?id=325.

[4]Henri Nouwen, *The Way of the Heart* (New York: HarperSanFrancisco, 1981), p. 27.

Chapter 3: Work Prayer

[1]For more thoughts on this, read Randy Woodley's *Shalom and the Community of Creation: An Indigenous Vision* (Grand Rapids: Eerdmans, 2012).

[2]Beth Shulman, *The Betrayal of Work: How Low Wages Fail 30 Million Americans* (New York: New Press, 2003).

[3]Ibid., p. 5.

[4]Robert B. Reich, *The Future of Success: Working and Living in the New Economy* (New York: Random House, 2000), pp. 111-12.

[5]Leighton Ford, *The Attentive Life: Discerning God's Presence in All Things* (Downers Grove, IL: InterVarsity Press, 2008), p. 23.

[6]Simon Chan, *Spiritual Theology: A Systematic Study of the Christian Life* (Downers Grove, IL: InterVarsity Press, 1998), p. 130.

Chapter 4: Contemplative-Rest Prayer

[1]Eugene Peterson was very affected by Abraham Joshua Heschel's book *The Sabbath* (New York: Farrar, Straus & Giroux, 2005). It transformed his thinking on the importance of keeping the sabbath, and he writes about it in *The Pastor: A Memoir* (New York: HarperOne, 2011).

[2]Thomas Merton, *Contemplative Prayer* (New York: Image Book, 1971), p. 89.

[3]Richard Foster, *Meditative Prayer* (Downers Grove, IL: InterVarsity Press, 1983), pp. 27-28.

Chapter 5: Prayer of Confession

[1]For a restoration of the communal nature of our faith see Soong-Chan Rah, *The Next Evangelicalism: Freeing the Church from Western Cultural Captivity* (Downers Grove, IL: InterVarsity Press, 2009).

[2]Ibid., p. 41.

[3]Leighton Ford follows this pattern and suggested it to me. He developed it and calls it "An All-Day Prayer."

Chapter 6: Blessing Prayer

[1]Larry Shelton, *Cross and Covenant: Interpreting the Atonement for 21st Century Mission* (Tyrone, GA: Paternoster, 2006), p. 219.

[2]International Workers May Day Portland 2011, www.youtube.com/watch?v=ElSsp51nZkM.

Chapter 7: Worship Prayer

[1]Lynda L. Graybeal and Julia L. Roller, *Prayer and Worship: A Spiritual Formation Guide* (New York: HarperOne, 2007), p. xviii.

[2]Alan Deutschman, "Change or Die," *Fast Company*, May 1, 2005, www.fastcompany.com/magazine/94/open_change-or-die.html.

[3]A current nonsmoking ad shows a grandfather reaching for his grandson who is learning to walk. When the baby gets to his grandfather's arms, he goes right through him. He has died and his sad face says it all.

[4]Thomas Lewis, Fari Amini and Richard Lannon, *A General Theory of Love* (New York: Vintage Books, 2001), p. 123.

[5]Ibid., p. 116.

Chapter 8: Daily Reflection Prayer—The Examen

[1]Chalcedon was the fourth and last ecumenical council. The focus of the council was the issue of Jesus' divinity and humanity.

[2]Barry Johnson, *Polarity Management* (Amherst, MI: HRD, 1996). A resource to explain the nature and value of polarity management.

Chapter 9: The Lord's Prayer

[1]For a more complete discussion of the divinity and humanity of Jesus read N. T. Wright's *The Challenge of Jesus* (Downers Grove, IL: IVP Academic, 1999), especially pp. 96-125.

[2]Jesus used the term *Abba*, Aramaic for "Papa" or "Daddy," explicitly in Mark 14:36. Recent scholars have refuted Jesus' exclusive use of the word *Abba* to address God. See James H. Charlesworth, "A Caveat on Textual Transmission and the Meaning of Abba," *The Lord's Prayer and Other Prayer Texts from the Greco-Roman Era*, ed. James H. Charlesworth (Valley Forge, PA: Trinity Press International, 1994).

[3]Joachim Jeremias, *The Prayer of Jesus* (Philadelphia: Fortress, 1978).

[4]Nicholas Ayo, *The Lord's Prayer* (Notre Dame, IN: University of Notre Dame Press, 1992), p. 29.

[5]N. T. Wright, "The Lord's Prayer as a Paradigm of Christian Prayer," in *Into God's Presence: Prayer in the New Testament*, ed. Richard N. Longenecker (Grand Rapids: Eerdmans, 2001).

[6]William D. Spencer and Aída Besançon Spencer, *The Prayer Life of Jesus: Shout of Agony, Revelation of Love, a Commentary* (Lanham, MD: University Press of America, 1990).

Chapter 10: The Servant Prayer

[1]Geoffry W. Bromiley, ed. and trans., *Theological Dictionary of the New Testament*, vol. 1 (Grand Rapids: Eerdmans, 1995), pp. 380-81.

[2]Grace Morillo, "Lord, Make Me an Instrument of Your Peace," *Latin America Mission*, www.lam.org/news/article.php?id=299.

[3]John M. Gottman, *The Relationship Cure: A 5 Step Guide to Strengthening Your Marriage, Family, and Friendships* (New York: Three Rivers, 2002).

[4]I could not find any books on prayer and servanthood, so I chose stories and prayers of people who are noted for being servants of Christ.

Chapter 11: Simplicity Prayer

[1]Ralph P. Martin, *Reconciliation: A Study of Paul's Theology* (Grand Rapids: Zondervan, 1989), pp. 32-47.

[2]For more on Randy Woodley's thoughts, read *Shalom and the Community of Creation: An Indigenous Vision* (Grand Rapids: Eerdmans, 2012).

[3]Joseph Heath and Andrew Potter, *Nation of Rebels: Why Counterculture Became Consumer Culture* (New York: HarperBusiness, 2004), pp. 98-101.

[4]From Barbara Kingsolver, *Small Wonders* (New York: HarperCollins, 2002), excerpted in *Discussion Course on Voluntary Simplicity* (Portland, OR: Northwest Earth Institute, 2005), session 7, p. 6.

[5]Richard Foster, *Freedom of Simplicity* (New York: Harper & Row, 1981), p. 12.

Chapter 12: Prayer in Play

[1]Bruce Malina and Richard L. Rohrbaugh, *Social-Science Commentary on the Synoptic Gospels* (Minneapolis: Fortress, 1992), p. 117.

[2]There are many excellent resources on fun games that help develop community with adults. One example is in the suggested book list for this chapter.

Chapter 13: Scripture Prayer

[1]Ben Witherington III, *The Jesus Quest: The Third Search for the Jew of Nazareth* (Downers Grove, IL: InterVarsity Press, 1995). See especially "Jesus the Sage, the Embodiment of Wisdom," pp. 185-96.

[2]William E. Phipps, *The Wisdom & Wit of Rabbi Jesus* (Louisville: Westminster John Knox, 1994).

[3]L. G. Perdue, *Wisdom and Creation* (Nashville: Abingdon, 1994).

[4]J. G. Gammie and L. G. Perdue, eds., *The Sage in Israel and the Ancient Near East* (Winona Lake, IN: Eisenbrauns, 1990).

[5]See ibid., esp. pp. 460-85.

[6]Ben Witherington III, *Jesus the Sage: The Pilgrimage of Wisdom* (Minneapolis: Fortress, 1994).

[7]Carol S. Dweck, *Mindset: The New Psychology of Success* (New York: Ballantine Books, 2006).

[8]Simone Weil, *Waiting for God*, trans. Emma Craufurd (New York: Harper & Row, 1951), p. 29.

Chapter 14: Relinquishment Prayer

[1]William David Spencer and Aída Besançon Spencer, *The Prayer Life of Jesus: Shout of Agony, Revelation of Love, a Commentary* (Lanham, MD: University Press of America, 1990), pp. 229-33.

[2]Jeffrey Kottler, *The Language of Tears* (San Francisco: Jossey-Bass, 1996), p. 11.

[3]Frederick Buechner, *Listening to Your Life* (New York: HarperSanFrancisco, 1992), pp. 236-37.

[4]Alan W. Jones, *Soul Making: The Desert Way of Spirituality* (New York: HarperSanFrancisco, 1989), p. 99.

[5]Ibid., p. 90.

Chapter 15: Forgiveness Prayer

[1]Miroslav Volf, *Exclusion & Embrace* (Nashville: Abingdon, 1996), pp. 153-56.

[2]Ibid., p. 154.

[3]Ibid., p. 152.

[4]Diana Fosha, "Emotion and Recognition at Work," in *The Healing Power of Emotion*, ed. Diana Fosha, Daniel Siegel and Marion Solomon (New York: W. W. Norton, 2009), p. 173.

[5]Ibid.

[6]Marcus Borg and N. T. Wright, *The Meaning of Jesus: Two Visions* (New York: HarperSanFrancisco, 2000), pp. 31-52.

[7]Marion Solomon, "Emotion in Romantic Partners," in Fosha, Siegel and Solomon, *The Healing Power of Emotion*, p. 236.

[8]Mary Sherrill, *Therapist's Encounters with Revenge & Forgiveness* (London: Jessica Kingsley, 2000), p. 146.

[9]Sarah L. Vasiliauskas, *The Effects of a Prayer Intervention on the Process of Forgiveness* (PhD diss., George Fox University, Newberg, OR, September 2010), pp. 4-5.

[10]Daniel Goleman, *Social Intelligence: The New Science of Human Relationships* (New York: Bantam Books, 2006), pp. 77-79.

[11]Solomon Schimmel, *Wounds Not Healed by Time: The Power of Repentance and Forgiveness* (New York: Oxford University Press, 2002), p. 96.

Chapter 16: Sacrament Prayer

[1]N. T. Wright, *Simply Christian: Why Christianity Makes Sense* (New York: HarperSanFrancisco, 2006), p. 213.

[2]Gerald L. Sittser, *Water from a Deep Well: Christian Spirituality from Early Martyrs to Modern Missionaries* (Downers Grove, IL: InterVarsity Press, 2007), p. 144.

[3]Michael Imediedu, "Personal Growth Through Prayer and the Sacraments," *African Ecclesia Review* 35, no. 6D (1993): 373.

[4]Wright, *Simply Christian*, p. 233.

Chapter 17: Prayer Language—Tongues

[1]*Perichoresis* is a Greek word literally meaning "contain around," and in trinitarian theology means "permeation without confusion" such as a dance. The term was used by the early church fathers, particularly John of Damascus (d. 749), to describe the intimate love relationship of the Trinity.

[2]Examples are found in Judges 6:34, "the Spirit of the LORD came upon Gideon"; Judges 11:29, "the Spirit of the LORD came upon Jephthah"; and Judges 13:25, "the Spirit of the LORD began to stir him [Samson]" (NIV 1984). A helpful resource on the Holy Spirit in the Old Testament is Christopher J. H. Wright, *Knowing the Holy Spirit Through the Old Testament* (Downers Grove, IL: InterVarsity Press, 2006).

[3]*Parakletos* is Greek from two words meaning "alongside" and "called" and is often translated "helper" or "advocate" and refers to the Holy Spirit in the New Testament.

[4]See pp. 121-29 in N. T. Wright, *Simply Christian: Why Christianity Makes Sense* (New York: HarperSanFrancisco, 2006) for a more complete explanation of the role of the Holy Spirit.

[5]Andrew B. Newberg, Nancy A. Wintering, Donna Morgana and Mark R. Waldman, "The Measurement of Regional Cerebral Blood Flow During Glossalalia: A Preliminary SPECT Study," in *Psychiatry Research: Neuroimaging* 148 (2006): 67-71. A synopsis of the report is in Benedict Carey, "A Neuroscientific Look at Speaking in Tongues," *New York Times*, November 7, 2006.

[6]Veli-Matti Kärkkäinen, *Pneumatology: The Holy Spirit in Ecumenical, International, and Contextual Perspective* (Grand Rapids: Baker, 2002), p. 47.

[7]Though the recording by Gavin Bryans called "Jesus' Blood Never Failed Me Yet" is in English, it is a powerful and moving example of spiritual singing. You can also find various examples of Christian prayers sung or spoken in different languages on YouTube, such as www.youtube.com/watch?v=rBkUz5YktDs, "The Lord's Prayer in Hebrew, Latin, Middle English, and Spanish."

Chapter 18: Conversational Prayer

[1]Elizabeth H. Pope, "A Longer Life Is Lived with Company," *New York Times*, September 11, 2012, www.nytimes.com/2012/09/12/business/retirementspecial/for-older-adults-close-connections-are-key-to-healthy-aging.html.

[2]Veli-Matti Kärkkäinen, *Pneumatology: The Holy Spirit in Ecumenical, International, and Contextual Perspective* (Grand Rapids: Baker, 2002), p. 33.

[3]Darrell L. Guder, ed., *Missional Church: A Vision for the Sending of the Church in North America* (Grand Rapids: Eerdmans, 1998), pp. 142-43.

[4]The inspiration for conversation prayer came from a little pamphlet written by Rosalind Rinker called "Aids to Conversational Prayer." In the suggested book section Rinker's *Learning Conversational Prayer* (Collegeville, MN: Liturgical, 1992) is the later book that presents her thoughts in more detail.

Chapter 19: Breath Prayer

[1]See books such as Antonio Demasio's *Descartes' Error: Emotion, Reason, and the Human Brain* (New York: HarperCollins, 1994) and Joseph LeDoux's *The Emotional Brain: The Mysterious Underpinnings of Emotional Life* (New York: Simon & Schuster, 1996).

[2]Laurence Gonzales, *Deep Survival: Who Lives, Who Dies, and Why* (New York: W. W. Norton, 2003), p. 65.

[3]This story is part of a wonderful article on breath prayer written by Dr. Bill Gaultiere, "Breath Prayers," Soul Shepherding, 2012, www.soulshepherding.org/articles/spiritual-disciplines/breath-prayers. He also has a list of breath prayers in the Bible.

Chapter 20: Healing Prayer

[1]Other texts include: John 15:7-8, 16; Matthew 21:20-22; and, somewhat similar, Luke 11:9-13. Remember to explore the texts in their complete contexts.

[2]Evelyn Frost, *Christian Healing: A Consideration of Spiritual Healing in the Church Today in Light of the Doctrine and Practice of the Ante-Nicene Church* (London: A. R. Mowbray, 1949). This book is out of print but the author did a detailed search through the early church fathers' writings to find every mention of healings, demonstrating its normalcy in the church.

[3]Bruce Malina and Richard L. Rohrbaugh, *Social-Science Commentary on the Synoptic Gospels* (Minneapolis: Fortress, 1992), p. 131.

[4]William Spencer and Aída Besançon Spencer, *The Prayer Life of Jesus: Shout of Agony, Revelation of Love, a Commentary* (Lanham, MD: University Press of America, 1990).

[5]Kenneth Woodward, "Is God Listening?" *Newsweek*, March 30, 1997, www.thedailybeast.com/newsweek/1997/03/30/is-god-listening.html.

[6]The term particularly refers to Lorenz's 1972 paper, "Predictability: Does the Flap of a Butterfly's Wings in Brazil Set Off a Tornado in Texas?"

[7]Another example is the "placebo effect." For many people just believing a medication will make them better

is enough to make them better, whether the pill is a placebo or not.

[8]Walter Wink, *The Powers That Be: Theology for a New Millennium* (New York: Galilee Doubleday, 1998), p. 184.

[9]Terrance Tiessen, *Providence & Prayer: How Does God Work in the World?* (Downers Grove, IL: InterVarsity Press, 2000), p. 337.

Chapter 21: Meditative Prayer

[1]There are many helpful resources on addictions. A good secular book is Lance Dobes, *Breaking Addiction: A 7-Step Handbook for Ending Any Addiction* (New York: HarperCollins, 2011). A classic book for Christians is Gerald May, *Addiction and Grace: Love and Spirituality in the Healing of Addictions* (New York: HarperCollins, 1998).

[2]Richard Foster, *Meditative Prayer* (Downers Grove, IL: InterVarsity Press, 1999), p. 9.

Chapter 22: Discernment Prayer

[1]Parker J. Palmer, *A Hidden Wholeness: The Journey Toward an Undivided Life* (San Francisco: Jossey-Bass, 2004).

[2]Ibid., p. 26.

[3]Danny E. Morris and Charles M. Olsen, *Discerning God's Will Together: A Spiritual Practice for the Church* (Bethesda, MD: The Alban Institute, 1997), pp. 12-13.

[4]There are several resources on clearness committees. The original use of these discerning groups occurred among early Quakers when two people wanted to marry. Some helpful books include Suzanne Farnham, Joseph Gill, R. Taylor Mclean and Susan Ward, *Listening Hearts: Discerning Call in Community* (New York: Morehouse Publishing, 2011); Parker Palmer's book already mentioned; and Rose Mary Doughtery, *Group Spiritual Direction: Community for Discernment* (Mahwah, NJ: Paulist, 1995). Guidelines are also found online posted by several Quaker groups.

Chapter 23: Watch Prayer

[1]Walter Wink, *Naming the Powers: The Language of Power in the New Testament* (Philadelphia: Fortress, 1984), pp. 11-12.

[2]N. T. Wright, *Evil and the Justice of God* (Downers Grove, IL: InterVarsity Press, 2006), p. 102.

[3]Ibid., p. 111.

[4]Chuck Lawless, "Prayer and Spiritual Warfare," in *Giving Ourselves to Prayer*, compiled by Dan R. Crawford (Terre Haute, IN: PrayerShop, 2008), p. 471. Lawless helped make the connection for me between prayer and evangelism.

Chapter 24: Rejoice Prayer

[1]Some of the more well-known thinkers in this field are Ed Deiner, Martin Seligman and Mihaly Csikszent-mihalyi. All have written several books on the topic.

[2]J. Shenk, "Finding Happiness After Harvard," *Wilson Quarterly* 33 (June 2009): 73-74. (The author wrote about George Vaillant's research results.)

[3]Alan Deutschman, "Change or Die," *Fast Company* (May 1, 2005): 2, www.fastcompany.com/magazine/94/open_change-or-die.html. Deutschman later wrote a book *Change or Die* (New York: HarperCollins, 2007).

[4]John Kralik, *365 Thank Yous: The Year a Simple Act of Gratitude Changed My Life* (New York: Hyperion, 2010).

Closing

[1]Emilie Griffin, *Clinging: The Experience of Prayer* (New York: McCracken, 1994), p 32.

[2]Some good prayer resources on the "dark night" include: Saint John of the Cross, *Dark Night of the Soul*, trans. E. Allison Peers (Radford, VA: Wilder Publications, 2008); Gerald G. May, *Dark Night of the Soul: A Psychiatrist Explores the Connection Between Darkness and Spiritual Growth* (New York: HarperSanFrancisco, 2004); Thomas Moore, *Dark Nights of the Soul: A Guide to Finding Your Way Through Life's Ordeals* (New York: Gotham Books Penguin Group, 2004).